Climbing the Himalayas of School Leadership

The Socialization of Early Career Administrators

Carol A. Mullen

ScarecrowEducation
Lanham, Maryland • Toronto • Oxford
2004

Published in the United States of America
by ScarecrowEducation
An imprint of The Rowman & Littlefield Publishing Group, Inc.
4501 Forbes Boulevard, Suite 200, Lanham, Maryland 20706
www.scarecroweducation.com

PO Box 317
Oxford
OX2 9RU, UK

British Library Cataloguing in Publication Information Available

Library of Congress Cataloging-in-Publication Data

Mullen, Carol A.
  Climbing the Himalayas of school leadership : the socialization of early
career administrators / Carol A. Mullen.
      p. cm.
  Includes bibliographical references (p.   ) and index.
  ISBN 1-57886-107-1 (pbk. : alk. paper)
  1. School administrators—Training of—United States. 2. Educational
leadership—United States. 3. School management and
organization—United States. I. Title.
LB1738.5 .M85 2004
371.2'011'0973—dc22

                                                        2003024418

∞™ The paper used in this publication meets the minimum requirements of
American National Standard for Information Sciences—Permanence of
Paper for Printed Library Materials, ANSI/NISO Z39.48-1992.
Manufactured in the United States of America.

To Sir Edmund Hillary and Tenzing Norgay,
in honor of their climb to the top of Mount Everest, May 1953

. . . and for those who dream about climbing the summit of school leadership and all who have already begun the ascent. The novice school leader, not unlike the distance hiker and the artist, "paints a canvas with a million strokes. Up close you may see only the rough brush strokes: the dust and fatigue, the heat, mosquitoes and rain. But unlike the artist, you cannot stand back to appraise your work. So you must depend on your vision, rather than your sight" (Ray Jardine, *Beyond Backpacking*, 2001, p. 465).

This is also for the WIT—Writers in Training—my Educational Leadership cohort at the University of South Florida, for contributing to this book and for committing to the summit of doctoral study.

Contents

Part 3: Climbing the Summit Using Signposts, Signal Flares, and Backpacking Tips

Figures and Tables

FIGURES

TABLES

Acknowledgments and Credits

This book explores the socialization of early career school administrators and was based on a longitudinal study in educational leadership that took place from 2000 to 2003. The quality of my experience and insights as a university professor in addition to the research story I tell were all greatly enhanced by my hiking companions and Sherpa guides.

No significant climb up a mountain takes place alone. In this spirit, a host of individuals, combined with several teams of trekkers, made noteworthy contributions to the book. On this challenging hike, I intentionally met many individuals along the way. Base camps were established at increasing heights of altitude with a fair number, all of whom turned out to be what one real mountaineer calls "angel hikers."

Regarding sources of financial support for this project, my appreciation goes to two parties: one, the University of South Florida's Research Council and Division of Sponsored Research, for the New Researcher Grant I received in 2002, and two, Professor Don Orlosky, retired chair of USF's Department of Educational Leadership and Policy Studies, for sponsorship of the Berbecker Fellowship that recognized faculty research productivity. This allocation was intended for use in funding the research assistance of a doctoral student in educational leadership. I selected Elizabeth Tuten.

Elizabeth Tuten, a high school English teacher and department head, stayed en route with me for six intensive months. She provided invaluable support that ranged from making contacts with potential participants to organizing focus group materials and reading my draft chapters. Because of her current experience at the school level in Florida and in the dual role she performs, she was able to help fill some of the gaps in my text. Our synergistic relationship transcended professor and student as we worked together to close the theory/practice gap in our own lives.

Another funded doctoral student, Carol Burg, who is also at USF, hiked a shorter distance that nonetheless made a difference by locating some of the educational references I consulted. She also provided a draft statement for many of the entries appearing in the *Annotated Bibliography on Early Career Socialization* (appendix B).

Along this trek, William Kealy, my husband, who is an Associate Professor at USF in instructional technology and a graphic artist, provided multifaceted assistance. He located relevant radio broadcasts and websites about mountaineering as well as landscape images. Of greatest significance were the original artworks he co-created for the book, designed with my ongoing input and his creative interpretation. Professor Kealy's research is in the area of learning from graphic displays used in instructional texts in addition to mentorship theory and practice.

Dr. Marc Shapiro, a Senior Associate at ICF Consulting in Washington, D.C., also supplied original mountaineering artworks. Among these is the magnificent image of the Himalayan mountain Manaslu, a favored trekking route in the Nepal region, on the cover. Marc specializes in environmental policy analysis and management on issues that include justice and children's health. Marc is also president of the Foundation for Sustainable Development and an adjunct faculty member of George Washington University's Public Policy and Public Administration program. In his rare free time, he likes to hike, trek, climb, and take photographs.

Regarding the texts used in this book, numerous academics and practitioners provided materials that have both an energetic and informing presence. All gave written permission. Massachusetts university educators Ellen Barber, Susanne Chandler, and Elaine Collins's excerpt is contained in chapter 2. Also, fifteen schoolteachers and leadership aspirants studying at the University of South Florida in Tampa, Florida, have contributed works. These energetic contemporary pieces are featured as case scenarios at the outset of chapters or as discussion points. In an editorial-pedagogical capacity, I have enjoyed working with this group of talented practitioner-scholars whose action research was produced in graduate courses: Frances Helfrich (see chapter 6); Linda Bayless (see chapter 8); Bonita Salsman Paquette (see chapter 9); Ashley Sullivan (see chapter 10); Sue Bouleris, Collett De Ette, Mike Mauntler, and Shirley Ray (see chapter 12); Laura Meadows (see chapter 12); Jeanette Buntin, Carrie Rovellada Gutierrez, and Carisa Spires (see chapter 13); Maryann Lippek (see chapter 14); Sonja Cairns (see chapter 15); and Pamela Llewellyn (see chapter 15). Change agent–principals Thomas Graves, Lynne Patrick, and Elaine Sullivan also supplied works, coauthored with me, that have been adapted for this text.

The manuscripts produced by all of the individuals named appear as citations in the References section.

I would be remiss to overlook the obvious: Without the contributions of the beginning school leaders—survey and focus group participants—some of whom I know but most of whom I do not, this book would not be here. They together enabled a journey that was rich and fulfilling. To the 115 participants who shared their thoughts and insights I express my heartfelt thanks. It is through their expert–novice lenses that the leadership mountain, revealed herein, has been "scaled" and from new angles.

My gratitude also goes to various trekking partners at ScarecrowEducation. Cindy Tursman, managing editor, helped bring this book into being. During our stimulating talk at the 2002 meeting of the University Council for Educational Administration in Pittsburgh, Cindy encouraged submission of a book prospectus. We agreed that the case study approach taken should be both rigorous and engaging and that artwork would provide visual support for the key ideas. Experts reviewed my prospectus in a timely fashion.

National Public Radio (copyright © 1990–2003) granted permission to paraphrase from transcripts of commentary on the Mount Everest ascent.

Additionally, the Florida Association of School Administrators (FASA) authorized the reprint of the map (figure 5.1) from the *Florida Education Directory*.

Photographs by Nova Development Corporation appear pursuant to its License Agreement for the Art Explosion library software that I purchased. The agreement authorizes use of clip art images in publication form (under "use of content," section 5) (http://www.novadevelopment.com).

The captions for all artwork in this book are mine.

Finally, in accordance with the University of South Florida's rule 6C4-10.109.B-6, I confirm that the opinions stated herein are my own, not the university's.

Foreword

Figure F.1.   Imagineering the Mountaineering Journey Ahead
Source: Nova Development Corporation

This is a creative, multifaceted, bold book. Using the concept of *imagineering*, Carol Mullen likens the early socialization of career school administrators to a mountain expedition, replete with the linking concepts and attendant vocabulary of mountain climbing. She weaves these images through her research of early career administrators in Florida, examining their reflections on their university preparation and what they consider to be the major tasks of the job, mostly as assistant principals.

The text is peppered with personal anecdotes that break down the walls that usually confine the "neutral" and "scientific" researcher. On the contrary, Mullen is an active participant in her mountain *imagineering* and her text. Passionate about her work, she has absorbed details from many realms, and these are skillfully applied to the canvas of the book.

While she has had many guides, Mullen's key Sherpas have been her students. It is clear that her relationship with them has been dynamic and that both instructor and student have grown immensely from the shared projects and experiences she recounts throughout the chapters.

The reader of Mullen's book is asked to break new ground by entering into the metaphorical trekking mind-set, shedding the customary passive-participant role for that of an interactive fellow hiker. The reader can't sit mentally still because Mullen presents stories that intersect and entertain. She negotiates some new rules of reality. We encounter Sherpa guides, hiking trails, base camps, climbing scaffolds, using a compass, and backpacking tips—all linked to the initial experiences of early school administrators coping with their sometimes overwhelming new responsibilities in schools facing escalating accountability challenges. Indeed, for the beginning school leader, the images of summit climbing will be cogent and real.

So get ready to do your own intellectual backpacking. Mullen's cognitive trails, reflections, ruminations, and celebrations leave one with a view from the top that is intense and mind expanding. Well worth the climb!

Fenwick W. English

Preface: How This Summit Expedition Began

Adventure isn't hanging on a rope off the side of a mountain. Adventure is an attitude that we must apply to the day-to-day obstacles of life—facing new challenges, seizing new opportunities, testing our resources against the unknown and, in the process, discovering our own unique potential.

— John Amatt, leader of Canadian expedition to
Mount Everest, 2000

Summit: The top point or utmost elevation, especially of hills or mountains; the highest point, e.g., of ambitions or achievements; the utmost elevation, as of rank, prosperity, etc.

—*New Webster's Dictionary and Thesaurus of the*
English Language, 1993

Real mountains vary in kind and difficulty, and the experienced mountaineer learns when and how to approach their summits. We are all, in a metaphorical sense, mountaineers climbing our own mountains, ranging from professional to marital to parenting mountains, as well as health, financial, and relationship mountains, and leadership mountains, such as that depicted in the trail map of Mount Everest that new expedition leaders often follow. It could take days, years, or even a lifetime to reach a summit, or just one afternoon—even a single moment!

But most mountains take a very long time to ascend; our "everyday Everests" are "harder to surmount than Everest" (Hobson and Clarke 1997, ix). You have probably already scaled a summit and even

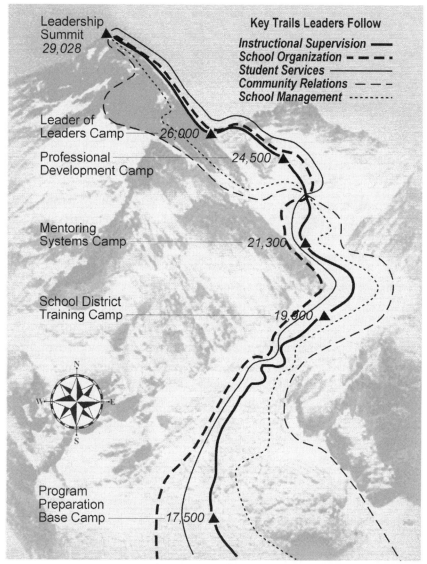

Figure P.1.   Trail Map for Climbing Leadership Mountain
Source: Carol Mullen and William Kealy

possibly a number of them by this time. Perhaps you are now n the process of again doing so. Among those peaks attained or sighted are such intellectual accomplishments as university degrees or diplomas, awards or programs, and career advancements or promotions. But in life, there are very few such occasions. Too few clearly designated

Figure P.2.   Different Kinds of Mountains Mark Our Lives
Source: Marc Shapiro

"summits" mark our successes, and some are invisible to others because they mark profoundly personal periods of growth in our lives. As mountaineers, Alan Hobson and Jamie Clarke (1997) explain that no one is ready to take our picture or shake our hand "when we get to the summit because there is no summit" (p. ix). And the loads we carry up our mountains are getting heavier by the day. While we contend with the metaphorical elements—wind, rain, and cold—the mountain keeps shifting. The leadership mountain that is the terrain of schools is certainly undergoing great change. And it can look more daunting than an actual one (see Kichke Himals, figure P.2).

Challenging climbs are not strictly of an intellectual or career-oriented nature. As mentioned, many reflect deeply personal goals, and some involve significant interpersonal experiences with families, colleagues, supervisors, teachers, students, and loved ones. We can even undergo tremendous struggle and change through our relationship with institutions, associations, agencies, and boards. Some of our greatest challenges are met, though, when we put our best foot forward, so to speak, personally, interpersonally, physically, and spiritually, and often because we have not made the trek alone.

SCALING THE SUMMIT

On May 29, 2003, the world celebrated the fiftieth anniversary of Sir Edmund Hillary and Tenzing Norgay's famous ascent to the peak of Mount Everest. At this time, I had my sights on a summit of a different nature—the completion of this book. Many have recognized the pioneering climb to the top of the world's tallest mountain as the greatest athletic challenge of our time (National Public Radio 2003b). Encyclopedias (e.g., *Compton's Reference Collection* 1995) claim it to be among the greatest achievements in history. This celebratory event dramatically sealed the comparison of expedition hiking and school leadership in this book. Just as the Everest team had gotten closer to the sun and moon than had any human being before, so too will new administrative leaders symbolically scale great heights to reach summits of their own.

The most rewarding expeditions in our lives require exertion, as well as the capacity to dream and envision, capitalizing on everything we can bring to the occasion, stretching us to a state of being only previously imagined. Perhaps this is why New Zealand adventurer Sir Edmund Hillary asserted, "It is not the mountain we conquer but ourselves" (Wiesel 2003). Some writers have described the state of being challenged and of challenging oneself as happiness. Similarly, as part of their makeup, it may be that administrators who are exemplary leaders feel most alive when challenged to improve the circumstances and quality of life of those within their charge (e.g., Mullen 2002c; Mullen and Patrick 2000). Schecter (2002), for example, recounts the experience of an Israeli principal whose effort to bring faculty and administration into a "communal deliberative process" proved invigorating in direct proportion to its considerable difficulty.

In this book we will metaphorically climb a summit together. This virtual trip will take you on an educational adventure through the Himalayas of school leadership. This adventure story is also a research story—it has been constructed out of the insights shared by newly practicing principals and assistant principals embarking on the journey of school administration. The results of this study have been visually represented in the trail map that launches this story, serving as the orienting schema for this book.

In brief, the following constitute the key trails that leaders follow, based on this study and the educational literature:

- Instructional supervision
- School organization
- Student services
- Community relations
- School management.

As chapter 5 ("Outcomes") explains, although there is no hierarchical distinction among these main (core) leadership areas for new leaders because context matters, there are different weights or values to be attributed to each. Instructional supervision, the thickest line (trail) on the orienting map, was the most heavily emphasized in the data collected for this research on the socialization of beginning school administrators. This area was closely followed by school organization, as indicated by the legend called "key trails leaders follow" on the map. Next, in order of importance as reflected in the new leader's time and energy, were student services, community relations, and school management.

The early career leader's experience of being a trekking guide for schools and of preparing for this role is the backbone of this book. Expert trekkers—our "mountaineers," school leaders, action researchers, and knowledge specialists—bring perspective to the discoveries made by these developing professionals. Early career leaders are referred interchangeably herein as beginning leaders and administrators, transitional leaders, expert novices, developing leaders, peer leaders, trekkers, team players, and imagineers.

The peak of early career administration can be imagined as the first part of the trek encountered on your entire journey of leadership, or it may be appreciated as a summit in its own right. We can assume that the first steps and the early years in any profession, especially educational leadership these days, require an awesome effort that continues beyond the first summits reached. Research on the socialization process of beginning school leaders (e.g., Crow and Matthews's [1998] *Finding One's Way* and Schmidt's [2002] *Gardening in the Minefield*) confirms that the climb involves much more than simply being an effective technician who can take the "right" tools from the knapsack to address and resolve situations as they arise.

TELLING THE APPRENTICE'S TALE

A story of beginning school leadership emerged from a personal revelation. I discovered that, in the company of one particular type of pathfinder (soon to be revealed!), my master's students felt energized, awakened more fully, and imagined scaling greater heights. While teaching in an educational leadership program, I gradually arrived at what may be a unique insight into the psyche of aspirants. I was seeing that many of these future administrators look intuitively to a particular leader for insight, leverage, motivation, guidance, and encouragement. This immediate role model is not necessarily the district superintendent, experienced principal, or former school leader. Instead, the leader who kindled my students' interest was that in-between, barely visible, and emergent entity—the newly practicing administrator, who is an assistant principal or principal.

As Nobel laureate Elie Wiesel (2003) has rightly impressed upon us, "Whoever survives a test, whatever it may be, must tell the story. That is his duty." Based on the responsiveness of novice (and experienced) leaders who spoke in my classes and dozens more who contributed to this study, it appears that many are willing to share their greatest insights through storytelling. Such information has value for socializing newcomers to the professional role of leader. How is it that these "backpacking hikers" or "apprentice leaders" (Kosseff 2003) who spin tales of a nitty-gritty nature induce such deep listening and the desire to follow?

Storytelling is how we transmit culture from one generation to the next. It is also how teaching culture is transmitted from faculty mentor to beginning teacher, and similarly how administrative culture is transmitted from experienced leader to novice practitioner (Crow and Matthews 1998; Mullen and Lick 1999). Educational stories assist the novice leader with the process of learning, remembering, problem solving, and decision making—information that can be stored and accessed under new or changing conditions (Williams, Matthews and Baugh, in press). A principal or mentor who might, for example, share an experience of extending instructional support and mentoring to veteran teachers could share the strategies used for seeking alliances with faculty who differ in their responsiveness and who have different needs, depending on the stage of their career (McDaniel 1999). Such stories could prove invaluable to novice leaders who may be younger or less experienced than their faculty or who have been promoted over others, now within one's charge.

The guests in my classes and the participants in my book all tell about survival as a freshly encountered challenge where problems have been diagnosed and the ability to cope and improvise has been tested. In this context, the story is not a past event that has already been lived and packaged for value but instead unravels—unfinished, rough, and raw. The teller, often still living the very story that he or she is telling, does not always know the ending. The listener is magnetically drawn to these peer mentors and their accounts. As expert-learners they come equipped with pragmatic know-how and campfire tales to share.

Although rare, a few other studies have alluded to the value of bringing school practitioners into university classrooms to "[tell] war stories from the field." In this way, aspirants interact and actively engage in problem solving when provided such prompts as, "How would you respond and why?" (Bratlein and Walters 1999, 98). School superintendents have testified that panel discussion and other opportunities for real-world exposure to administrative life are key to viable graduate education because they integrate theory with practice (Bratlein and Walters 1999; Mullen et al. 2002). This is the closest that many administrator candidates get to an internship or field practice within their graduate degree programs.

In my students' eyes, beginning school leaders have legitimacy in their role because they experience firsthand what it means to administer and lead in today's climate. And they have already gained some intimate knowledge of how to maneuver through the briar patch of school life. Stories of "being there" that feel immediate, real, and sensory especially make this figure very popular. Descriptions of the job and even of daily work have particular appeal. Anything that can be learned about "the ropes" of administration fuels interest. Future leaders seek knowledge about how accountability standards can best be met, as well as curricular programs implemented, school events organized, classroom instruction supported, alliances forged with parents and other community groups, stakeholder encounters effectively managed, and school policy implemented, especially in the areas of student discipline and teacher performance.

These master's groups do not hold back from soliciting techniques from their more experienced counterparts for addressing a range of interpersonal situations and for actively addressing curricular and behavioral challenges at the classroom and school levels. They do not feel threatened—these newly practicing administrators who were recently in their shoes can presumably identify with their circumstances and concerns. The administrator apprentice who grapples with life "in the trenches" has already reached a summit in my students' minds. Cast as a peer mentor who has bridged the precarious stream between theory and practice, these Sherpa leaders guide those wishing to place their own feet on the school administrative trail.

Watching this scenario unfold semester after semester, it suddenly dawned on me that I needed to challenge myself to dig deeper. I then conducted a statewide study that would bring to preservice (or prospective) leaders all of the insight and information I could muster from practicing administrators about their role and adaptation to it, as well as their graduate preparation experiences. This book is the product of that research adventure, where participants from Florida's school districts have provided feedback and shared stories. In the same way that the practicing novice administrator gained visibility in my courses, this barely visible entity has also become audible in this text. About this issue of voice, one of the members of a focus group session for this project wrote,

> As an assistant principal [AP] I am truly in the "middle management" role. Rarely does anyone want to hear or care about my opinions or those of my colleagues (other APs). It was nice to share my experiences with someone who is interested and who will put the information to use to serve other administrators. (Workshop evaluation form, April 2003)

LEARNING TO LOVE THE GAPS

Bring along your own sense of adventure and school stories as you vicariously live this leadership narrative that is, of necessity, incomplete in scope, riddled with tension, and open to alternatives. Uncertainty and flux are the norm now in the field of educational administration—a world not exempt from postmodern, even whirlwind changing conditions of life

(Diamond and Mullen 1999a; English 2003c). There is no "big picture" or whole view of the mountain anymore, and no one knows how everything works. Learn to love the gaps.

A career in school leadership these days means recognizing that you will be called upon to make critical decisions based on partial information. You may even feel as though you have to climb one summit after another of complex decision making without even knowing how the previous trek turned out. Or, you may feel as though you will never come to know the whole mountain because of the time spent exclusively on the east, west, north, or south side. Florida elementary principal McDaniel (1999) claims that "with this role came many . . . 'hats to wear' and the rush against the clock that I experience playing many mentoring roles each day" (p. 119). And as English (2003c) adds, these experiences of fragmentation, multiplicity, and ambiguity are all common.

Rarely will there be "the answer" or "right solution," only a plethora of choices that can approximate better and worse decisions. This requires an open attitude toward the work, and a deep appreciation for context and understanding situations on their own terms. The administrator who can cope with such uncertainty contrasts with those poised with certitudes: those who are fixed in their ways and closed to input and critique, who are rarely invigorating travelers, and even may be among those new to their campsite. Set your own sights on being a different kind of administrator, one whom McDaniel (1999) describes as a mentoring leader—encourager, synergist, and liaison—a list to which I add, "guide."

THE METAPHOR'S ORIGINATING SOURCES

The mountaineering metaphor appearing throughout this book originated in part from the master's courses I teach at the University of South Florida. In my educational leadership courses, writing teams tackle leadership topics of interest and produce data-based narrative accounts. The student groups approach their new learning as a mountain to be scaled. The curriculum they encounter exposes them to a series of mountaineering exercises, metaphorically staged as a trekking expedition. Teams give a name, such as "Unity," to themselves, and they work synergistically to reach the goal of developing models (like units to address diversity issues arising from terrorism threats) that have been informed by school contexts and are designed for application.

Those studying in my course all face the same important task—they must decide just what to put in their backpacks (actually cardboard illustrations and objects). In teams, they identify what tools they think are essential for the hike that lies ahead, such as a map for plotting out directions, and then they create icons, along with the other symbols selected. This is how we begin.

The other origin for my metaphor is the actual trekking I have done in Ontario, Hawaii, Arizona, and Italy through wilderness, on mountains, and in canyons. Illustrations of some of these experiences appear wherever the research participants' words or my associations with them have jogged memories, sending me back to the videotapes and photo albums.

DOCUMENTING YOUR TREK

As you trek along here, consider keeping a journal—just as trekkers do! Add new chapters to help fill in some of the gaps. If you are an experienced leader, whether in a school or university, you will have material to contribute. You may even learn "new approaches to thinking about your work" (Kosseff 2003, 2), especially when it comes to reaching out to newcomers. If, on the other hand, you are a preservice administrator, many gaps can be expected between this text and your own experiences. The new administrators who participated in this project are currently on a learning curve in their own summit expeditions, so it only stands to reason that you may find what they have to say supportive of your own growth and goals. Like Kosseff's (2003) guide to outdoor leadership, this text should give a head start to anyone "just starting out."

Lastly, during this book expedition, mentoring scaffolds will be identified for educators and leaders to use. At the end of our trek, a gift—a summit stone—will be offered in the hope of further inspiring your own journeys and those of others.

Part 1

MOUNTAINTOP VIEW OF THIS RESEARCH TRAVELOGUE THROUGH HIGH-POWER BINOCULARS

Chapter One

Trekkers: Travelogue Benefits and Landscape Features

Figure 1.1. Trek Your Own Mountaineering Path
Source: Marc Shapiro

When you look back, you see a clear path that brought you here. But you created that path yourself. Ahead, there is only uncharted wilderness. In the final analysis, it is the walking that beats the path. It is not the path that makes the walk.

—A. de Gues, *The Living Company*

In this section, the benefits to virtual trekkers (spectators) in taking this journey are discussed along with the landscape (design) of this text. Although I have created paths for you to walk alongside other trekkers (practicing school leaders), it is ultimately your own "beating" upon it—or how you make sense of and use this book—that lends credibility to this journey (Hargreaves and Fullan 1998).

RESEARCH TRAVELOGUE BENEFITS

Filling a Gap

This book attempts to address a gap within the educational leadership, mentorship, and school improvement literature. Currently, the core issues—as these germinate from and directly affect beginning school leaders—tend to be overlooked as a significant area of study. Ironically, from the career school leader's perspective, little is known about the nature of the work of school leadership itself and, subsequently, the knowledge and abilities critical for prospective administrators. It is what beginning school leaders have construed as important foci in relation to both their administrative roles and preparation programs that are the nucleus of this book.

Importantly, schoolteachers aspiring to administration can also realize benefits from insights offered by a crucial peer leadership group—a welcome change. Teachers and administrators who carry mentoring, evaluative, and instructional, or staff, development responsibilities may also profit. They will probably glean new insights from the descriptions of school leadership that have been interpreted in relation to deeper issues of context, culture, socialization, adjustment, survival, and success. Similarly, policymakers can draw ideas from new school leaders and construct educational themes on the basis of their input. The results can be used or built upon for informing legislation that accounts for this stakeholder group's viewpoints, experiences, and recommendations on how to improve preservice training programs.

Finally, graduate university instructors and school-based personnel trainers, as well as those located in district centers, can make gains for their own purposes from a text on school leadership that has been grounded in the field.

Going Wider

It is anticipated that the work and experience of new school leaders in Florida could have value beyond the state level for both our nation and perhaps others. Where appropriate, the outcomes can be reflected in future research, program content, and policy reform. An urgent call at the Florida state level, for instance, has signaled that university faculty must take responsibility for reforming our university preparation programs. A major goal of this text involves addressing possibilities grounded within practicing leadership for improving administrative training programs at the state and national level. Readers' own connections and contributions to this theme could give this project an impact beyond its immediate effects.

Moreover, as one significant consequence, the least effective of these educational leadership programs could be eliminated in Florida, as they have in North Carolina (*Effective Leaders for Today's Schools* 1999). This book could help obsolete programs move forward. It is expected that preservice administration programs will be aligned not only with the goals of our universities, policy-making bodies, and the public, but also with the needs of school districts, administrator candidates, and practicing school leaders (Mullen et al. 2002).

However, this position is not beyond critique. The outcomes-based standards that U.S. accreditation bodies have established to conform university preparation programs to national criteria have been seriously questioned (e.g., English 2003a, 2003b). With the recent adoption of the ELCC (Educational Leadership Constituent Council) national standards, which are NCATE (National Council for Accreditation of Teacher Education) aligned, professors who teach university preparation courses are now bound by the standards in order that programs qualify for accreditation. Because of this regulatory practice, a lack of accreditation amounts to putting some preparation programs out of business (English 2003b). The suggestions I have made for revising American leadership preparation programs should also be debated, as practicing school leaders from around the nation and other countries (such as Mexico) will likely have different cultural perspectives (e.g., Slater et al. 2003).

Going Deeper

Teachers seeking insight into the role of administrator look to the "real thing" for assistance during their coursework. And many long for guidance from those "living in the trenches" or who are best apt to present this picture (e.g., Crow and Matthews 1998; Schmidt 2002). But these leadership students cannot be "given" the real thing or even come to know the "big picture." The onus will be on them to construct the big picture they seek and to contextualize their knowledge in response to particular situations. That they cannot seize upon that which is not fixed and knowable is a source of frustration for those who see their higher education programs as a delivery system responsible for delivering the "right science" (English 2003c). Alternatively viewing these as a venue for professional empowerment, preservice administrators could go deeper into their own education. One example, the exclusion of schools from the standards debate and policy reform agenda, could be confronted (Mullen 2002a, 2002c). The high-stakes testing pressure placed on school districts underscores an instrumental and competitive view of education that many practitioners think is unfair or unjust.

Nevertheless, better simulations of problem solving that provide clues about real-world contexts can be created (Mullen et al. 2002). The answer is not simply the clinical internship for assisting the learning and socialization of future administrators, as this vehicle has been fraught with problems for some graduate programs throughout the United States (Mullen and Cairns 2001). This realization impresses upon professors and students the need for expanded, if not imaginative, group-based fieldwork simulations, such as the Monet Project (see chapter 2) and the mountaineering knapsack activity (see chapter 6).

Supporting Educational Leaders

In addition to benefiting aspiring leaders, this text should also prove informative to school-based personnel, including beginning leaders, peer mentors, and other institutional figures—anyone who takes seriously the task of socializing, empowering, and learning from newcomers. Principals and other school leaders, such as supervisors, personnel trainers, district office administrators, consultants, regional and state administrators, and school superintendents are all part of the target audience. Curriculum developers constitute yet another spectator group because of their interest in designing materials to aid the acquisition of relevant knowledge and skills for administrator interns and school leaders. Finally, this book is for university leaders and policymakers whose approaches could be strengthened by better understanding of the challenges that recent university graduates face as they lead schools in today's accountability climate.

Those teaching in educational leadership or principal preparation programs are of particular interest as an audience because, as Clark (1999) attests, the primary purpose of "graduate programs in educational leadership [is] to prepare school administrative personnel" (p. 231). But this statement begs the question, To do what, exactly, and from whose stakeholder perspective?

A text that is both research-based and practical holds promise for all constituencies involved in the preparation of future school leaders, thereby reducing the theory/practice gap that dominates our educational landscape. Based on my own instructional experiences, relevant graduate courses for this book include educational leadership, the principalship, clinical internship, practicum, case studies in school administration, curriculum and instruction, policy studies, management, mentor training, school improvement, and organizational analysis and change.

TEXTUAL LANDSCAPE FEATURES

Providing a Research-Based Lens

Integrated and scholarly research is a major feature of this book. Not much research has empirically solicited the feedback and simultaneously exposed the reflections of this particular school leadership population. At best, the literature provides overview statements and case scenarios concerning the transitional experiences and critical reflections of new school leaders—but without evidence of having engaged them in a rigorous collaborative inquiry process. Chapters 4 and 5 describe the research-based lens of this book, with emphasis on the process of this study and its outcomes.

Capitalizing on the School Leader's Voice

A unique feature of this book is the Sherpa-like stature that the beginning school leader fulfills as a spokesperson for newcomers to the field. However, data do not speak for themselves. In the company of school practitioners, I have taken steps beyond my own analysis to reinterpret the survey data. Through this cooperative group process I have deepened and extended my interpretations of the survey information, encompassing quantitative and qualitative feedback. At times I also step away from conveying the impressions formed about the new administrator's ways of introducing critique and alternative ideas. (See, e.g., chapter 16, "Lantern: Knowledge Source.")

Given these caveats, the beginning school leader guides the journey with support from other trekkers—outdoor leaders, researchers in educational leadership and teacher education, and authors from various domains, namely literature and the arts. We will hear them talk about (1) the nature of their work in Florida schools, and (2) the quality of formal preparation they have experienced. Because my understandings of the data and results were partly informed by the responses of emergent leaders, readers will hear beginning leaders speaking at all levels of the text, in the form of metaphors, images, quotes, themes, and outcomes.

Constructing the Author as Interpreter

In an effort to capitalize on the school leader's voice, I have assumed the role of interpreter. By clarifying and expanding upon the information received, I will be able to provide insights, some thought provoking. As a controversial example, not unlike other developing leaders in the United States, my study participants seem to believe that "if skills, knowledge and technology are applied [to problems], educational conditions will improve" (Slater et al. 2003, 51), thereby supporting the value of instrumental learning, which English (2003c) asserts is a leftover from the prescriptive "behavioral science era" (p. 34). My intention is to offer any such insights from the literature while valuing the developing expertise of the school leaders who contributed to this educational leadership project.

Translating Leadership Ideas into Metaphor

The overarching mountaineering metaphor was developed to reflect salient areas of leadership identified by the study participants. For instance, one such area that characterizes aspects of their work is mentoring scaffolds, which support effective school administration rooted in a caring pedagogy as well as university preparation. This area was matched with the backpacking image of the rope in order to structure the relevant thematic patterns in the data that pertain to mentoring, support, and teamwork.

Integrating Experiential Text

Part 2 is organized around case scenarios, some fictitious and some real. The cases generate sections on Reflection and Discussion, Summit Data and Analysis, Lessons, and Backpacking Tips and Leader Activities. Master's students, teachers who are aspiring school leaders, not university scholars, have written the ten case scenarios. These are to be adapted for use wherever possible.

Chapter Two

Perspectives: Backpacking with Binocular Vision

B—Benevolence
A—Accountability
C—Context
K—Kindling
P—Practice
A—Adaptability
C—Conditioning
K—Knowledge
I—Imagineering
N—Navigation
G—Group

Anyone who backpacks through any type of wilderness will see life differently on the trail (e.g., Kosseff 2003). In the outdoors, long-distance hikers say they experience "synergy in motion," a freedom of movement wherein connections occur spontaneously and reflections deepen (Jardine 2001, 40). While traveling in this mode, "activities that produce a state of flow are, to the person involved, totally engrossing and present constant challenges to be met with appropriate skills" (Kosseff 2003, 108). Although one may trek for a relatively short time, "the journey tends to expand in many directions—outward, inward and upward—as much as it reaches ahead and behind" (Jardine 2001, 456). The miles clocked will matter less than the quality of experience that the trekker constructs through making observations and connecting these to patterns.

Figure 2.1. Bridging Theory with Practice
Source: Nova Development Corporation

BRIDGING THEORY AND PRACTICE

It was just this kind of nonlinear flow that a team of university educators in Massachusetts described in the article, "Using Monet to Teach Leadership."

After the students [in the administration program] had already spent one week discussing leadership from a variety of scholarly perspectives, they were directed to assemble in an art studio rather than their usual classroom. . . . As students slowly took their seats, [the university professors] distributed to each 1/12th of a reproduction of Monet's *Water Lilies and Japanese Bridge*. . . . Students were not told what the "big picture" was, although some had an idea that it was a Monet. . . . Given something relatively concrete and intriguing with which to begin, students became more eager. They went to the center table and selected paints. . . . More than one student tore up a be-

ginning attempt only to begin again with less structure. . . . No student in the
administration program considered her or himself an "artist." . . .

Students knew that they each had only a piece of the whole artwork. They
conferred with each other in an effort to discover how the pieces might fit
together. The context of conversation changed from concern with the need
for prediction and control over the process ("What do *you* want?") to *questions* about how to create patterns and meaning within and among the
pieces. Excitement about the *emerging* process . . . mounted. . . .

The students still had no idea what they were actually creating, and
this ambiguity led to frustration for some of the participants. When the
groups stepped back, however, they could see the bridge and its environment in each of the four large recreations. . . . Amazingly (for all of us)
the bridge. . . . was clearly evident.

As students stepped back to admire their creations, they discovered that
each piece held the whole picture, and that each piece was critical to the
whole. . . . Michael commented, "Everyone contributed from her or his own
perspective. Even with no one in control, we still arrived at a bridge that we
each had invested in—and it was incredible." (Barber, Chandler, and
Collins 2001, 28–31)

As this segment illustrates, Barber, Chandler, and Collins (2001) created
the conditions for a group of prospective administrators to engage more
openly in and about their own learning. The objectives of this life lesson
were to immerse oneself in an organic process, to make unplanned connections individually and collectively, and to reflect critically on the experience. More shared leadership and organic learning experiences could be
incorporated within graduate school to benefit preservice administrators.

Let us consider more closely what happened as the group gained significant reflective mileage through the unanticipated gateway of an arts-based,
experiential activity. The particular meaning of this narrative for our purposes is that it provides a glimpse into how any interested practitioner can
integrate theory and practice in group settings or applied contexts. As Schön
(1987) asserts, "university-based professional schools" that house, for example, leadership programs and academies "should learn from such deviant
traditions of education for practice as studios of art . . . and apprenticeship
in the craft, all of which emphasize coaching and learning by doing" (p. xii).

Theory and practice can and should be perceived as interdependent, co-
existing lenses or frameworks. Neither is the "deviant" paradigm. Based

on my own understanding of the Monet Project, the realization of this mutual relationship for the learners seemed to depend on an organic approach to learning reinforced by a reflexive engagement in constructivist activity. Many of us better understand theories of educational leadership, whatever they might be—change theory, social role theory, professional learning communities, systems thinking, organizational culture, learning styles, collaborative mentorship, or transformational leadership—through application, and application through reflection.

Further reflecting on this teaching/learning scenario, we can see that prior assumptions faded for the preservice group as new possibilities emerged. The Monet Project revealed that students could form impressions of their own rather than simply accepting those of others. As the graduate students engaged in this project, the frustration over how to predict their teacher's wants decreased along with the desire to control the process and its outcomes: "*Questions* about how to create patterns and meaning within and among the pieces" were overshadowed by "excitement about the *emerging* process." While the individuals' contributions (i.e., segments of the image) came together to form a whole picture—of Monet's "Bridge"—the students realized how "people perceive things differently." Each segment of the bridge had been painted using a somewhat different style (e.g., combination of colors and brush strokes), underscoring the importance of individual *and* collective meaning making within a social group context. One participant noted that she now thinks about her relationships with colleagues differently, partly in terms of who she believes them to be and what possibilities they have for becoming.

Through reflective discourse, this group of future administrators created a more empowering view of learning and leading, self and other, theory and practice. The members gained perspective by talking about "the engagement of self in the project, interpretation, multiple perspectives, and coherence of the art project with readings they had prepared earlier in the program" (Barber, Chandler, and Collins 2001, 31). Integral to this process, the class had incorporated a "critical frame," grappling with the ideas in the readings and those assumptions implicit in each other's responses. They challenged one another to look at problems and situations from multiple perspectives and to reach tentative solutions through shared discovery, always "remembering the bridge" and the crucial insights gained from the activity. Critical thinking and problem solving can be taught in educational leadership programs in creative ways, using constructivist techniques with cooperative learning groups (Shapiro 2000).

The vision of the Monet Project as a powerful "bridge" for connecting theory and practice resulted from my own experiential encounter. During the year before the article appeared, I attended an Eastern Educational Research Association conference in Clearwater, Florida. University educators Ellen Barber, Susanne Chandler, and Elaine Collins had altered the formal space, creating roundtables instead of rows and paint stations at center stage—foreshadowing the idea of teaching and leadership as an "art form." Clearly there would be no formal talk or panel discussion— this was an invitation to engage or disengage in new learning, depending on one's response. After being handed a part of the Monet landscape to reproduce, I began painting the section, registering my inexperience with the paintbrush as primitive strokes awkwardly formed. I glanced up at the other attendees as some asked questions, others hesitated, a few fled. But then the group got busy, lost in time without knowing what would come from what we were making but somehow trusting the process.

Once finished, we placed our panels together side-by-side on the floor and stepped back. The large-scale bridge emerged across the unique strokes and various colors of our individual panels. Standing together, this group of academics, who had just recently been strangers, shared an awakening, not about any hidden truth that got revealed, but about what we could meaningfully create as a social unit, through art and discourse on the process. Many questions remained unanswered at the workshop, however, perhaps because any such big picture emergence does not necessarily eliminate ambiguity and complexity (English 2003c). In fact, the Monet Project only perpetuated endless possibilities, despite our bridging (literal and metaphorical) of theory and practice, as such "indeterminate zones of practice" are "central to professional practice" (Schön 1987, 6–7).

A generative teamwork process supports such *synergy*, wherein members produce, through their shared efforts, a total effect that is greater than the sum (result or outcome) of their separate efforts (Mullen and Lick 1999). Of course the challenge becomes not how to create such workshops within the university or school setting so much as how to extend the feeling of synergy generated to benefit others. This creative group process has the potential to be a powerful learning tool for many educators and administrators. As such, the partnership model that fosters positive synergy is an example of benevolence.

SEEING WITH BINOCULAR VISION

Because it affords them "magnifying power," some hikers use binoculars on walking tours (Logue 2000). Binoculars have two glass lenses contained by a frame. But for the purposes of this experiment, first picture two lenses, one called "theory" and the other "practice," neither contained by a frame. Look through each lens separately, concentrate for a few minutes, and then jot down what you have observed. For example, I imagined moral leadership (e.g., Sergiovanni 1992) for the *T* lens, and for the *P* lens I recalled a grave but hopeful situation involving a low-performing school in Alabama that developed support systems for the children through a whole community effort (Mullen and Patrick 2000).

Now place the two lenses side by side. Notice the gap between your *T* and *P* lenses, obviously lacking a fundamental and intrinsic relationship

Figure 2.2.   Theory–Practice Integration as Binocular Vision
Source: Carol Mullen and William Kealy

to one another. How might we approach or overcome this "gap"? How can the two paradigms—theory and practice—be reconciled? Let us change our viewing angles.

Next, imagine fitting the same two lenses into a set of binoculars, having labeled them *T* and *P* accordingly. Or, better yet, try this test with a pair of binoculars, placing small sticky notes, one cut into a *T* shape and the other a *P*, directly onto each lens.

My own results underscored the following three observations: (1) The eyeglasses or lenses function optically and optimally when part of a larger system; (2) the two encased lenses (not those from the smaller side your nose sits on, but the larger end) suddenly converge into one—it is as though one is peering through a *single lens* as distant objects become instantly larger, and (3) the pasted *T* and *P* disappear as though they never existed—not a rudimentary trace of them is detectable, an instantaneous effect of the magnification.

What might we infer from this experiment? As one possibility, because the two eyepieces of the optical instrument are functionally connected as part of a larger system, the *binocular* system is conceptually integrated. Similarly, the "lenses," or theory and practice constructs (*T* and *P*, respectively), are functionally and conceptually an integrated part of a whole. For our purposes, the binocular system is, symbolically, the administrative leadership field wherein theory and practice already naturally occur. It is the quality of thoughtfulness and experience involving how we construct these "lenses" that is the issue.

When theory and practice are integrated, we may not consciously attend to this mutuality or coexistence, in much the same way that visionary convergence occurs unthinkingly when we peer through a set of binoculars. Yet, the lenses of theory and practice offer far less value individually than together. As part of a larger apparatus or system, one synergistically supports the other. However, while glass lenses enhance vision, the process of seeing is not objective, in that "seeing" is inseparable from the observer's frame of reference, including one's belief systems, values, and cultural experiences, as well as interpretations of ideas and events. While there is the possibility of a "singular lens" that connects otherwise disassociated lenses, this does *not* imply that a single understanding of a situation therefore follows or that objectivity guides vision for the observer by copying reality.

CONCEPTUALIZING BINOCULAR SCHISMS

Binoculars enable us to take advantage of our innate binocular vision. As cognitive scientist Hoffman (1998) writes, we all have the extraordinary gift, quite naturally, of visual intelligence that is put to the test in countless ways from birth and in everyday living. Within any professional domain, theory and practice are pervasive constructs. These entities or paradigms cannot be separated from the professional domain any more than the bee from the flower. If you take one away from the other, neither can perform its essential function.

Because metaphors and analogies are a good way to explain complicated concepts or key issues, let us stay with the flowers and bees. Without theory, we have no practice and, without practice, we have no theory. Consider what it is that fertilizes the flower—the bee. Similarly, practice nourishes theory by providing us with experiential knowledge from which we can see ideas, taxonomies, constructs, logical relationships, possibilities, and connections. Conversely, without flowers, there are no bees. Remove theory, and practice itself would become random acts lacking meaning and coherence. Individuals would operate on the basis of chance, bereft of guiding principles and vision.

To illustrate with a school-based scenario: A revolutionary reform that has been transforming education for the better in the United States is the New Millennium High School program in Florida, and, more broadly, the career academy school movement. In this program, secondary schools strive to meet the increasing demands of a changing world through the integration of academic and vocational curriculum at the systems level (for a comprehensive case study exemplar, see Mullen 2002c). This practice seems to have benefited from Dewey's vision of education that promotes a "whole-school reform strategy . . . for mend[ing] the curricular schism" (as cited in Mullen with Kohan 2002, 655). However, this deeper originating source for framing integration within educational systems was not necessarily recognized at the policymaking or applied level.

This implies that, while theory and practice can be effectively integrated in real-world settings, there may be different levels of consciousness achieved in reaching this goal. But then again, sometimes theory is subconsciously applied. Judging from the actions of many seasoned administrators (e.g., Mullen with Sullivan 2002), one's decision-making practices can reflect theory that has been internalized or is subconscious, a process that philosopher Polanyi (1962) attributed to tacit knowing. Similarly, curriculum researchers Connelly and Clandinin (1985) claim that "actions are not merely performances; they are minded, knowing actions" (p. 178). In other words, school practitioners embody "practical knowing," the very tension that exists between theory and practice in education.

Indifference to the connectedness between theory and practice is to be blinded to our own capacities as a "theoretician of modes of knowing" and a "practitioner of teaching and learning" (Connelly and Clandinin 1985, 175). This attitude may only serve to reinforce the ineffectiveness that many complain about in educational administration preparation and practice. An analogy is a situation involving a person who wants to learn how to drive a vehicle. Certain principles need to be understood and applied in real time in order to perform this task well, even though the tendency may be to just step on the gas. Theory may be seen as an impediment that serves only to keep trainers (i.e., researchers or practitioners) employed. Similarly, novices to school administration (or, conversely, educational research) may think that knowledge unnecessarily delays getting one's hands "on the steering wheel."

Practice at practicing (English 2003c) is equivalent to spinning one's wheels without a sense of direction. The novice trekker may believe that hiking only involves putting on one's boots and getting on the trail, without learning the "hard skills"—terrain navigation, equipment needs, camping techniques—and the "soft skills"—human caring, decision making, and conflict resolution—both critical aspects of the climb (Kosseff 2003). Some individuals must get lost, or even injured, before they realize the value of prior theory, conditioning, and training.

The perception of a "theory/practice gap" in our educational profession, then, held by many to be natural or inevitable, communicates that the objectives of research and reality are fundamentally and irreconcilably at odds. The majority of the early career participants in this study felt that their educational leadership programs had largely proven inadequate for preparing them for the reality of school administration. Their current frame of reference seems to favor school-based, practical knowing that "mirrors" reality rather than a deeper integration with theory that "constructs" reality: "My graduate program did very little in preparing me for the experience as principal," and "My degree did not prepare me! The only course I felt gave me directly applicable information was school law." Consequently, connecting theory to practice should probably be a major target for reform in graduate school education.

Read differently, my participants' concerns underscore that the theory/practice gap is being perpetuated in graduate schools. Many researchers echo the critique expressed by these novice school administrators, arguing that not only is practice missing from leadership preparation but also that theory is actually espoused at the expense of any useful application (e.g., Malone 2001). Simply put, the artificial separation of theory and practice seems to be a "fish to water" syndrome within traditional preparation programs (Murphy and Forsyth 1999). Regardless, many practitioners and scholars alike argue persistently for adequate training opportunities for aspiring principals through longer and more rigorous internships, mentoring and shadowing practical experiences, and instruction by model practitioners (Bloom and Krovetz 2001; *Effective Leaders for Today's Schools* 1999; Lumsden 1992; Mullen and Cairns 2001; Mullen et al. 2002; Schmieder, McGrevin, and Townley, 1994).

Some practitioners have even gone so far as to claim that the insufficient attention paid to practical knowing and relevance within university programs is not only unrealistic but dangerous when it comes to school emergencies, especially those inciting violence (e.g., Llewellyn 2004; Mullen and Cairns 2001). School crisis management planning can foster the integration of theory and practice by aligning terrorism preparedness with diversity awareness training through studies of different cultures (Mullen 2004). If university-based principalship programs are to increase student satisfaction and survive mounting competition (Orozco 2003; Creighton 2003), the normative view is that hands-on, problem-solving experiences must address the actual needs of schools (e.g., Hopkins 2000). However, missing from this particular worldview is the integrative role of theory.

McCarthy and Kuh (1997) propose that educational leadership programs have yet to effectively combine "leadership theory, education research, and craft knowledge" (p. 262). This implies that neither theory nor practice is being well handled within the principalship program culture, let alone effectively incorporated. Perhaps leadership preparation programs have either unsuccessfully integrated practice, or the *P* lens through which theory is being introduced is being misunderstood or possibly de-valued.

In educational administration, the theory/practice gap, asserts English (2003c), will remain "a permanent fixture of the landscape because it is embedded in the way we construct theories for use" (p. 228). He believes that the problem is not that we need more practice, notably, fieldwork and internships, in our educational leadership programs but, rather, that we need to produce "different and better theories which predict the effects of practice" (p. 228). This perspective is contradictory to the pervasive crit-icisms previously discussed. Very few of the beginning administrators in my study expressed a constructivist view of the theory/practice issue. But someone did state: "Just like in teaching, the theory taught doesn't always mirror the real-life experience. You can't always teach the good judgment needed in crisis situations and everyday problem solving but we can do a better job of guessing what this might look like." In other words, we will need to rise to the occasion of creating and recreating the relationship be-tween theory and practice, and through this process test the possibilities and limitations of knowledge.

The theory/practice gap is deeply reflected, I believe, in the conceptual schisms that, John Dewey long ago warned, haunt education at its root. The "legacy of dualisms," alive in university and school systems, contin-ues to be perpetuated by how our practices are organized into knowing and doing—as in academic and vocational tracking. Educational institu-tions are entrenched at all levels in such fragmentations of theory and practice (Mullen with Kohan 2002; see also Schön 1987). However, ho-listic models of education such as that promoted by the career academy school movement signal hope and renewal (Mullen 2002c; Mullen with Sullivan 2002).

EXERCISING BINOCULAR VISION, BODHISATTVA-STYLE

The Sherpa guide is a knowing porter or, in more majestic terms, a bod-hisattva. In Tibet, this is a benevolent person who declines Nirvana to mortally assist others in achieving enlightenment. Even the experienced mountaineer Sir Edmund Hillary had a Sherpa companion (Jones 2003), which means that any of us at any time may choose to lead or be led. This also means that in climbing a mountain the effort is not to "conquer" it but to develop the capacity for reflection that brings into conscious awareness the quality of experience and relationships we have with others, the environment, and ourselves. This may help explain why the Tibetans call the Nepal–Tibet mountain "Chomolungma," which means "Goddess Mother of the Earth."

The novice practicing school leader has been selected as our guide—to serve as the preservice administrator's Sherpa trail guide. Although the depth of insight and explanatory power of each individual novice leader varies, just as it did for the research participants, as a collective force the visionary strength of this trailblazing novice shows promise. Just as our Sherpa guide will prove invaluable for helping us to adjust our own lenses (i.e., biases, assumptions, and entrenched habits) at the individual and programmatic level, so too will analysis and review play a role in elaborating or challenging our guide's ideas.

In the real world of trekking, the Sherpa steers the trekker to follow well-marked trails where possible and to forge new paths. Our Sherpa guide (e.g., mentor principal) can also assist with the act of reflecting itself. Reflection is necessary while engaged in activity and on that which has been performed; otherwise the novice trekker can get lost in daily minutiae, failing to recognize patterns in the work and landscape itself, and within people's behaviors (Kosseff 2003; Mullen et al. 2002). Similarly, the new practicing leader will need to exercise what Schön (1987) calls "knowing-in-*practice*" where activities and types of situations within institutional settings are organized into a professional body of knowledge (p. 33). The process of "knowing-in-*practice*" can form a theoretical backing for the expert novice, one that is constructivist and thereby authentic to one's experience.

In other words, while *doing* seems to fill the gap in the education of the new administrator, the issue of *knowing* will drive the impulse to organize activity into theory and within a body of knowledge. It does not mean that the summit is being climbed just because one is very busy or that much has been accomplished in any given day, week, or month. (Similarly, "busy work" will not amount to much in graduate school without a program that scaffolds the learning, integrating the theory and the practice.) Consequently, beginning leaders who are reflective practitioners will be faced with the dual challenge of "fostering forward movement (vision) while coping with day-to-day realities that promote both school improvement and school management" (Mullen et al. 2002, 160).

As backpacking expert Logue (2000) says, it is not just a matter of reaching the top, but how we get there that matters. Kosseff (2003) adds that helping others reach their summits determines the success of our own rise. For school leaders, one's ascent entails fostering the growth and assistance of teachers, students, and other stakeholder groups. The essential capacity for leadership that concerns "what is best for children/youth" should influence decision making at the school level as well as professional preparation at the university level (Mullen et al. 2002, 160). Beginning school leaders are seen in this book as *emergent* guides because they can feel "in the dark" about the deeper call of this mission. Yet, they are expected to accomplish an ascension each year, and with responsibility for maintaining the welfare of an entire "village." Consequently, those anticipating the job or who are new to it often feel ill trained for leading their school-communities.

Regardless of the caveats on their capacity as role models, there are at least four compelling reasons why the *beginning professional* has been selected to be our guide. First, the fresh viewpoints of newcomers in any field can offer highly valuable information for assisting new inductees. Generally speaking, however, "The socialization literature tends to emphasize uniformity of socialization . . . [and] ignore . . . the smaller group or subculture contexts that influence socialization processes" (Crow and Matthews 1998, 31). In other words, beginning administrators have a particular subculture and specific understandings of their own socialization and learning. This subculture needs to be recognized and studied, with implications for the improvement of preservice graduate education.

For this book I have sought insight into this somewhat invisible yet crucial substratum of socialization while emphasizing that any understandings developed cannot be overly generalized. As the focus group participants who contributed made resoundingly clear, what may seem important to know as a new school leader at one level (i.e., elementary, middle, and secondary) and within one context does not necessarily hold across all levels and contexts (e.g., urban, suburban, and rural). (See chapter 5 for an elaboration on the value of context.)

Consider, for example, the following exchange between two beginning school leaders in response to an item on my Early Career Administrator

Survey. It conveys the value of context through a scenario focused on assisting teachers with instructional planning:

> "What is really important to me on this survey is 'assisting teachers with instructional plans.' I gave it a '5' because I've walked into so many elementary teachers' classrooms and found no plans and that they would get in front of students unprepared. And when there is a sub-teacher, no plans have been left. Also, I have seen teachers who have problems managing their classrooms because they run out of things to do. Kids get bored; you can't just pull out a worksheet. When I make sure that teachers have a plan to follow on a daily basis, things work out fine. They can use the guide the next time for that lesson. This process helps the teacher become a better instructor, which is important."

> "Yes, but that's another difference between elementary and secondary schools because I'll show you plans that are down to the minute. I tell you when I taught high school, I did my plans at the end of the year—most of us did."

A second reason for the selection of our guide is that the transitional stage of entry into beginning school administration, which extends through the first three years on the job, offers a veritable forest for discovery about the complex life of leadership. The survivor of this phase can serve as a model for the aspirant whose ability to adapt to context will be put to the test.

A third reason is that the beginner's entrance itself into the field demonstrates success to the aspirant, showing that leadership is indeed possible. This bigger point seems to be communicated even though the new leader is under great stress to achieve and impress his or her co-leaders and faculty. The aspiring party relates synergistically to those living the very lessons being shared, those for whom the sweat of living on the trail is readily apparent rather than recollected. Storytelling and advice also aid aspirants who believe they can better prepare for their school leadership careers by following those immediately ahead on the same rocky footpath.

And a fourth reason concerns the *comentoring* or collaborative structure of learning, which suggests that individuals who relate well to others are more successful. This form of partnership can be extended to a group context. School practitioner teams that exhibit a range in learning expertise can exceed what an individual or pair can accomplish through shared purpose and commitment (e.g., Mullen and Lick 1999). Similarly, the cumulative effect of the feedback from the research population (practicing novice school leaders) also offers rich insight.

As many of us know, in practice in the school, the beginning administrator may not be seen as anything close to a Sherpa guide and may not even have access to a mentor. We will try to compensate for these realities by hiking together across the Himalayas of school leadership with experienced porters—practitioners, professors, and researchers—who will expand our capacities for binocular vision or global perspective.

Administrator candidates will receive some guidance from this trekking team but will also be called upon to interpret the journey for themselves. Reflection and pattern-making are the key! Be prepared to assemble your own backpack, decipher guidebooks and signposts along marked trails, document your journey, and use your ingenuity for survival and growth. There is no tool or person who will simply show you the way, as the journey is yours to take and, besides, "following a compass bearing is made difficult by the obstacles that block walking along a straight line over rugged terrain" (Logue 2000, 230).

The emergent role model is a figure that I have created through a social science inquiry process. Actualized from multiple data, our novice Sherpa guide will reveal some of the most salient aspects of administration in elementary, middle, and secondary schools. As the writer, I also play the roles of climbing partner, "conduit," and interpreter through which more than a hundred beginning assistant principals and principals from Florida speak, sometimes in their curricular and disciplinary roles.

RESTING, BEFORE FORGING AHEAD

Before proceeding, it is worth re-stating that your visual ability to interact with this text, according to Hoffman (1998), is innately powerful. I feel that I can count on your creative capacity to relate to the trekking metaphor as we go, developing it in your own terms and to suit your personal objectives. Your translation of the mountaineering metaphor—Sherpa guides, hiking trails, climbing scaffolds, and slippery footholds—could significantly contribute to your understanding and practice of leadership.

As you turn your binoculars toward the school and university landscapes that follow, you may also learn some new ideas and techniques for exercising your visionary powers or those of others. In this chapter, notably, we learned about the theory and practice of educational leadership and how these constructs can become powerfully connected in new ways for informing our thoughts and actions.

POSTSCRIPT

The visual acronym *backpacking* appearing at the outset of this chapter is being "unpacked" throughout the book—the key words embedded within it (e.g., imagineering) will be defined in context. This tool was inspired by Mount Everest climber–author–motivational speaker John Amatt's (2000) *adventure* acronym (Amatt 2000).

Additional specialized terms for this book appear in the School Leadership Expedition Glossary (see appendix A).

Chapter Three

Orientations: Charting the Course at Base Camp

Self-awareness is critically important for you as a leader because people may sign on to follow you through stormy seas, over desiccated deserts, or up to extremes of altitude. Effective outdoor leadership is built on a foundation of self-awareness.

—A. Kosseff

The reflective time we spend at "base camp," whether in the world of mountain climbing, school leadership, or educational research, helps us better understand the deeper orientations that influence the course ahead. In chapter 2, the theory/practice gap that characterizes educational administration and its perennial challenges put this journey into perspective. In this chapter, I describe three orientations of my own combined with those of other scholar-practitioners that have influenced the values and assumptions, and lenses and possibilities, of this book: *imagineering the new school leader as expert novice; constructing the beginning school leader's voice;* and *identifying socializing influences of administrator inductees.*

IMAGINEERING THE NEW SCHOOL LEADER AS EXPERT NOVICE

To *imagineer* is to imagine (or dream) and simultaneously engineer (or design) something new or familiar from a different angle. One example is the somewhat radical notion of regarding beginning school leaders as expert

26

novices and their developmental learning processes as integral to the educational leadership field. Broadly speaking, the process of *imagineering* is the art or science of creating practical applications using a combination of imagination and knowledge (O'Callaghan 1999; see also LeBoeuf 1980).

Toward this end, *expert novice* may seem oxymoronic. However, the great potential for this construct, borrowed from cognitive psychology (e.g., Bereiter and Scardamalia 1993), is its value as an alternative and empowering lens for school leadership. New school administrators are often immediately expected to lead as experts, with the skillful grace and know-how of champion climbers. This probably has something to do with the fact that they have recently graduated from a university administration program and are presumed to have the "latest" training. It looks, however, that for administrators "on the job" training is what matters to leadership success—a perennial issue. Consequently, even the most talented beginning imagineers will need time, resources, and assistance as they apply their impressive knowledge-building capacities to complex problems and decisions. As one participant who completed a survey for my study commented, "This year has been a challenge because the need to strive for perfection in every area is overwhelming."

In contrast, experts in any profession have already developed the adaptive strategies necessary for accomplishing something against all odds (Bereiter and Scardamalia 1993; see also, Kosseff 2003). Often taking the form of groups that combine expert and novice professionals, persevering leadership teams forge new pathways by creating a shared vision that mobilizes change of the sociocultural context itself (Mullen and Lick 1999). Faculty-administration teams have, for example, created family intervention programs that address the needs of homeless minority students living within disadvantaged communities and the resiliency of the school culture (Mullen and Patrick 2000). Expertise can come in many brands and can take forms that are social, cultural, and political, not just managerial or technical.

One cannot overlook the fact that novice professionals who are on "an expert track of development" have to continually strive "against the limits of their competence" (Bereiter and Scardamalia 1993, 175). For beginning administrators of schools, this means that the formal training they receive could assist or hinder their "climb." Lumsden (1992) implies that even the keenest of their aspiring colleagues in graduate training programs will probably have to struggle all the way to the top: "As practicing administrators will attest, the match between formal pre-service training and the actual demands inherent in being a principal is not a particularly good one" (para. 1). Again, we see a need for "on the job" training in graduate school.

But there is much that formal programs can do differently to better prepare future trekkers for the long distances they will no doubt travel on the path to proficiency. In the parallel world of outdoor sports, avid backpacker-educator Kosseff (2003) emphasizes that one must put in "hundreds of days of practice" before assuming the role of leader and much more time developing and refining the necessary expertise (p. 54). Time is necessary not only for learning but also for applying the relevant concepts and skills, reflecting on the effects, and making constant adjustments to one's practice.

Paradoxically, beginning administrators—overwhelmed with the quality of work expected for even an adequate performance—are, to varying degrees, experts and nonexperts at learning. In their first few days, months, and years on the job, any assistant principal's or principal's level of expertise will be affected by the phase of adjustment itself, which is why the term *early career administration* has validity even though practitioners' expertise probably varies dramatically. One respondent to my survey claimed to have barely survived the first day as an assistant principal, which underscores the issue of adjustment itself: "My first day I was shocked at how busy I was and how little time I had to make decisions. I dealt with a range of duties from buses to hall to lunch, and to bus duty again, and then with discipline issues and teacher concerns in between." Whew.

Notably, to smoothly navigate leadership's rough terrain, one must have progressively complex problem-solving skills and the ability to approach difficult situations as matters that will not readily conform to a fixed set of rules. A successful administrator has the ability not only to multi-task but to interpret situations. As Bailin (1988) asserts, critical thinkers "go beyond the confines of the given information, supplying imaginative constructs" instead of simply "pass[ing] definitive judgment on isolated arguments, actions or pieces of information according to clearly-defined criteria and using specifiable techniques" (pp. 124–25).

In contrast, "nonexpert learners" treat information as disparate tasks to be performed, failing to make meaningful connections as critical thinkers would. And they tend to feel disoriented when learning something new or transferring what has already been learned to a new skill, concept, or situation (Bereiter and Scardamalia 1993). Not surprisingly, they may seem "scattered" and their mentoring efforts disorganized and ineffectual. A theory-organizational base would help this transformation.

Expert novices, on the other hand, can integrate new information in ways that are not merely analytic but also constructive (Bailin 1988). They have the ability to take the next step in developing vision at the personal or institutional level, and in contributing to their own deeper programs of learning. In essence, these individuals demonstrate what has been called "expertise in learning" (Bereiter and Scardamalia 1993, 179), defying cultural stereotypes of "novice" and "expert."

Despite this description, there is no easy way to identify the *expert learner-novice* in any institutional place. This individual's capacity for demonstrating expertise in learning cannot be neatly correlated with the amount of time put into the job, with having satisfied any particular credentialing or professional development requirements, or with having met any other institutional or technical criteria.

In Schön's (1987) worldview, the expert novice would probably exhibit "knowing-in-*practice*." As chapter 2 describes, this process occurs as the individual conceptually organizes activities and practices into units and types within a professional knowledge system. An example of an expert learner-novice whom I know is Thomas Graves. In his first two years of the principalship, he led a middle school in Florida through a series of significant cultural changes that birthed a new vision of school improvement that researchers identify as *democratic accountability* (Mullen and Graves 2000). Another whose transformative work I have studied is Elaine Sullivan, who used a whole-school reform strategy with her administration-faculty team to turn their Florida site into a New Millennium High School. This career academy model enabled academic study and vocational training for every learner, which led to increased academic achievement and expanded life options for students (Mullen with Sullivan 2002).

CONSTRUCTING THE BEGINNING SCHOOL LEADER'S VOICE

We need to hear what practicing novice leaders have to say. Hearing them is a process fundamental to "imagineering" beginners as expert novices in

Florida's schools and elsewhere. And we must strive to represent their assessments, ideas, and practices in educational leadership and policy circles. We should especially extend opportunities for school leaders to be
heard when policy on all pertinent matters is being created and changes
formulated, especially given the perception that the solution to educational improvement lies with teachers and schools (Scott and Dinham
2002). More attention in general should focus on the role of exemplary
school leaders as state and national figures; they have informed opinions
about issues ranging from professional teaching standards to the high-
stakes testing of students. The educational movement in North America
continues to be in an early evolutionary phase when it comes to reform activism and honoring practitioners in a leading role as knowledge sources,
policy advisors, and change agents (e.g., Mullen 1999, 2002a, 2002d;
Scott & Dinham 2002).

Few studies reveal what new administrative leaders are actually doing
in their jobs, how they are adjusting, and what insights they could share
with aspirants (exceptions include Oliver 2003 and Rallis and Goldring
2000). Instead, trends in the leadership literature highlight strategies for
effective leadership, most often in the form of advice from former principals (e.g., Schmidt 2002; Schumaker and Sommers 2001). When researchers impart the thoughts and actions of early career leaders without
representing their "voices," a credibility problem results. (To a lesser degree, this claim can also be made about experienced school leaders who
overlook the value of what their novice counterparts offer.) In terms of research, when a theory builds upon an existing body of literature without
field-based study, the problem is compounded. One solution is to rebuild
knowledge from the inside out, placing at the forefront practicing school
leaders and their ideas, as I have attempted to do. Insight and advice from
new leaders are offered in this text, but uncertainty will also prevail, as the
perspectives are not simplified or homogeneous. Hearing the "authentic
voices" of administrators may be an important first.

Empirical case study is one method that can be used for constructing
the knowledge, experience, perspective, voice, and authority of new leaders. Leadership surveys, combined with focus groups that bring together
elementary, middle, and secondary level administrators in their early
years, provide a means for accessing this population. Comprehensive efforts at formulating networks of beginning school leaders combined with

deep approaches to conversation and analysis can help us to learn more about critical educational issues, including school leaders' adjustment in the workplace.

On the one hand, war stories and how-to handbooks dilute the voices of novice practicing leaders, offering only surface perspectives that have not helped the credibility of university preparation programs and the educational leadership field itself. On the other hand, existing research on the new school leader tends to subsume the issue of voice in favor of such abstract concepts as socialization and problem solving. While case studies provide an alternative, these rarely go beyond a single person or group, are often limited to site comparisons, and sometimes have even been fictionalized to make a point. Mayer, Mullens, and Moore (2000) add that it becomes difficult to monitor school quality given that "most of our understanding about school leadership comes from case studies that can only suggest what might be true in a broader application" (p. 38). If researchers were to build their orientations using comprehensive methods of analysis that promote the administrator's perspective on the critical areas of leadership, knowledge of the principalship could be enhanced, and even perhaps achieve the authority that has been missing for many school personnel. Toward this visionary goal, this book takes a step.

Concerning our focus here, in some case studies the *voices of leaders* are present, but not always, and often at a surface level. The objective for most case writers is to depict complex dilemmas in education and society that readers can respond to by generating possible solutions and keeping these open (Merriam 1998). Problem-solving skills need immediate work in graduate programs and at school sites. The aspiring administrator is not necessarily developing knowing-in-*practice* or even actively tackling issues in education. However, if he or she does, different ways of thinking about problems can be pursued and the various options available for resolving them internalized. The university educator who works with groups of future administrators in these constructivist problem-solving ways will probably capitalize upon their voices.

"Voice" per se is not an explicit issue in the case literature, but various creative scholarly techniques (e.g., direct quotation, paraphrase, anecdote, practitioner writing, and even coauthored publication with participants) have been used to bring integrity to an issue (see, e.g., *Journal of Cases in Educational Leadership*; Mullen and Lick 1999). The voices can then be generalized, albeit cautiously, over a large population. Research that is permeated with the voice of practicing leaders can in turn "give" voice to aspirants, with the effects of encouraging deeper reflection and discourse on relevant issues, bringing theory and practice close together, and de-centralizing the dominating power of universities, policy boards, legislative bodies, and school districts. Fullan's (1999) definition of hope would probably encompass such processes of change.

Ann Lieberman's challenge to become more inclusive by incorporating the issues and voices of school practitioners in our studies (as cited in Glaser, Lieberman, and Anderson 1997) urges researchers to go to the source, as I have done. Qualitative research on school administration practice that captures practitioner knowledge and actions in context-specific ways may be a wave of the future (e.g., Labaree 2003; Mullen 2000; Schechter 2002). As Lincoln (1997) asserts, the process of constructing the voices of participants in research requires that a transformation in the university researcher's own identity occur. As part of a deeper gestalt, "We will have to find ourselves and our voices, since breaking out of our scholarly 'native languages' and learning new ones to match our new commitments will not be easy" (p. 42).

The solution of "giving voice" to practitioners is an antidote to external forces that Sarason (1993) says work *on* instead of *with* schools. One consequence of being worked *on* is that newly practicing administrators have not traditionally had the opportunity individually or as a professional group to publicly represent their own issues and perspectives. How can we better represent the critical aspects of the school administration profession than by *going to the source* itself and to seeing through the transitional leaders' eyes?

Climbing the Himalayas of School Leadership has emerged out of an empowering and authentic epistemology by having directly gone to the source and theorized about why this is important to do. My study used a variety of methods to uncover insights about the early years—written and oral feedback, storytelling, and focused commentary. Support for constructing the beginning practicing leaders' voices has also come from three areas—the data collected from new administrators, the literature on educational leadership and administration, and my experience teaching in an educational leadership and policy studies program.

IDENTIFYING SOCIALIZING INFLUENCES
OF ADMINISTRATOR INDUCTEES

Socialization is defined as "the process by which an individual selectively acquires the knowledge, skills, and dispositions needed to perform adequately a social role (in this case the school principalship)" (Parkay and Hall 1992, 286). This presents a paradox: formal, standardized degree programs are the primary means of socialization for principals (Begley and Campbell-Evans 1992; Mullen and Cairns 2001), yet these do not seem to meet current needs for a changing repertoire of school leadership. And if a principal or assistant principal is unwilling to help the "novice," socialization is stunted. With the expanding diversity of students, teachers, and school leaders, traditional leadership programs are likely to meet fewer and fewer needs of future leaders (Begley and Campbell-Evans 1992).

Schmieder, McGrevin, and Townley's (1994) survey-based study of 450 principals and superintendents found socialization to be critical to the preparation of school leaders. There is some evidence that *organizational socialization* (the learning a principal experiences in a new job) has a greater influence on the development of new administrators than *formal socialization* (university degree programs and training situations), and in fact moderates the effects of previous learning (Heck 1995). In addition, previous job experience and even established colleagues apparently provide less support than expected in socializing beginning leaders in a new job, partly due to role conflict (Adkins 1990), lack of reward, and differences in power, status, and function.

This indicates that professional socialization at the new school site is the most important stage of principal socialization, and yet graduate degree programs and familiar support systems tend to provide inadequate support for the new principal. Certainly this contributes to feelings of isolation and powerlessness reported by assistant principals and principals alike (Cantwell 1993), especially women and minority leaders (Hart 1991; Parkay and Hall 1992). Constraints of formal socialization programs include a tendency to reproduce leadership styles, suppress innovation, and promulgate a custodial orientation in the new inductee (Cantwell 1993; Crow and Glascock 1995; Hart 1991; Schein 1985).

Although not much has been reported on informal socialization processes, there is congruence in the literature on its ubiquity and alleged importance and efficacy (Goldring and Rallis 1993; Hart and Bredeson 1996; Heck 1995; Marshall 1985; Nalls 1994; Parkay and Hall 1992). Schein (1985) asserts that informal teaching and coaching mechanisms are more powerful than formal. The socialization of school administrators, characterized as a "sink or swim" experience for many, has been further construed as not only informal but random as well (Greenfield 1985).

Duke, Isaacson, Sagor, and Schmuck (1984) suggest that professional socialization includes a transitional period of about one year. Some of my survey respondents validated this perspective: "This year it was like being thrown in the deep end of a pool. I arrived and the principal left and the new principal never had been a principal." Importantly, Hart and Bredeson (1996) and Schein (1985) see cultural stories occupying a vital place in the socialization of novices. Mentor programs could thus be a means of remedying inadequate professional socialization and support, but the efficacy of these initiatives for new administrators needs further investigation (Hart and Bredeson 1996; Mullen and Cairns 2001). Some researchers suggest attenuating existing mentoring programs into ongoing professional support relationships (Daresh 2001a; Glickman, Gordon, and Ross-Gordon 1998). Another idea for reforming current formalized socialization programs is giving in-depth attention to the planning of training programs (Crow and Glascock 1995; Daresh and Playko 1992; Hart 1993; Mullen and Cairns 2001).

A U.S. national government forum on effective leadership similarly believes that aspirants need more exposure to practical leadership opportunities, including time for reflection and discussion and making research a practice domain of leadership (*Effective Leaders for Today's Schools* 1999). Hay (1995) suggests that a "developmental alliance"—"a relationship between equals" in which those involved identify alternatives, initiate action, and develop themselves—is necessary (p. 40). In this kind of alliance, the needs of the mentee take precedence over the organization, and a goal of the mentoring relationship becomes eliciting the learner's tacit knowing and building upon it.

Specific interventions for improving preparation programs and the socializing influences of new leaders inundate the literature. For example, Milstein, Bobroff, and Restine (1991) discuss how a recurrent "learning cycle" should be implemented for new inductees. A longer initiation period, they suggest, could prove beneficial for covering a range of administrative functions. Goldring and Rallis (1993) expand on this notion. To them, socialization should be a "revolving door" with multiple entry and exit points over time, providing ongoing professional development and renewal. This tends to be how teacher preparation works, so why should it not be utilized for administrators?

Additionally, problem-based learning experiences for new principals, including computer simulations, have been seen as a possible solution (e.g., Lumsden 1992). Hart (1993) believes participant observation, peer coaching, and organizational analysis are all practices that expand the effectiveness of principal preparation programs. Schmieder, McGrevin, and Townley (1994) reported years ago that longer and more rigorous internships, mentoring and shadowing experiences, and instruction by practitioners are among the top changes needed for principal preparation, and many other empirical studies have since concurred (e.g., Malone 2001; Mullen and Cairns 2001). In support of these goals, Cantwell (1993) has described a beneficial intervention: The SuperCenter Model in New York featuring on-the-job mentoring, small group seminars, retreats, consultation, and networking events.

Giving urgency to all such modifications to educational leadership programs is the rapid pace of change in American society. Diversity, political climate, and external turbulence, including threats of terrorism and bioterrorism, all impact school culture (Goldring 1992; Mullen 2003a). These challenges pose novel, constantly changing issues for schools, requiring new sensitivities and orientations to leadership.

For example, one newly emerging leadership model is *transformational leadership*, an innovative approach that treats school culture as something to be built through shared decision making and collaborative problem solving (Leithwood, Jantzi, and Steinbach 1999). Similarly, *shared leadership* is administered by teachers, parents, and possibly other community personnel (Barr and Bizar 2001). Another emergent model is *environmental leadership*, which emphasizes the need for sensitivity to surrounding cultural and global events (Goldring 1992; Snyder, Acker-Hocevar, and Snyder 2000). A new branch of leadership known as *comparative educational administration* uses the concept of culture and cross-cultural analysis to promote a rigorous approach to globalization rooted in critical reflective practice (Walker and Dimmock 2002; see also Begley 2002).

Finally, a significant socializing influence that has been affecting the quality of transition for administrator inductees is the impending shortage of leaders. This mirrors the dire state of teachers, too. As the need for principals increases, this problem has inadvertently truncated or even bypassed the tenure of an assistant principal in many school systems across the United States (Bloom and Krovetz 2001). As never before, this is occurring in more and more states, giving rise to alternative, profit-making delivery systems, such as the recent National Association of Elementary School Principals' (NAESP) Nova University collaborative (Creighton 2003). These compete vigorously with university preparation programs as a new socializing vehicle for preservice administrators and teachers alike. As Linda Orozco (2003), former president of the California Association of Professors of Educational Administration, confirms, "Candidates for leadership positions can bypass comprehensive leadership preparation, and instead satisfy one of a host of alternative routes" (p. 5).

At least five alternative routes to certification of the principalship and superintendency, beyond traditional university programs, now exist: These include, with California in the lead, internships conducted by local school districts, county office preparation, and private, profit-run agencies (Creighton 2003; Orozco 2003). What this signals for some is "a departure from viewing school leadership as a profession" to "a skills-based occupation" (Orozco 2003, 5). The skills-based emphasis permeates the results from my own study of early career administrators' views of the profession. For others, such as Theodore Creighton, the 2003 Executive Director of the National Council of Professors of Educational Administration, this signals that the "university professorate" is no longer in charge of framing its own profession.

Numerous "new breeds" of high-powered Sherpa guides that offer tempting, alternative ways to get to the summit now populate the leadership mountain. These younger guides have grown strong very rapidly, bypassing our traditional Sherpas who grow weak, suffering from a declining reputation and old age. One new powerful porter—the NAESP/Nova Southeastern University (NSU) partnership—now offers two doctorates, one in Educational Leadership and another in Organizational Leadership, which will be completed online at NSU for scholarship-funded working principals (NAESP Principal Online 2003).

Just as Creighton (2003) was anticipating the reality of Internet-bound doctorates forthcoming in the leadership field, following the footsteps of

Figure 3.1.   Unexpected Avalanches Alter the Leadership Mountain
Source: Marc Shapiro

teacher education, the new NAESP/Nova program option was already under way. This underscores how quickly the established trails and weather conditions have been changing on our leadership mountain—as unexpected avalanches for the unprepared competitor.

Things are not always what they appear: Some of these young, robust porters and their alternative systems train non-educators in the role of administrative leader. This means that fully prepared, licensed candidates now compete with far less qualified individuals. In Florida, the latter may have completed "four educational leadership courses" and "pass[ed] [a] test to become an assistant principal" (Orozco 2003, 5). Twenty percent of the Florida respondents who filled out my administrator survey had not received their graduate degree as part of a traditionally recognized formal degree program (e.g., Master's degree in Educational Leadership). In such cases, the "other" category was not completed, so there is no way to determine where they completed their programs and no way to assess the quality of their advanced degrees.

A SUMMITEERING GLIMPSE

However, for a host of reasons, Orozco claims that the availability of alternative routes is not the only thing affecting the decisions of many who are fully qualified to administer but who choose to continue teaching or to pursue other professional summits altogether. Her question "*Who* shall be eligible to lead schools?" (p. 4) jolts us into recognizing that new countercultural (or nonstandard) forces are currently at work, indefinitely impacting the cultures of schools and universities. The same reaction can be attributed to Creighton's question, "Who is framing the nation's understanding of Educational Leadership and preparation?" (p. 1). There now exist many short routes to the professional summit of school leadership that will have a ripple effect beyond what can be imagined at this time.

Chapter Four

Snapshot: Research Travelogue Summary

Snapshot. A photograph taken instantaneously, with a very short exposure.

—New Webster's Dictionary and Thesaurus
of the English Language, 1993

The research travelogue snapshot provided in this chapter outlines the footsteps of my research journey and includes updates and adjustments. For an elaboration on the results, see chapter 5, "Outcomes: Topographic Research Patterns."

THE SNAPSHOT DEVELOPED

I. Preliminary Steps—Charting the Route
   A. Inspiration for study and selection of beginning school leader as Sherpa guide [For an elaboration, see preface]
   B. Literature review (completed in 2000 and updated 2002 and 2003) on school leadership and administration (specifically, early career principal socialization; school culture and work contexts; mentorship and collaboration; professional development and training; and the implications of role learning for aspiring school leaders in graduate school). Relevant web-based databases included the Educational Resources Information Center (http://www.eric.ed.gov); OCLC FirstSearch (http://www.newfirstsearch.oclc.org); Questia's online library (http://www.questia.com); and the U.S. Department of Education (http://www.ed.gov)

The Journey in a Snapshot

Select a knowing guide for inspiration (Sherpa)

Decide a research issue to investigate (route)

Design questions to study (systems for charting)

Survey parallel practitioner group (charting plans)

Analyze the data and seek patterns (research journal)

Incorporate peer assessment of data (hiking guides)

Re-analyze the data for new insight (research journal)

Share outcome with peer assessors (hiking guides)

Ponder meaning of results (mountaineering wisdom)

Figure 4.1   The Journey in a Snapshot
Source: Carol Mullen

C. Research issue: What matters most for beginning school administrators to know?
   1. *Questions to be investigated*:
      a. What are the most salient areas of administrative leadership (e.g., supervision of instruction) currently performed by beginning school leaders in Florida?
      b. How can university preparation programs be improved to better socialize aspiring school administrators for their future role?
D. Financial support secured (research grant and fellowship for research assistant)
E. Institutional review board (IRB) application approved
F. Identification of beginning school leaders (those within their first 2 years) as potential survey respondents. Consultation of the Florida Association of School Administrators' (2002) resource, *Florida Education Directory by FASA, 2002–2003 school year* (FASA).

II. Phase I: Preliminary Data Gathered on the Administrator Survey

  A. Survey designed in 2000 with focus group 1 (master's class of 10 teachers and acting administrators that confirmed the accuracy of the instrument created by the principal investigator and a teacher); it was piloted in the community by those who completed and critiqued the instrument)

   1. Piloting of survey instrument—validation received from beginning school administrators in Tampa Bay area on the administrator duty items selected, with support from empirical studies in leadership (Mullen and Cairns 2001)

   2. Improvement of the instrument based on the feedback received about the survey items and qualitative, open-response portion

III. Phase II: Survey Instrument Revised and Distributed to Schools

  A. Improved survey instrument distributed to 271 Florida schools; 91 completed surveys returned from early career administrators

   1. Numerical and qualitative data analyzed by researcher and assistant; corroboration of the results established at this level

IV. Phase III: Peer Assessor Critique Solicited through Group Participation

  A. Focus group protocol completed—questions and activities designed for facilitating validation, critique, or expansion of the study results

   1. Focus group facilitation (with focus groups 2 and 3, in 2003)

   2. Validation and critique of the survey data built into different stages of collection; process documented via audiotaping and note taking; discourse thematically analyzed for insight

V. Data Analysis—Journaling the Results

  A. Analysis of survey data conducted, framed by two research questions appearing as response items on survey's commentary section

   1. Analysis of numerical ratings from survey—section topics (e.g., school organization) and survey items (e.g., design master schedule, including specials); additional analysis of written commentary, which focused on administrator tasks performed on the job and quality of university preparation. (For the survey instrument, see appendix C, and for the numerical outcomes, see appendix D)

   2. Corroboration of survey results established independently by researcher and assistant researcher

B. Focus groups 2 and 3 conducted as strategy for validating or critiquing study process and results of survey (as well as building research skills among new administrators and prospective doctoral students)
  1. Group 2 (Hillsborough County) reviewed survey instrument, data, and analysis. Members analyzed preliminary data set based on survey results (numerical and qualitative) and provided formative evaluation of data and thematic patterns (e.g., mentoring scaffolds). (*Formative evaluation* means, using Verma and Mallick's [1999] definition, an assessment carried out in the early phase of a study for critiquing the process and implementing any changes, such as in the meanings attributed to the data)
  2. Group 3 (Pasco County) analyzed survey data and validated comments received and themes. Members reflected on the complete survey set and provided summative evaluation of data and thematic patterns (e.g., mentoring scaffolds). (By *summative evaluation*, the understanding established with the group was that the thematic patterns already developed would be reviewed to critique and enrich interpretations of the survey data)
C. Focus group data (transcription and journal entries from two different groups) analyzed and organized into thematic categories; corroboration of results established independently with assistant
D. Evaluations from focus group members on workshops (analyzed and organized into thematic categories); corroboration of results established independently with assistant
VI. Metaphoric Interpretation—Imagineering the Results
A. Re-analyze survey data (using focus group 2's insight into "timing" as variable accounting for fluctuations in administrator's most important functions in calendar year)
B. Trekking metaphor
  1. Learn about trekking and mountaineering to strengthen metaphor of summit climbing (occurred throughout study)
  2. Create parallels: Interpret data analysis (thematic categories) in context of trekking metaphor while preserving integrity of study itself (i.e., thematic analysis and participants' words)

VII. Thematic Outcomes—Exhibiting the Artifacts (see chapter 5 and part 2)
  A. Administrator survey: Core areas of leadership deemed most important due to time spent on the job and value attribution, relative to the top 20 administrator tasks performed, is as follows: supervision of instruction (60%); school organization (60%); student services (40%); community relations (30%); and school management (10%)
  B. Focus groups (transcription, note taking, and participant workshop evaluations)
    1. Focus group 2 (Hillsborough County): Useful research tools (e.g., interpreted data using mixed-methods and qualitative strategies) learned for application within school and university contexts; authenticity circle created among various school districts and across school levels (e.g., elementary, middle, and secondary); and critique of thematic (coded) analysis of preliminary survey data collected
    2. Focus group 3 (Pasco County): Use of focus group as a reflective tool for research and validation of study process and content with peer assessors (school leaders and teachers); responses on survey viewed as context-dependent, varying from one school to another and especially from one level to another, in addition to generalizable beyond single sites based on cultural patterns of structured leadership activity
  C. Thematic results (represented in part 2, "What Practicing School Leaders Have to Say about Their First Administrative Trek and Then Some"): Conditioning Preparation; Inventory Survey; Direction Indicator; Basic Know-How; Real-World Experience; Knowledge Source; Mentoring Scaffolds; Emotional Expression; Coping Skills; Accountability Climate
  D. Final check: Research outcomes and book manuscript shared with selected focus group participants to confirm resonance for reader and check accuracy of claims about school administration context relative to Florida

Chapter Five

Outcomes: Topographic Research Patterns

People who are afraid of heights need to work at this problem step by
step, day by day, climb by climb.

—Zoe Bundros

Every mountain climb requires significant exertion, including careful
step-by-step planning. When you reach the summit, you will need to ask
yourself, "*How* did I get here?" so other hikers may learn from your reflections on the journey. As applied to the process of writing this book, the
effort is manifested as successive, overlapping phases, with a few intentional changes to accommodate the unexpected, rather than straightforward, sequential steps. Several teams of trekkers contributed to this longitudinal research project along the way, and the quality of my experience
and this research story were consequently greatly enhanced. No trekker in
the academy should travel alone.

This overview documents the discoveries resulting from investigation
into what new school administrators believe they need to know and be
able to do in order to perform their role. While part 2 of this text is devoted to a detailed discussion of the results, this section provides a
macro view of them. The trail map appearing in the preface oriented the
trekker-reader visually. In mountaineering language, the following journal entry describes the broad topographic patterns or outcomes of my
book expedition.

THE JOURNEY'S OUTCOMES, FROM START TO FINISH

Annotating the Route

After the school leadership study topic and the research questions were decided upon, subsequent research mapping focused on designing the instruments (appendixes C, E, and F) and piloting the Early Career Administrator Survey (appendix C). Other steps involved collecting the data, conducting the analysis, and identifying the outcomes, or—in the metaphoric terms of trekking—gathering the rocks, journaling the observations, and exhibiting the artifacts.

Successive Phases

This longitudinal study was carried out from 2000 to 2003 in three successive phases: Preliminary Data Gathered on the Administrator Survey (Phase I); Survey Instrument Revised and Distributed to Schools (Phase II); and Peer Assessor Critique Solicited through Group Participation (Phase III). In all, 115 beginning leaders from the same number of Florida schools participated, 91 as survey respondents and 24 as focus group members.

For Phase I, a group of school practitioners (ten graduate students at the University of South Florida) participated in developing the survey and critiquing the piloted results obtained from practicing assistant principals (APs) working in the Tampa Bay area.

In Phase II, the revised version of the administrator survey was mailed (with a prepaid return envelope, Institutional Review Board (IRB) consent form, and project description) to 271 beginning administrators throughout Florida's urban and rural elementary, middle, and secondary schools. Postal service was required by the IRB regulations that, for this study, required participant signatures on the consent form.

For the discussion that followed in Phase III, two new focus groups (three for the entire study) were formed and met with the research team. Six members, primarily from Hillsborough County, critiqued and expanded upon the survey results, thereby providing a formative assessment.

A third focus group, consisting of eight members, mostly from Pasco County, also critiqued the data set but in its entirety, providing a summative assessment independently of the research team.

The orchestration of the focus groups was adjusted from the original design because it proved difficult to sustain the work of any particular team for the seven anticipated sessions. Three separate focus groups were alternatively formed, and twenty-four individuals participated, once each. Two positive offshoots occurred: (1) the time spent in focused discussion with the peer assessors (for all three phases) turned out to be twelve hours instead of the expected seven, and (2) reflective activities (individual and collective) served as an active learning tool for manifesting the expected discussion points (outlined in appendix E).

Mixed Methods

The information provided in this book (especially part 2) should prove empirically and experientially relevant because it was obtained by mixed methods. I drew upon both quantitative and qualitative strategies to formulate the research design and develop the thematic results. In other words, this text and its results were not informed strictly on the basis of numbers (survey instrument) or stories (discussion group), but rather through a synthesis of both. My own experiences and orientations as an educator have also been incorporated where relevant to beginning administrative leadership.

For analysis purposes, the research assistants were trained to use qualitative methods for coding the transcript data and tracking the numerical information in table form. With two doctoral researchers, one in Phase I and another in Phase III, I independently coded all of the data so that I could monitor my own analysis and results for utility in educational leadership. Because it was important that the analysis be credible, objective, and thorough, we each applied established coding procedures (Miles and Huberman 1994) in addition to Merriam's (1998) data analysis process for blending common ideas into themes. Thematic patterns emerged, and the data were color-coded for the researchers' ease of comparison and for sharing with Phase III discussion participants. The patterns we constructed evolved from the identification of key words and phases within "chunks" of information (on the commentary section of the survey, the transcriptions of dialogue from the focus groups, and the participant workshop evaluations).

Field-Based

The data collected were field-based, focused on the views of practicing school leaders themselves as opposed to a more distant party, such as practicing superintendents, who would have to infer the knowledge and skills necessary for aspiring leaders to perform leadership roles.

Consensus-Building

A further point of substantiation is that the perspectives on the data were developed through a consensus-building, validation process not only by the principal investigator and author—myself—but also by two teacher leaders and three focus groups over a three-year period. The outcomes, formative for Phases I and II, and summative in Phase III, were developed, refined, and confirmed through ongoing and reflective analysis with various practitioner-based focus groups and partnerships. These field-based, preliminary inquiries turned into published scholarship on this study's related topics of formal administrator preparation and capacities necessary for effective leadership and school reform (Mullen and Cairns 2001; Mullen et al. 2002).

Specifically, validation was accomplished with the study participants through the processes of dialogue about and critique of the administrator instrument (appendix C), in addition to the survey response ratings (appendix D) and thematically coded data (outlined in "Thematic Outcomes," this chapter). For this purpose, the thematic patterns were derived from the survey commentary section that elicited open-ended responses. By the engagement of critical reflection with school practitioner groups that paralleled the survey respondents, validation also occurred through the process of peer assessment. Formative and summative evaluations of the preliminary and complete data sets, respectively, were thus thoroughly met.

Process-Based

The process-based planning and outcomes were geared toward soliciting feedback from a group of school practitioners that was similar to my study respondents. The objective was to obtain a comprehensive sense of whether the research process and content "rang true" for school practitioners, who constitute not only the participants of this study but also the primary audience for this book.

In the traditional approach to qualitative research, the researcher's meanings of the data and conclusions may be verified or authenticated with a sample of the study participants. In contrast, my study participants functioned as peer assessors, their feedback was built into successive phases of the research, and their critical as well as clinical understandings contributed to insights and modifications from start to finish (e.g., see "Context Matters," below).

The school leader was placed at the center of this journey, then, as a Sherpa guide in the form of inspirational source, survey participant, peer assessor, clinician, and critic. Perhaps for this reason, the focus groups developed into authenticity circles propelled by active learning through which the reflective practitioner's voice was heard at all levels, beyond the survey data collected. In these ways, I was better able to bridge or integrate my own theoretical understandings as a university professor with the current practical understandings from the field.

CONTEXT MATTERS: PRACTITIONERS BRIDGE THEORY

Context is a valued lens or variable in a qualitative study; in fact, both the survey respondents and the discussion groups drew attention to this issue. This insight is consistent with increasing criticisms of educational leadership and administration. As Walker and Dimmock (2002) assert, "It is clear that a key factor missing from many debates in educational administration and leadership is context" (p. 2). English (2003c) believes that educational administration's perpetual state of "context denial" means that the "concept of human agency" has been reduced to a "knowledge base," one that reifies skills and behaviors (p. 44).

Here I examine the issue of context or particularity, which emerges as a dynamic, mediating influence of significance in the psyche of the administrator. To not report this phenomenon is to overstate the technical, organizational, and managerial sides of educational leadership that resulted from this study. This oversight would also make my results seem monolithic, when in fact there were many caveats, sidebars, fluxes, and serendipitous moves at play in the interpretation represented in this chapter and book. In other words, this study depended upon "human agency" combined with sensitivity to context as primary forces in the research, which shaped and reshaped its directions.

School Level Relevance

One salient theme emerging from the data was that the different educational levels of the school and the client base (i.e., public school student) affect the outcome of the administrator's duty. Participants reflected on this information in ways that suggested awareness to context:

> It was interesting to learn from my colleagues how our roles as administrators differ by factors such as level (e.g. primary or secondary), and geographic area.

> I noticed that the priorities we gave to the survey items differed within our group, depending on the level of school in which we administer. We all had our own ideas about certain data (i.e., which administrative duties were more important in an elementary school versus a high school) based on the situations in our own schools. We all backed up our opinions with concrete examples.

Contextual Responses to the Survey

Context is pivotal in understanding the situation that administrators encounter and experience, a sentiment many of my respondents expressed. To this effect, a new school leader wrote in the open-response section, "My answers on your survey are dependent upon my particular needs for this particular school." An assistant principal for curriculum shared this thoughtful reflection that united the practice of school leadership with the preparation for the role, "While it's very important for administrators to review and enforce the curriculum, I don't think it is *that* important for leadership students to learn because the curriculum is so varied depending on the school site."

The issue of context was evident even in terms of how the survey itself could be interpreted and rated. Accordingly, three survey recipients phoned the researchers and asked, "Do you want me to rate the survey items in terms of what I think is important or what I do that's important?" They had experienced this uncertainty despite the instruction—"rate each item . . . that best represents the nature of the work and tasks you perform as a beginning school administrator." The instructions did not ask them to rate in terms of what they *thought* was most important but what they themselves *actually* perform. However, they wanted to be certain to fill out the instrument as intended so that the research results would prove helpful to educational leadership practices and programs (Mullen 2003b). Perhaps ambiguity was unavoidable in this situation, even where the written instructions had been explicit, especially as the broader context and goal of the study had also been stated in the instructions: "Hopefully a picture will emerge from the survey data that answers [the] pertinent question . . . what matters most for Florida's school administrators to know? What's least important and what's most important?" It may have been better to separate this larger picture from the instructions on the survey to minimize confusion.

On a different matter relating to the context, the issue of differentiation in the leader tasks carried out by beginning assistant principals and principals is noteworthy. According to Oliver's (2003) 2000–2002 survey-based study of the entry-level assistant principalship in Orange County, California, a difference in responsibilities and, implicitly, status is evident: The school principal generally focuses on "leadership activities associated with instruction and programs," while the assistant principal is allocated "management oriented tasks" (p. 38). A major implication of Oliver's research is that the new assistant principal's development (and prestige) could be enhanced by a better balance between instructional and administrative duties.

Although in my study this categorical breakdown, though apparent, was less prominent, it supports Oliver's recommendation that schools must be vigilant about designing and extending mentoring opportunities for administrator apprentices. The assistant principals I surveyed, like the principals, attributed high value to the instructional leadership domain overall. However, the ratings received on the leader tasks within this area varied somewhat from that of the vice principals, who ascribed a lower overall score to the following instructional duties: "assist teachers with instructional plans"; "interpret test results for teachers"; "develop instructional guides/resource materials"; "observe levels of questions used in instruction"; and, most clearly, "develop a monthly bulletin, spotlighting effective teaching." In fact, a sporadic pattern was evident among these particular leader tasks at the beginning assistant principalship level.

However, this does not imply that they valued these tasks any less than their principal counterparts or held them in less regard. As strong possibilities, it may be that the assistant principals have not yet carried out the particular duties listed and therefore have less of a "feel" for their relative importance or that the duties of the assistant principalship are themselves hierarchically separated. Some of the assistant principals' comments on the survey hint at this reality, as revealed by this remark: "For the first two years I dealt with discipline nearly all day. This year we have a dean who handles discipline. I now have time to observe and help teachers grow." The assistant principals of discipline in Florida are not given much exposure to the instructional domain, as someone else clearly explained:

> Although a great majority of the items listed in your survey are vitally important, my district provides each middle school with an assistant principal of discipline and an assistant principal of curriculum. Therefore, those tasks related to curriculum are of most importance to me because I am responsible for them, but my colleague who is accountable for discipline matters gets no experience at all.

Timing and School Cycles

Differences in survey ratings were apparent over the course of the study. Several survey items (e.g., "assist in interviewing and hiring potential faculty and staff") organized under the various topic sections (e.g., supervision of instruction) had varied in participant response—two quite significantly. During Phases II and III, which lasted from January until May 2003, the response ratings for certain survey items escalated and de-escalated. For the purpose of brevity, this discussion will be limited to the status change of two particular items in terms of their relative importance in the administrators' minds and within the "big picture." They illustrate how opinions change over the course of the school year.

First, as critical background information, the focus group that met in June 2003 observed the possibility of fluctuations in survey responses over time. This cooperative learning process stimulated new insight into the meanings that could be constructed and inferred about the data. Of particular interest was that some items would likely have more or less importance depending upon the time of year the instrument is completed, as well as at what schooling level (e.g., elementary). In other words, the person filling out the survey may have been engaged in one activity of importance at the beginning of or during the academic calendar but then attended to another that emerged later.

In returning to the survey data matrix from February 2003, the researchers reviewed the listing of all the topic sections/survey items and the individual ratings. We did the same for the second matrix (dated June 2003), which contained the complete numerical information. For the first matrix, fifty individuals' responses were tracked; for the second, ninety-one. We examined the two matrixes to record any changes occurring in the "5" responses, as these denoted the "most important" tasks or responsibilities being carried out according to the administrator respondents, with implications for content focus in educational leadership programs.

From this comparison of the time-sensitive matrixes, it became apparent that the most important item (administrator task) identified on the survey had shifted. In February 2003, "design master schedule, including specials" received the highest tally on the surveys. But by June 2003 "assist in interviewing potential faculty and staff" moved into first place. This signaled no small shift but rather a complete one, away from the core leadership area—school organization—to instructional supervision as the place beginning leaders were devoting much of their time and energy.

The focus group participants from the June meeting speculated on this change: During May each year it could be expected that the hiring of new teachers and noninstructional staff was well under way within the schools. They emphasized that all administrators have a role in either recruiting new faculty members or interviewing potential hires. The prominence of this item/task is not peculiar to Florida schools, they added, as the traditional academic calendar is similar from one state to another. However, based on this reexamination of the survey data from the two matrixes, there appeared to be only two items (i.e., "design master schedule" and "interviewing and hiring of potential faculty and staff") that suffered from the time/importance effect. In fact, most of the items seemed to grow exponentially.

Considering that the surveys had been sent to beginning leaders in various Florida counties over the course of five months, it seems logical that timing was a factor in the rating of at least some of the items. This explanation leads us to consider how shared cycles and rhythms of structured human activity occur in schools (Connelly and Clandinin, 1986). From one school to another, across school districts, regions, and states, patterns of school and leadership activity connect one child to another, one teacher to another, and one administrator or school or another. Society itself adheres to "temporal symmetry as a formal pattern of organizing our lives. In other words, we have developed a tendency to do many things in our lives at the same times as everyone else" (Zerubavel 1981, 65). Schedules and calendars in school and social life have always been built upon the premise that life can be predicted and activity patterns followed.

It can also be inferred from the analysis of the survey data that two different realities may simultaneously exist for schools and those who lead them. This could account for the tension experienced by the school practitioner who feels that while his or her context has unique (or nontransferable) aspects, it also has generalizable (or transferable) elements:

> *Reality A—nontransferability*: "The idea that a beginning leader might not rate something as a priority because she personally did not have that responsibility to perform at her school was something I had not thought of until now." (April 2003, *Focus Group Participant Evaluation Form*)

> *Reality B—transferability*: "We spent a lot of time during the group discussion relating the administration duties on the survey to our own situations (elementary, middle, or high school) and to seeing that we share much in common across levels." (April 2003, *Focus Group Participant Evaluation Form*)

Inferring the Mountain

Some, despite the inherent limits on their own role or job, viewed the survey as inclusive of the work of the new school leader: "In my school I am one of two APs. I do not have some of the jobs you asked about, but these jobs are important." In addition to further validating the instrument once in the hands of the statewide respondents, this reflection is more thought-provoking than at first glance. These first-, second-, and third-year administrators see the role of school leadership unfold everyday, and those wishing to become principals sometimes accept roles and duties of the principalship that can be cited as "hands-on" experience in future interviews.

Although early career professionals can be burdened by what they do not know—analogous to failing to fully see the mountain for the trees—some can still imagine "the whole." That is, it is possible for a new leader to have knowledge of and insight into the principalship beyond his own immediate situation and particular tasks or responsibilities, as well as status. The "whole" mountain is a modernist concept anyway; no single or absolute picture of reality, truth, or life is possible or desirable, at least in the minds of postmodernists (e.g., Diamond and Mullen 1999a; English 2003c). As a related possibility, those assistant principals who administer within Florida's large school districts are often specialized in their role, known in technical terms that signal organizational value as Level 1 (discipline) AP—the most basic—and Level 2 (curriculum) AP—the more advanced. But they also have the opportunity to learn vicariously and hence more expansively through the administrator role performed by others. In all such ways, we can begin to "imagineer" how beginning school leaders might be able to perform as novice experts.

Culturally Situated

This survey is not exhaustive of all the roles or even core leadership activities that a new school leader may perform in Florida, let alone throughout the nation. As discussed elsewhere in this book, this study is culturally situated and determined, a reality that extends to the survey instrument itself, which was based on the current literature and variables that coalesced at a particular time (the year 2000).

Further, those who participated in this research and in the formation of the piloted survey instrument wear particular cultural lenses. Slater, McGhee, Capt, Alvarez, Topete, and Iturbe (2003), as well as Walker and Dimmock (2002), Begley (2002), and English (2003c), are among those leadership professors who have compared the views of aspiring school leaders studying educational principalship in the United States with those in other countries (e.g., Canada, Mexico, Russia, Sweden). To summarize, future school leaders in America are believed, generally speaking, to have the following cultural perspectives:

- An individual over a collective approach
- An instrumental view of improving education that stresses skills and knowledge
- Value of practice or "real world" application over preparedness and rigor in research

- Ethnocentrism over a more global perspective concerning the influence of politically powerful forces in school leadership
- People-oriented or interpersonal skills above broad management skills and vision

One inference is that practicing school leaders in America have critical insights and essential information to share, but only within a culturally bound system. This caveat should be noted for understanding the outcomes discussed in this book, as the nature of early career administration, and the implications for improving university preparation programs and district training, are all culturally and contextually situated.

Still, the concerns and hopes expressed in the survey responses for future improvement in the kind of graduate education offered to aspiring administrators seemed very fresh and honest. Over the telephone, on the survey, and within the focus group sessions, many participants expressed interest in being able to help improve the design and delivery of educational leadership programs in Florida. Although it was not a theme within the actual quotes from these educators, we inferred that despite the gaps in their knowledge—and there are gaps in every professional's knowledge—they appear nonetheless to be trying to better themselves and the practice of the education craft.

What Counts as Administrative Experience?

Another contextual issue involving a few of the administrators' survey responses arose from the question of how many months or years they had spent in their current posts. The *FASA Directory* (formally known as the *Florida Education Directory by FASA, 2002–2003 School Year Florida Statewide Education Directory* [2002]), produced by the Florida Association of School Administrators (FASA), was scoured for administrators who were within two years of their hiring as assistant principal or principal. So it seemed odd that approximately 10 percent answered "three or more years" when queried about their time spent in administration.

However, two possibilities came to mind: (1) These more experienced leaders were referring to all of their administrative experience, which was not necessarily at the formal rank of assistant principal or principal. To explain, a department head in English or another subject area who is a teacher is also a member of the administrative staff (although the salary received will be a teacher's, not an administrator's). This is also generally the case in Florida for public relations specialists, career specialists, counselors, and other faculty who carry out various administrative roles. An individual starting in any of these posts and working up to assistant principal and eventually principal may "count" all of his or her administrative years toward time spent in rank. (2) Another possibility concerns the mobility between counties and states. School administrators frequently relocate. In these cases, an individual may have had experience in another state prior to being listed in the *FASA's Directory*. Carryovers between counties were sought and some connections were found, but those who migrated from different states would have slipped though the cracks.

ADMINISTRATOR STUDY:
NUMERICAL AND THEMATIC OUTCOMES

Primary Data and Survey Results

Instrument and Rating

Selected respondents—beginning assistant principals and principals within their first two years of the position—completed and returned the Early Career Administrator Survey subtitled "What matters most for Florida's school administrators to know?" The instrument contains a three-part format: (1) basic demographics of participants (numerical data); (2) matrix representing the nature of the work and tasks new leaders may perform (numerical data); and (3) open-response commentary on experiences as a beginning school administrator and/or as a graduate student preparing for the experience, and critique of the instrument itself (qualitative data). The summative matrix results of the survey for all Florida counties are provided in appendix D.

Survey respondents in Phase II (following the piloting of the instrument and validation of it) rated items in each of the topic sections from "0" to "5." This six-degree Likert scale was reflected directly in the matrix where the numerical responses were recorded (separately from the commentary that was thematically analyzed). The descriptors of the rating categories used the familiar range of ratings from "No Importance" (0) to "Most Important" (5). These differentiations allowed the new leaders to more specifically pinpoint the value of a particular task in their work duties.

Table 5.1. Florida Districts: Surveys Sent and Returned

	S	R		S	R		S	R
Alachua	4	1	Hamilton	3	0	Okaloosa	3	0
Baker	2	1	Hardee	2	0	Okeechobee	4	0
Bay	2	0	Hendry	2	0	Orange	5	1
Bradford	0	0	Hernando	3	3	Osceola	7	3
Brevard	19	2	Highlands	3	0	Palm Beach	6	3
Broward	10	4	Hillsborough	18	16	Pasco	9	8
Calhoun	0	0	Holmes	0	0	Pinellas	16	15
Charlotte	10	1	Indian River	2	1	Polk	0	0
Citrus	6	1	Jackson	2	1	Putnam	3	2
Clay	4	1	Jefferson	1	1	St. Johns	2	0
Collier	12	2	Lafayette	0	0	St. Lucie	5	2
Columbia	2	0	Lake	9	1	Santa Rosa	6	1
Miami-Dade	9	1	Lee	9	8	Sarasota	5	1
Desoto	3	1	Leon	0	0	Seminole	2	0
Dixie	0	0	Levy	4	2	Sumter	2	0
Duval	7	1	Liberty	0	0	Suwannee	2	0
Escambia	4	0	Madison	1	0	Taylor	1	0
Flagler	0	0	Manatee	5	1	Union	1	0
Franklin	2	0	Marion	8	3	Volusia	2	0
Gadsden	3	0	Martin	6	0	Wakulla	1	0
Gilchrist	4	0	Monroe	3	1	Walton	0	0
Glades	0	0	Nassau	3	1	Washington	0	0
Gulf	2	0						

S = Sent (271); R = Returned (91)

The survey was mailed, from January to May 2003, to 271 individuals identified as new school leaders in 56 out of 67 districts/counties in Florida. (Some of the counties did not have any new administrators at all.) All of the new administrators were contacted via telephone to confirm identification and to encourage participation in the study. Most also confirmed receipt of the surveys. (Overall, fifteen of the newly practicing administrators throughout Florida declined to participate and twelve could not be reached, some having left the position.) Table 5.1 provides a record of the surveys sent and received to the various Florida school districts.

On the survey, the administrator respondents assessed the following core leadership areas:

- Instructional supervision
- School organization

- Student services
- Community relations
- School management

These five areas were integral to the concepts and results communicated within the educational leadership literature (e.g., Mullen et al. 2002), in addition to feedback elicited from Phase I participants. The survey was therefore not only informed by and derived from several credible sources but also validated through this process. Each topic section contained a varying number of survey items, as the list in table 5.2 shows. The results indicate that all of the domains proved important to varying degrees and noteworthy in the lives of practicing school administrators.

To begin, when considering the most salient administrator duties (e.g., "assist in interviewing and hiring potential faculty and staff," and "participate in PTSA/SAC involvement") selected in 2003 by the Phase II respondents, instructional supervision received the top billing and was emphasized overall. School organization and management received prominence only in relation to single items/tasks that were selected, with weight given to faculty meeting attendance and budget management, respectively (see table 5.3).

Conceivably at a time of economic expansion and growth, the primary concern of an organization would be personnel: Finding appropriately and

Table 5.2.   Core Leadership Areas Performed: Survey Outcomes for Top 20 Tasks

Leadership Area	Weight	Total Items	Item/Task Most Highly Rated
Supervision of Instruction	60%	12	Assist in interviewing and hiring faculty/staff
School Organization	60%	13	Attend faculty meetings selectively
Student Services	40%	15	Attend parent–principal conferences
Community Relations	30%	5	Participate in PTSA*/SAC** involvement
School Management	10%	9	Manage budget (e.g., for instructional supplies)

*PTSA = Parent–Teacher–Student Association
**SAC = School Advisory Council

Table 5.3. Administrators' Top Selections of Core Leadership Areas

Total	Item (Administrative Task) Most Highly Rated	Core Leadership Area
Primary Tier		
63%	Assist in interviewing & hiring potential faculty/staff	supervision of instruction
63%	Participate in PTSA/SAC involvement	community relations
53%	Attend faculty meetings selectively	school organization
52%	Manage budget (e.g., for instructional supplies)	school management
52%	Advise teachers regarding classroom management	supervision of instruction
52%	Observe teacher–student interaction	supervision of instruction
52%	Communicate *every* school employee supports instruction	supervision of instruction
52%	Attend parent–principal conferences	student services
51%	Supervise and assess evaluations, fire, & tornado drills	student services
49%	Interpret standardized test results with/for teachers	supervision of instruction
Secondary Tier		
47%	Assist teachers with instructional plans	supervision of instruction
47%	Review and enforce school safety program	student services
44%	Attend principal/assistant principal meetings	school organization
42%	Design master schedule, including specials	school organization
41%	Plan staff orientation/school-opening activities	school organization
41%	Relate to youth with disabilities	student services
40%	Plan open house	community relations
38%	Newsletter (student/staff accomplishments)	community relations
36%	Review curriculum documents	school organization
33%	Serve on a school committee	school organization
Tertiary Tier		
31%	Review & enforce attendance/tardy policies	school management

highly qualified persons to accomplish the work of the organization. However, currently this is certainly not a time of economic advantage for public schools in Florida. Yet, the value placed on instructional supervision was nonetheless maintained in this study as a significant priority for the new leaders. On a deeper level, the results from this research suggest that despite the budgetary restrictions that are worsening and continuing to affect Florida's public educational institutions (Mullen and Applegate 2002)—and the obvious tensions that this implies for schools—the tendency is for new leaders to extend themselves beyond the managerial function in favor of a supervisory role (as reinforced by table 5.3).

The results from my study indicate that new school leaders devote more time and energy to instructional supervision than anything else in their buildings, including financial operations (see chapter 8). This outcome has significant implications for professional accountability, which extends far beyond financial responsibility for school administration. Based on the survey results, instructional leadership involves new administrators in such areas as faculty hiring, classroom management, teacher–student interaction, whole-school ownership of instructional support, and standardized test interpretation. Based on the top ten administrator tasks selected in this study, then, instructional supervision achieved prominence as the major focus of responsibility—it was chosen 50 percent of the time as "most important" in relation to the five items/tasks just listed.

Open-ended comments on the survey and in the focus group transcripts reinforced this picture with specific strategies that instructional leaders model for creating a climate of academic achievement, particularly within disadvantaged sites: classroom visits, curriculum assistance one-on-one and in small groups (including feedback on lessons), technology infusion, computer-based learning in laboratories, and FCAT (Florida Comprehensive Assessment Test) training. In comparison, student services appeared in 20 percent of the top choices, and school management, school organization, and community relations just 10 percent each, equivalent to a single selection (see tables 5.2 and 5.3).

Interestingly, although community relations had attained only 10 percent significance within the context of the core leadership areas, one of its items/tasks—participate in PTSA/SAC (Parent–Teacher–Student Association/School Advisory Council) involvement—received the *same* rating (by 63 percent of the participant pool) as the top candidate within supervision of instruction. While this community relations' task proved to be a "contender" of equal weight or value to the instructional supervision task in and of itself, this was not the case when the survey results were viewed holistically and systematically. Just as the weight given to the management duties that involved attending faculty meetings and budget operations did not hold up across the core leadership areas (and entire data set), this was also the case for the community task. In other words, supervision of instruction proved to be the most important administration domain in this study while community relations was the least, albeit nonetheless salient on the continuum of priority areas. (For an explanation of the PTSA/SAC task and its value to schools seeking outreach with the community, see chapter 13.) In the context of the data collection as a whole, then, instructional supervision had more influence for administrators than any other core leadership domain.

Considering the pattern revealed by a second tier of choices (the next ten) as displayed on table 5.3, school organization clearly moved to the fore. This was chosen 50 percent of the time as the core leadership area. Student services and community relations followed, each with an overall 20 percent rating. Supervision of instruction was given a 10 percent weight only, although the item itself (i.e., "assist teachers with instructional plans") competed for popularity with the highest rating in the secondary tier.

Taking the primary and secondary tiers together, the weight given to the five core leadership areas (relative to the top twenty tasks performed) is as follows:

- Supervision of instruction (60 percent)
- School organization (60 percent)
- Student services (40 percent)
- Community relations (30 percent)
- School management (10 percent)

A third tier contained only one item (i.e., "administering attendance policies"), achieving second place within the school management domain. However, this also received less emphasis than any other priority task in terms of the total number of selections made (see table 5.3).

Survey Weight Distribution

Moreover, the attention that had been given to the core leadership areas on the survey was intentionally unequal, meaning that these had not been equally represented or emphasized. The differences among the five categories, including the varying number of related items/tasks reflected within each, was supported both in the educational leadership literature as well as the Phase I piloted feedback. Current North America studies have highlighted (as does my survey) the vital role of instructional supervision and leadership at the level of the principalship (e.g., Cole, Squire, and

Cathers 1995; Glickman, Gordon, and Ross-Gordon 2001; McCarthy 1999; Mullen et al. 2002).

Notably, the current school leader has increasing responsibility for student performance and teacher development, and in the capacity of facilitator, mentor, and coach. School administration is expected to promote teacher development, proficiency, and reflection, ranging from principal-teacher interaction about instruction to more proactive forms of peer coaching (e.g., Blasé and Blasé 2000), in order that gains in student achievement can be met. Classroom learning and effects on changes in teachers, programs, instruction, and student outcomes are all part of a larger emphasis on transformational leadership and school restructuring (e.g., Leithwood et al. 1993). In line with these results, McCarthy (1999) has recommended that leadership preparation programs be adjusted to focus on the centrality of learning for students and teachers within the context of broader educational goals, and that the corresponding accountability of school leaders be addressed in this light.

Broader Thematic Patterns:
Socialization Patterns and Values

Analysis of the complete study data (i.e., survey ratings and commentary and focus group transcripts, in addition to secondary sources) highlighted salient areas of leadership. These broader areas, derived from written and oral exchanges with the study participants, subsume the survey results displayed in tables 5.2 and 5.3. Ten areas in which the beginning school leaders are being socialized or attribute value can be summarized as:

1. *Conditioning preparation:* Training program, preparation, learning curve, conditioning (e.g., cultural, social, conceptual, political, and physical).
2. *Inventory survey:* School inventory and management (equipment monitoring); self-inventory; school improvement via data-gathering instruments (e.g., school management).
3. *Direction indicator:* Instrument, person, document, process, program, committee, professional meeting, or educational resource.

4. *Basic know-how*: Routine administrative tasks requiring basic know-how and competency with essential skills.
5. *Real-world experience*: Leadership capacity development via on-site exposure and alliance building outside schools.
6. *Knowledge source*: Real-world application, theory relevant where operationalized, and especially practical knowing.
7. *Mentoring scaffolds*: Peer networks, teams, effective mentors, and role models; effective mentoring systems, apprenticeships, and coaching strategies (e.g., supervision of instruction).
8. *Emotional expression*: Stress, challenge, and excitement; convey or document feelings and experiences; discern behavioral patterns and promote growth.
9. *Coping skills*: Ability to understand, manage, or resolve a problem; others turned to for support; practice coping as a skill, daily conditioning or training.
10. *Accountability climate*: Professional accountability, high-stakes national testing, school grading, effects on school culture, curriculum, and student achievement.

This list, critical to the book, has been expounded upon as items for the traveler's knapsack in chapter 6 and as case exemplars and narrative descriptions throughout part 2.

Secondary Data Outcomes

The previous thematic patterns were also identified based on secondary data sources: participant workshop evaluations and researcher journaling (during focus group sessions, telephone conversations, and research meetings with assistants). The earlier section concerning contextual responses to my survey is an example of how information, based upon informal telephone exchanges, has been cited from the journal that my research assistant and I each kept throughout 2003.

Judging from the quality of reflections and the insights attributed to the group discussion, significant learning was kindled for the peer assessors in Phase III. Most importantly, based on analyses of the data sources (e.g., participant workshop evaluations), six benefits were derived for the participants:

1. The survey proved valid, with some amendments suggested and made to the survey items (e.g., value placed not just on "review the school safety program" or any other but on actually enforcing such policies at the building level).
2. Thematic results of the survey (the ten areas listed in "Primary Data and Results") were authenticated, further explained, and contextualized (see "Context Matters" in this chapter).
3. Useful research tools (e.g., numerical and qualitative processes of documenting school issues and change) were learned for application within school and university contexts (e.g., dissertation writing, with a focus on developing and implementing methods).
4. Cooperative learning groups created among various school districts and across school levels (e.g., elementary, middle, and secondary).
5. Use of practitioner focus group throughout the project as a tool for refinement and validation of the research process and content.
6. Survey responses were seen to be context dependent and somewhat varied from one school to another, and especially from one level to another (e.g., secondary).

These outcomes support the use of authenticity circles and a participant feedback loop in research, known as a process-based outcomes approach.

IDENTIFYING NEW SCHOOL LEADERS: FASA'S DIRECTORY

A strategy was needed for comprehensively and thoroughly identifying Florida's beginning school administrators within their current role. As previously indicated, for this purpose FASA's *Directory* (2002) proved invaluable.

All building-level beginning administrators in Florida were first telephoned to confirm their status and establish whether they would be willing to complete a survey. When someone could not be directly reached, a second communication occurred. Most indicated interest, receiving, within the week, the Early Career Administrator Survey, abbreviated project description, and consent form. Given the positive reception received to the survey and its goals, it was expected that the response rate would be much higher than 34 percent. On the other hand, the telephone calls to all respondents probably helped to make the databased aspects of this study possible.

After consulting with seasoned administrators in Florida, I gained insight into the probable forces that had influenced the response rate. For one thing, the survey, which had been distributed over a five-month period, overlapped with the school year closing in May 2003. This would have made the process hectic for those planning to respond. For another thing, the extra steps required by IRB for respondents to fill out the survey and return it with a signature on a separate form may have discouraged some from making the effort even after expressing interest, especially for anyone more electronically inclined. Finally, and perhaps most importantly, the FCAT (Florida Comprehensive Assessment Test) cycle occurs during the spring months each year, which requires fastidious management by school principals. The testing timeframe had overlapped with my survey distribution. Also, for the first time in Florida's history, third graders were required, in the spring of 2003, to take the FCAT Reading and Mathematics (Florida Department of Education, July 2003, online). This development may have complicated the lives of elementary administrators planning to contribute to my study.

In total, twenty-nine districts were represented by the completed surveys that were returned. Participating counties were Alachua, Baker, Brevard, Broward, Charlotte, Citrus, Clay, Collier, Miami-Dade, Desoto, Duval, Hillsborough, Jackson, Lake, Lee, Levy, Manatee, Marion, Monroe, Nassau, Orange, Osceola, Palm Beach, Pasco, Pinellas, Putnam, St. Lucie, Santa Rosa, and Sarasota. The highest return for the surveys occurred within the Tampa Bay area (e.g., Hillsborough, Pasco, and Pinellas), in part because I was better connected to this area. In fact, some of the respondents were my colleagues who had taken my courses. However, because I anticipated a higher response rate from the west-central region, the "outlying" districts (i.e., north, south, and east)—those farther from the Tampa Bay area—were contacted first. This gave the new school leaders unknown to me more time to complete the surveys than those within the radius of the university and Tampa.

SCHOOL DISTRICT PORTRAIT: FLORIDA CONTEXT

It may be helpful to see the Florida school district map used for this study, so it is included as figure 5.1. A full-color version is available at the FASA

Figure 5.1.   Florida's School District Map
Source: *Florida Education Directory by FASA, 2002–2003 School Year*

website, complete with hotlinks on each of the districts that include information about the schools within each county (Florida Department of Education [Florida Information Resource Network, or FIRN]).

In order to get a picture of how Florida's districts are structured, with emphasis on those that responded to the survey, an overview is provided here, followed by a more detailed description in appendix G. Additional data are available at the FIRN website: While it covers facts relevant to the districts' schools, teachers, and students in relation to racial/ethnic group, graduation rates, comprehensive test assessment data, and teacher salaries and experience, among other factors, there is no information pertaining to the population of school administrators—it has been overlooked, statistically speaking, by the Florida Department of Education's representation of the state's school system. Interestingly, this oversight reinforces my critique that the beginning school administrator is a barely visible entity in educational systems, a fact that will need attention if schools and universities alike are to achieve greater potency in their improvement efforts in areas of leadership.

Florida School Law: Overview

Florida consists entirely of single-district counties, a setup that is unique in that a district equals a county in this state, whereas in other states, such as New York, there are typically a few or many districts in a single county. For this reason, the words *county* and *district* are used interchangeably in this book, owing to the structure of Florida's school governance. A number of other southeastern states also have some single-district counties. For example, Tennessee has many single-district counties, although it also has independent city districts within some counties (Benjamin 2003).

Here is the relevant Florida school law concerning the configuration of counties at the district unit:

> Each county shall constitute a school district and shall be known as the school district of _____ County, Florida. Each district shall constitute a unit for the control, organization, and administration of schools. The responsibility for the actual operation and administration of all schools needed within the districts in conformity with rules and minimum standards prescribed by the state, and also the responsibility for the provision of any desirable and practicable opportunities authorized by law beyond those required by the state, are delegated by law to the school officials of the respective districts. (The 2002 Florida Statutes, Statute 1001.30, FIRN website)

District Structure: Description

As of 2003, the most recent demographics provided by the FIRN website were for the 2000–2001 academic school year. The information shared in this section is a précis, tailored to the districts that returned the surveys and the school cultures in which the administrator respondents worked. Because the website does not contain any information about the administrators per se, the circumstances and perhaps school culture in which they work can in part be inferred from the contextual information provided. For purposes of organization, the discussion of the districts is based on their geographic region—north, south, west, east, and central (see appendix G).

One thing that can be deduced from this Florida school district portrait is that the counties that responded serve both diverse, multiethnic student populations (e.g., Hillsborough) and a majority of white students (e.g., Pasco), even within the same district. In other words, the administrators who lead Florida's schools serve within sites that vary in degree of diversity, with increasing numbers of ethnic/racial groups. Related to this, the predominately white student populations served by many of the counties have been gradually changing, largely because of the influx of Hispanic families.

SCHOOL LEADER PORTRAIT: SURVEY RESULTS

The beginning administrator of Florida's schools is most often a white female from 36 to 55 years old, working at the elementary, middle, or secondary level. More specifically, in my survey sample of assistant principals and principals, 30 percent of the females were employed in elementary schools, 12 percent in middle sites, and 18 percent in secondary establishments. Regarding the males, 18 percent were working in elementary schools, 4 percent in middle sites, and 18 percent in secondary establishments. This statistical picture is generally consistent with Spencer and Kochan's (2000) finding that underscores a recent increase in females entering the principalship in Alabama. Moreover, it suggests that more women may be working in secondary sites, and more men in elementary sites, than is traditionally the case.

Frequently, in Florida this school leader is from an urban or suburban area, primarily an assistant principal but also principal, with up to two years of administrative experience (and often less than one year). Not surprisingly, his or her professional goal most often targets the principalship and, to a far lesser degree, county office administration or the school superintendency. (These results are consistent with the trends reported in the literature.) This individual typically holds a master's degree in educational leadership, with principalship certification from the state of Florida. Very few already hold a doctorate in education, but many show some promise of pursuing this advanced degree.

Demographic Characteristics

Basic demographics were compiled for the respondents: geographic area, level of the school where they administer, administrative title, time in rank, gender, age, professional goals, and formal degrees and programs.

Geographically, 67 percent of those responding identified their school communities as "urban" and 33 percent, "rural." Within this participant pool, 36 percent lead at the elementary school level, while 33 percent work at the middle level and 31 percent in secondary sites. Regarding their formal administrative titles, an almost equal response was obtained from successive principals, as 50 percent were assistant principals, 45 percent, principals, and 5 percent, "other." (The "other" designation was chosen to encompass school leadership roles not identified on the survey or formerly identified in the research.)

It was important to establish the time spent in rank in order to confirm that the subject pool consisted strictly of beginning administrators. For less than one year, 45 percent had been serving in their current role, whereas 19 percent had functioned at their level for one year, and 36 percent had held their position for two years. These figures clearly established that the beginning leader only would inform the worldview expressed from "the trenches" of schools.

More female leaders (60 percent) than males (40 percent) responded to the survey, which was unexpected. According to a report prepared for the U.S. Department of Education, only 39 percent of all principals from 1993 to 1994 were women, and 14 percent belonged to a racial/ethnic minority group (Henke et al. 1996). (Although racial/ethnic demographics were not pursued on the survey, the predominance of white and female was evident from the configuration of the three focus groups and the master's classes

in my educational leadership program.) Although gender and racial im-
balances that traditionally prevail among school leaders show improvement in the nation, it is important to view this trend in perspective. The
workforce of principals is still largely male and white (see, e.g., Spencer
and Kochan 2000, for a statistical analysis of 550 principals of all stages
surveyed in Alabama), though gradual increases have been occurring in
the representation of women and, less so, of minority principals.

Regarding age, the majority of Florida's school leaders surveyed fell
between 46 and 55 years of age (35 percent) and, to a lesser degree, at 26
percent, in the 36-to-40 range. Another 14 percent were between 41 and
45. Additionally, 10 percent were 25 to 30, and another 10 percent were
31 to 35. Only 5 percent were over 56. As one possibility, more principals
at a younger age may be seeking early retirement via the state system's
drop programs (Mullen with Sullivan 2002).

For the question involving professional goals, the new leader checked the
appropriate box; some provided a statement. The career goal selected by the
majority, 52 percent, was that of principal. Two individuals indicated the desire to remain as an assistant principal, while 19 percent aspired to a position in the county office. Others (12 percent) expressed the goal of district
superintendent. One person hoped to become a curriculum supervisor, shifting from being an assistant principal in charge of discipline.

The formal degree and program were also identified from a list. The
majority (63 percent) held a master's degree in educational leadership,
and three, a doctorate of education. Ten new leaders had earned degrees
in curriculum and instruction with certification in educational leadership.
Twenty individuals who could not be classified according to these categories marked "other." The reason for a majority with master's degrees in
educational leadership, as opposed to other fields, namely curriculum and
instruction, seems obvious enough: Florida's world of K–12 leadership
currently requires that potential leaders be certified via the state Department of Education's Florida Educational Leadership Exam (FELE).

IMPLICATIONS FOR EDUCATION AND LEADERSHIP

Getting a master's degree in another field and then completing certification
in educational leadership is a two-step process, whereas the master's de-

gree in educational leadership involves only one step. The issue of certification and quality of preparation is clearly a challenge at the state and national levels. For, as Orozco (2003) explains, because of the nationwide vacancies in the principalship, comprehensive leadership preparation within colleges of education is increasingly being bypassed in favor of "short-cut solutions." Reports about school climate reinforce that many qualified school administrators choose "to remain in the classroom or change professions entirely"; in California this translates into the majority (62 percent) of qualified school leaders. This signals that not only is there a "critical shortage of administrators for current vacancies" but also that "qualified and licensed educational candidates" have left education in droves for other professional fields (Orozco 2003, 4, 6). In Oliver's (2003) California-based survey study of entry-level assistant principals, this leadership mountain proved less drastic, as "the majority of the respondents (78 percent in 2002) indicated they intended to stay in administration" (p. 40).

Assuming the accuracy of this account, there is a hopeful note struck in this study. From the statistics obtained for the professional goals of Florida's new school leader, the assistant principals primarily think of the educational principalship as a finite career goal. Moreover, 31 percent of the respondents (assistant principals and principals) expressed aspirations for a position outside the building level and at the county or superintendent's office. However, one way of interpreting this picture is that the new leaders I surveyed were still in the "honeymoon" phase of the summit climb, similar to Oliver's study respondents but unlike those qualified leadership candidates in Orozco's (2003) account who decided against entering administration. Another possibility is that no one in my participant pool had his or her professional sights set on a summit outside education—all wished to leave footprints upon the Himalayas of school leadership. This is the more hopeful interpretation.

Chapter Six

Knapsack: What to Pack for Your Virtual Trek

Backpacks come in many different makes and models, and choosing the right one can be perplexing. But do we really need all the gadgetry? More importantly, do we need to carry huge loads? I think that most of us could get by quite nicely with a simple rucksack fitted with a couple of straps. Grandma Gatewood [illustrious 80-year-old mega-hiker of the U.S. continent] would probably have suggested that we don't even need the straps.

—R. Jardine

As a new or practicing leader anticipating the trek ahead, certain "items" will come in handy for your backpack while others, perhaps initially helpful, may dim in importance (Logue 2000). In our case, the anatomy of a knapsack that evolved, to suit our purposes to the extent possible for the particular leadership trek ahead, comprises ten metaphorical necessities: mountaineering boots, map, compass, Swiss army knife, rope, journal, first-aid kit, ax, tarp, and lantern (see figure 6.1 and table 6.1). However, there is no one *right* knapsack or set of items to pack for this journey, just as the tools that school leaders need will vary. Administration requires a flexible, versatile, and adaptable approach in order to be effective. And there will certainly be better and wiser choices, depending upon context and variables such as the political climate of the time, the type of school and its particular profile, and the individual's vision and comfort level with risk. All in all, your knapsack and its contents will likely evolve as a reflection of your capacity to lead, learn, collaborate, and accept new challenges.

If school leaders were preparing to climb the Himalayas in reality, it would not be difficult to imagine the serious organizational and psychological effort that Montgomery and Krutulis (2002) say is required. Similarly,

Figure 6.1.   Anatomy of a Knapsack
Source: Carol Mullen and William Kealy

those seeking to enter school administration must thoughtfully if not vigorously prepare for the challenge awaiting them. And those currently practicing will need to work continuously on self-improvement by reflecting upon their own role and life challenges.

GETTING THE KNACK OF KNAPSACKING

How the students in my graduate program decide what to put in their expedition packs is not unlike the planning that goes into any journey. Because they and their teammates will literally and metaphorically carry their knapsacks throughout the semester, decisions are vital. While most teams pack such obvious items as a compass and map, few at first recognize the value of including, say, mountaineering boots and a journal. Such objects offer invaluable benefits for trekkers who must condition both their physical and intellectual muscles.

The benefits of developing the capacity for reflection in graduate school become apparent in this context when my students' packs change as the semester wears on. This occurs naturally as the learning deepens, the sense of the task sharpens, and members' decision making improves. In the hiking world, expert backpacker Jardine (2001) attributes just such a change to a positive attitude and amenable outlook on the unknown. In contrast, "a negative or fearful outlook" is demonstrated by a hiker who insists on carrying "a magnum-sized backpack full of heavy-duty gear" (p. 16). In my courses, the students learn that initial decisions may be superficial and that these will probably change where one is steeped in a reflective inquiry process that involves a team's mutual effort and shared goal. All such learning can be transferred to the schools to benefit a variety of situations where collaborative reflective inquiry can produce a positive outlook on the unknown.

On a lighter note, when my husband and I were preparing for our hiking trip to Italy in 2001, we faced the challenge of also having to pack for the three-week trip to Europe itself. So we packed one suitcase each for Europe and brought along a rucksack that was shared on the daylong hikes. We trekked the return trip across eighteen kilometers (approximately eleven miles) of Cinque Terre's mountainous range, connecting what are known as the Five Lands. Instead of a journal, we opted for a lightweight video camera for the hike. I wanted to be able to document my trekking metaphor for this book—a related but different context—and so my voiceover was recorded in relation to particular landscape images (e.g., signposts, obstacles, narrow passageways, thorny bushes, rough waters, and rocky slopes).

The process of selecting the images and turning them into analogies for school leadership proved much more challenging than the hike itself. In essence, I was able to transfer the learning. Moreover, the conceptual and art-making process of *interpreting* the trek for what I imagined to be a parallel universe was *the climb*. Similarly, the preparation program from which one graduates may be the "hike" but the experience of becoming a school leader will be the momentous climb.

As these various scenarios illustrate, the knapsack metaphor can be used as a device for exploring any purpose where discovery is valued, and on levels that range from the personal, practical, and professional, to the cultural, social, and institutional, and finally to the intellectual, imaginative, and spiritual.

REDUCING CUMBERSOME LOADS

Novice school leaders will probably communicate wisdom to others as they shift from carrying "a magnum-sized backpack" to a load that does not detract from the quality of their experience — working smart, not hard! They learn to recognize what tools (styles or approaches) work best in which situations and what connections can be made among tasks or situations. Leaders who develop "pattern-recognition abilities" will have a better chance of making informed decisions about the problems they face. They will have learned how to group information and observations and consolidate the tools needed for making decisions, as opposed to becoming overwhelmed or lost in the details and options.

Principals and other school leaders can develop this cognitive skill by comparing their awareness of a day's events with others. Kosseff (2003) claims that such tactics enable one's awareness skills to deepen and sharpen. As we make conscious attempts to create pictures out of a myriad of clues, this process ironically enables "further layers of details" to be constructed as part of the "eye-opening experience" (p. 76).

Metaphorically speaking, cumbersome baggage equates with, for example, unresolved issues, outdated mind-sets, obsolete traditions, poor planning, ineffectual decision making, impoverished self-awareness, defensiveness, fear of the unknown, and mistrust. Other signals of

excess baggage are rationalization, scapegoating, regression, and repression. Individuals or leaders who exhibit such behaviors tend to be
isolated or form cliques that bond through negativity and ostracizing
others (Kosseff 2003).

Excess baggage is always negative. It keeps individuals from seeing the
critical issues in administration that require personal time and effort. Also
cumbersome is ethnocentric or culturally bound thinking, which is a form
of blindness that can be manifested in some individuals' decision making
or actions. For such individuals, "the value orientations of others" exist
outside the radar of what Begley (2002) describes as "Western-centric"
persons and schools, despite the increasing diversification of institutions
in the United States and the United Kingdom. In trekking terms, *ethnocentric* may be equivalent to *topocentric*—a perception from a specific
point on earth. As an example of how different cultural assumptions can
be manifested, consider that where one school culture may value consensus among educational stakeholders, another may not, valuing the perspectives of elite or senior parties only. In effect, leaders who are unaware
of their own sociocultural assumptions may not understand the role their
own values play in assessing people and situations. It will prove much
more difficult to reach the summit of "sophisticated and sensitive educational leadership practice" (Begley 2002, 47) under the strain of any such
personal or shared cultural overload.

KNAPSACKS THAT FOSTER LEADERSHIP CAPACITY

Based on responses of practicing school leaders and comments of specialists from school administration and outdoor sports, the following
"items" are possibilities for your own knapsacks. Although various experts have informed the descriptions, they consistently reflect the perspectives gathered from beginning administrators in Florida. Each particular leadership capacity and skill (e.g., conditioning preparation)
represents a thematic outcome of my study that has been matched with a
corresponding metaphorical backpack item (e.g., mountaineering boots).
To visually aid access, these research results first appear as a graphic display and then a chart that provides some detail. (See part 2 for the fuller
descriptions of outcomes.)

Table 6.1.   Packing a Capacity-Building Knapsack

Backpack Items	Capacities and Skills	Purposes and Benefits
Mountaineering Boots	*Conditioning Preparation*	Condition muscles (physically and intellectually) and develop training and routines for handling exertion and the unexpected. Anticipate a learning curve and daily challenges ahead. Condition for these long hikes by building up to them with shorter walks (e.g., basic duties and staff training). *Conditioning preparation* occurs at all levels, including cultural, social, conceptual, political, and physical. Learn the district, state, and national policies that govern schools; consult student and faculty handbooks to learn the local culture and aid conflict resolution and decision making, and become familiar with the school's history by getting to know the influential people within the school community.
Map	*Inventory Survey*	Provide direction and reduce chances of getting lost. Two general kinds of maps are self-inventory (e.g., reflective journaling) and school inventory (e.g., equipment budget). Maps can assist with assessing the specific behavior and performance of practitioners, as well as with monitoring overall activity, routines, patterns, and change. Action research (along with survey instruments) provides opportunities for reflection and evaluation on individual or collective levels.
Compass	*Direction Indicator*	Provide direction in the form of an instrument, person (e.g., peer coach), document (e.g., how-to guide), process (e.g., informal support system), or program (e.g., graduate preparation). Direction can occur vis-à-vis faculty meetings, administrative planning, school committees, professional meetings, workshops, and educational resources (e.g., curriculum guides).
Swiss Army Knife	*Basic Know-How*	Routine administrative tasks (e.g., designing a master schedule, planning staff orientation/ school opening activities, working to reach consensus in a group) require basic know-how that takes time to develop. Specialized tools (Swiss army knives, or multitools) symbolize effective approaches to obtaining competency with essential skills.
Tarp	*Real-World Experience*	A facility with school crisis planning and emergency procedures is just one example of the many ways in which real-world experience is essential to developing school leadership capacities. The tarp, unlike the tent, symbolizes exposure to natural elements, not being sheltered *(continued)*

Table 6.1.   Packing a Capacity-Building Knapsack *(continued)*

Backpack Items	Capacities and Skills	Purposes and Benefits
		from them. One is "exposed" by virtue of being *inside* the school setting where the action and decision making are taking place and by taking appropriate risks. One is also exposed when *outside* the school, making alliances that meet the school's needs and propel its vision. Internships and apprenticeships offer real-world experience to administrator candidates, as do action research, panel discussions, and simulated activities.
Lantern	*Knowledge Source*	Sources of knowledge that matter for practicing leaders can be applied in real-world contexts. Theory plays a role where it can be operationalized. But preservice training programs tend to underemphasize the value of practical knowing and application and therefore function short of being "lanterns" themselves. Candle lanterns offer a particular type or quality of light—one that is more diffuse than kerosene lamps and flashlights. The analogy is that beginning school administrators may value being able to see more broadly or globally over spotlighting issues in depth or detail.
Rope	*Mentoring Scaffolds*	Come in multifarious forms, such as peer networks, teams, effective mentors, and role models. Effective mentoring systems, apprenticeships, and coaching strategies offer solutions for socializing leaders and professional opportunities for growth. The rope secures or binds a school team, through such mechanisms as mission building and shared vision, and protects leaders from falling.
Journal	*Emotional Expression*	Emotional expression is associated with the stress, challenge, and excitement of being a new leader. Administrators convey feelings of a personal, direct, and emotional nature. Professionals can benefit from documenting experiences and feelings to discern behavioral patterns and promote growth. Experienced trekkers recommend that a journal be used on a daily basis and that patterns be identified and analyzed to aid improvements in performance.
First-Aid Kit	*Coping Skills*	Needed for effectively approaching, understanding, and resolving a problem or managing a complex situation. A person, unit, or institution can demonstrate coping skills. Administrators cope by trying to make the best decisions possible. Learning how to cope means turning to others

Backpack Items	Capacities and Skills	Purposes and Benefits
		for support when appropriate. It also takes practice and is a skill that can be acquired through daily conditioning or training. Administrators who are recent graduates will have deficiencies that must be compensated for through expedited learning and mentoring scaffolds. Expert trekkers recommend an appropriate level of first-aid training. The first-aid kit is a toolbox that helps with finding solutions for special needs or problems, but the user must know how to employ the items and should avoid carrying too many in it.
Ax	Accountability Climate	Professional accountability for schools has become entangled with high-stakes national testing that affects school culture (e.g., morale, reputation, reward structure, graduation rates) in very real ways. Student achievement and "teaching to the test" have become almost synonymous in response to this educational reform. Alternatively, an accountability climate that fosters improvements in teaching and learning would not use standardized test scores as the "end-all-and-be-all" measure of educational quality. The ax is not intended to be a danger to anyone; to the contrary, it helps trekkers cut through icy patches and negotiate difficult passages where sliding can occur.

LITERARY ADDITIONS TO YOUR KNAPSACK

So far you have enclosed ten items in your knapsack. You have probably already noticed the high value I place on texts, especially those with enriching perspectives on leadership and administration, regardless of whether they have been produced from within the traditional field of education. There are some essentials that you may wish to enclose, in addition to your own choices, which will probably be modified over time. The contents of your backpack will reflect your own changing outlook, national cultural issues, emerging leadership frameworks, and the various contexts in which your trek takes place. By packing some critical texts that offer relevance without trading off rigor in our development as school leaders, we will have expressed our willingness to close the theory/practice gap in our own lives. This is the hope for the future of graduate preparation.

I have often found it mind-expanding to view our professional field anew by sizing it up from another slope (e.g., outdoors sports) and to use this creative method in both my teaching and writing. Before continuing on this traverse of the Himalayas, then, I encourage you to pack texts that can act as a compass. It is to be expected that none will provide any absolute direction, only general ranges to be forged into pathways. Always you will be making meaning by carving out your own paths as you progress, not simply following a path that already exists (see chapter 9).

The conflicting values that permeate educational leadership cannot be overlooked when we make literary selections for our trek. Begley (2002) summarizes the problem this way, "Practitioners can be rather insistent about the need for relevance. Scholars, on the other hand, tend to focus on a need for rigor" (p. 50). He explains that this discrepancy in values is manifested in the "low tolerance" that many practitioners have "for abstract models and theoretical debate that stray any distance from the practical problems of the day" (p. 50). Of course, the same text that seems watered down or superficial to a scholar may to a practitioner appear even more valuable for having avoided extraneous concepts and information that do not directly pertain to school life, or for having escaped the use of academic jargon. Some aspiring leaders have told me that they experience jargon not only as cumbersome baggage but, more importantly, as a mechanism that keeps conversation closed, or alive only among university researchers.

In an effort to bridge the chasm between theory and practice in our own professional landscape, we will need to cope with the value differences that exist at the macro level between university professors and school practitioners (Begley 2002). By doing so, the objective becomes to produce a reciprocal, as opposed to a top-down, process of knowledge creation (Mullen and Lick 1999). Scholars and writers who reflect on the current issues of school leadership using personal school-based experiences, collaborative project initiatives with administrators, research-based comprehensive explorations, and multisite case studies seem to offer the most useful guidebooks.

Toward this end, the leadership development of the new school leader can be enhanced by texts that deal explicitly with the socialization and survival of beginning administrators. However, the focus in the leadership literature is on the principalship without much emphasis on the assistant principalship, for which this work attempts to compensate. This work also offers data, whereas most other texts on school leadership seem to be a collection of real-life stories—an administration narrative—a point that Mayer, Mullens, and Moore (2000) make when discussing the limitations of case histories where research is not evident. Theory and practice meld better in the presence of hard data and a concern for measurable change.

Regarding the principalship, helpful texts for getting ready for practice are Crow and Matthews' (1998) *Finding One's Way* and Schmidt's (2002) *Gardening in the Minefield*. Both of these "how-to" survivalist casebooks are "candle lanterns" in that they offer a broad or diffuse view of particular issues that preoccupy the school leader and aspirant.

In *Finding One's Way* the authors look at the experiential aspects of leading as stages of entry and adjustment to school administration. They frame leadership and socialization issues using a case story format that focuses exclusively on mentoring situations and dynamics that have school-wide relevance. By 2004, *Finding One's Way* will have been on the market for six years. It is worth noting that during this relatively short time, the sociopolitical climate of the United States has changed rather dramatically. Public schools have become increasingly complex sites of accountability, safety, and security; the preparation of leaders has consequently dealt much more with educational standards, high-stakes testing, and high performance. The increased expectations of schools for supporting academic performance now place a premium on stakeholder involvement and research documentation showing evidence of student and school improvement.

Gardening in the Minefield presents a broader terrain of leadership with a focus on "best practices" for hiring and motivating staff, distributing leadership, problem solving, and various other inherent functions of the job. Schmidt's survival guide offers new school administrators a tool for exerting control over the unknown and managing crises. It neither relies upon the feedback of new school leaders nor builds concepts from collected and analyzed data; instead, the author extrapolates from her own experiences as principal and uses humor to do so.

Another data-rich practical book, *Directions in Mentoring* (Mullen and Lick 1999), resulted from collaboration among professors, school and university leaders, and new and experienced teachers. This Partnership Support Group endeavored to mend the theory/practice gap. We used reciprocal mentoring (instead of traditional top-down mentoring) as the solution for creating an authentic partnership between school and university practitioners and for resolving cultural differences inherent within hierarchal, bureaucratic structures.

Walker and Dimmock's (2002) edited collection, *School Leadership and Administration*, embodies complex global and cultural perspectives. For instance, in Western societies we emphasize gaining the necessary technical skills for leading schools, but elsewhere, as in Chinese communities, leading is associated more with the process of modeling and influencing behaviors in desirable ways. Integral to any summit climb is reflection upon who and what we are and expanding our potential as critical thinkers.

Depending upon your own professional sights, you may want to pack *Case Studies of the Superintendency* (Short and Scribner 2002), a well-researched specialist text that focuses exclusively on the superintendency. I have learned from my master's groups of inservice teachers over the years that few teachers overall—and very few women—plan on becoming superintendents and fewer actually do. According to Schmidt (2002), America's schools still resemble "the traditional family," with only 4 percent of females accounting for school superintendents; fewer women than might be expected—35 percent—are actually principals (p. 23). Most graduate programs do not even include a superintendency course, let alone an entire training program. Instead, leadership preparation programs have their sights set on the principalship, in line with the demands of student bodies and state departments of education (Mullen et al. 2002). But this narrow emphasis on the principalship is out of step with "non-mainstream" school administrative positions, such as districtwide curriculum specialists. Focus group participants who fill such proliferating positions in Florida emphasized this point and their own subsequent marginality.

Other books that may be placed into your knapsack include Cole, Squire, and Cathers' (1995) *Supporting Beginning Teachers: A Handbook for School Administrators*. Such texts respond to the continued support that beginning teachers desperately need from administration for survival and improvement. Accountability and assistance to personnel in the core areas of teaching, learning, and curriculum are viewed as a major jurisdiction of school administration (e.g., Walker and Dimmock 2002). The mentoring and supervisory support roles for which administration—principals, assistant principals, program administrators, lead teachers, and district leaders—is increasingly responsible cannot be overlooked.

Hargreaves and Fullan's (1998) *What's Worth Fighting For Out There?* connects the sights of school leaders to the external summit—the community and policy environment—that influences daily operations. As administrative and faculty teams reframe their relationships to the outside, they will in effect strengthen their institution's internal resiliency and goals by having proactively engaged in "bridge-building" wherein "entire *systems*" (e.g., schools, universities, families, neighborhoods, businesses, and agencies) are "the focus of change" (p. 113).

Space Saving Tip

Finally, instead of enclosing a seemingly endless stack of books in addition to other documents in your knapsack, you can refer to the Annotated Bibliography on Early Career Socialization (appendix B) for additional ideas. This is a "space saving" educational tool designed to lighten the weight of your knapsack.

RESTING, BEFORE THE NEXT ASCENSION

We have now completed the first significant part of our journey and anticipate moving onto the next ridge (part 2), which will be of higher altitude and greater risk. It is best to seek shelter now, as the winds are buffeting and the temperature has dropped. An impeding storm as also been reported. Even Sir Edmund Hillary and Tenzing Norgay, storing energy before ascending the icy slope on the way to the summit, found themselves huddled in a tent twenty-eight thousand feet up Mount Everest (National Public Radio 2003a). So, put up your tarp, record your day's events by the candle lantern, and apply the ointment from your first-aid kit to those blisters. Wrap yourself in extra layers to stay warm in preparation for your own ultimate challenge.

Our mountaineer—the beginning school leader—will guide us even more vigorously on the next administrative foray. Expect to hear real-life stories by aspiring and practicing school leaders along the way. You will also learn how to use the essential equipment for a successful climb and to practice conditioning your muscles and capacities as a developing leader.

Part 2

WHAT PRACTICING SCHOOL LEADERS SAY ABOUT THEIR FIRST ADMINISTRATIVE TREK AND THEN SOME

Chapter Seven

Mountaineering Boots: Conditioning Preparation

By strengthening our bodies we become more capable in handling the exertion of hiking. Thus, we reduce the hardships and discomforts, both physical and mental, and we increase our chances of success. The training forays also help us develop patience and persistence, and they go a long ways in helping us overcome lethargy [and provide] respite from the daily rut and from any beleaguering pressures and worries. And the exercise, fresh air, and increased blood circulation will stimulate vitality and productivity back at our jobs or studies.

—R. Jardine

CASE SCENARIO

The Creation of WOW (Weight Off Wisely)

As the wellness chair on special assignment at a suburban Florida high school this year, Frances Helfrich had a goal: to build a strong wellness team for the adults. With this in mind, she knew it was imperative to develop a vision and mission statement. In order to accomplish this task, her wellness committee sent out a survey to determine how it could best meet the needs and desires of their faculty and staff. The results indicated a demand for the improvement of morale, increased teamwork, established fitness programs, and better food choices, including the availability of purified drinking water. The needs assessment led the group of teacher leaders to create their pointed mission statement: "to encourage a healthy lifestyle."

Coincidentally, the committee's school goals aligned with the Healthy People 2010 fitness objective to improve health, fitness, and quality of life through daily physical activity (President's Council on Physical Fitness and Sports [PCPFS], March 2001). With this new knowledge, the coordinators were able to design and implement a program that was multifaceted, one that could help meet the needs their faculty considered important.

WOW Implementation

Everyone at the school site was invited to join the WOW program. As of February 2003, seventy-five members (out of a possible 125 teachers) joined and paid the $10.00 membership fee. In addition, the program was point driven and team based; all members were placed into teams of three to instill collaboration and promote motivation and teamwork. The committee's intention was to inspire healthy habits, such as eating wisely and increasing exercise. People at all fitness levels joined the program, though—not just those wanting to lose weight.

The members were required to weigh in during the first day of the twelve-week program; for every 1 percent of body weight lost they received one point, and for 10 percent, an extra ten bonus points were awarded to help build team cohesiveness. For example, in the allotted time, a 150-pound person would receive one point for every 1.5 pounds he or she lost, and an additional ten bonus points for fifteen pounds or more, for a total of twenty points for the team. In addition, one exercise point was given for each twenty-minute interval of continuous aerobic or anaerobic exercise (only one point could be earned daily for an anaerobic activity). At the culmination of the program, the team with the most points would receive a $750.00 reward.

The administration, in full support of the WOW program, generously donated $400.00. These extra monies allowed the wellness committee to sponsor weekly competitions and rewards. In addition, fact sheets were placed in people's mailboxes, along with the next week's competition.

WOW Results

In retrospect, Frances believes the success of the program was largely due to the empowerment of the participants. Their input was essential for designing and implementing a workable program. Moreover, the WOW program changed the culture of their school. The attitude of the faculty seemed more upbeat and positive. There now exists a community feeling where there once was none. One assistant principal even commented on how refreshing the conversation in the faculty lounge had been since WOW.

Many faculty members' energy levels have significantly increased. They as a faculty body managed to shed over three hundred pounds in four weeks! Surprisingly, Frances has noticed her students modeling some of the adults' new behaviors, such as drinking more water (less soda) and eating "healthier"; some have even told of their new or improved exercise habits. With the way this program has caught on, staff participation in WOW cannot help but yield better results than anticipated (from Helfrich 2004).

REFLECTION AND DISCUSSION

Interpreting the Case

In Administrative Analysis and Change, a master's course at the University of South Florida, Frances Helfrich conducted an assessment of the school-based Weight Off Wisely program known as WOW. This wellness committee chair developed and assessed a team-oriented health program that is rare in a high school. The teacher-led initiative was funded exclusively through staff members' fees and the financial donation of the building level administration. Frances's case study focused on the design and implementation of the WOW program and its preliminary effects. Through this action-based inquiry process involving survey design and analysis, she learned some vital information about the program and its effect on school culture.

First of all, Frances discovered that "the team approach was instrumental in the positive outcomes the faculty had observed." Additionally, it had become essential "to continually inform the teams of health-related issues and concerns." Furthermore, "the point driven system has been an effective tool; however, more points (100) should have been allotted for those individuals who lost at least 10% of their weight because they had significantly changed their eating habits."

Interestingly, her insight into people's motivation illustrates the focus of whole-school training: "I originally thought the use of rewards and placing a monetary value for the winning team would be a motivating strategy, but the opposite became obvious—intrinsic motivation is the key to success. In fact, the extrinsic motivators have caused some friction between teams and team members." Based on this outcome, next time she expects to "establish other tangible motivators such as before and after health screenings, which would be more valuable and personal for the participants." Lastly, this wellness coach reported that most of the school teams expressed the desire to have the program continue for a longer period of time, as a reflection of its "favorable outcomes."

Warm-Up Stretches

Novice mountain hikers actively undertake basic training and conditioning programs before embarking on a journey (e.g., Jardine 2001; Kosseff 2003). One must *get ready* for a hike.

Mountain climbers are often pictured hanging from ropes or struggling up a wall of rock, but in order to climb a mountain it is necessary first to get to it. For this reason, the basic skill required for mountain climbing is hiking, and anyone interested in the sport should develop the strength and stamina to walk long distances without tiring. Strong arms and legs support a climber's weight, making physical strength essential.

If you will be trekking long distances—as you can expect to do, both literally and metaphorically, in schools—you will need to do all you can to prepare.

According to expert trekkers, a hike is not simply a long walk—it belongs to a different class because it is much more strenuous. For example, it is one thing to observe, as an intern, a parent–teacher conference, and quite another to handle this yourself as the school leader. You may find yourself in the difficult situation of having to explain to a parent why her "troubled youngster" requires "professional support outside the scope of services the school [can] provide" (McDaniel 1999, 118). The first situation is, analogously, a walk, and the latter, a hike. But even in this context, you can seek the assistance of the teacher and guidance counselor and approach the parent as a team, equipped with the relevant documentation and a caring attitude.

SUMMIT DATA AND ANALYSIS

For the beginning school administrators who contributed to this study, university preparation programs ranged in quality from weak to satisfactory to strong. While many had not gotten the "extra support" expected, others had. On this subject, the results were mixed. Nonetheless, the survey respondents and focus group members viewed the actual school site as the most valuable training ground.

This is where the administrator, adapting to his or her new role, experiences conditioning preparation to an escalated extent. Even for those participants who considered themselves well prepared, the process of on-the-job education necessitated more knowledge. A typical comment to this effect was, "Despite going through a leadership training program and substation as an assistant principal and learning a great deal, I was not prepared for the amount of knowledge I would need."

As part of this leader conditioning, a learning curve almost seemed to take on a personality of its own in the data—it was instantaneously activated and permeated the work. Consequently, the "learning curve syndrome" was expressed by almost everyone: "My graduate program prepared me well, but then each school specializes in so many different things that there's always a huge learning curve," and "My experience as an AP prepared me tremendously, but it is still a learning curve once you get into the job."

Interestingly, *learning curve* did not appear as a term on the Early Career Administrator Survey (see appendix C), yet new leaders from different districts used it. This suggests the ubiquity of a learning curve for new careerists in at least two senses, as the projected knowledge base needed for learning a new set of skills and as the escalated growth cycle.

Regardless of how much conditioning you may actively pursue through, say, clinical internship, practicum, shadowing, or action research for breaking into your future career, it may be essential to embrace this study's basic message: "Expect each day to be a whole new learning experience." A new day, another summit to climb. The scope of the job and the deeper and more comprehensive patterns in school activity take time to develop. The newcomer will have to construct these complex knowledge banks with the assistance of reflective inquiry (e.g., action research) and ongoing training (e.g., professional development) throughout their career.

When Tom Graves became a first-time principal at a middle school in Florida, he had a strong belief in developing school culture by exercising self-initiation and teamwork. He subsequently applied his philosophy to a number of schoolwide initiatives embedded in ritual. For example, "Rambo Day" was organized to introduce the school to a new conditioning process that would

> communicate the importance of teamwork in achieving our objectives for the year. Rambo Day was an inclusive team-building event that took place at an outdoor center before the school year had started. Each activity (e.g., the big-shoe walk where everyone tried to move together on the same plank using strung ropes) involved participation by all teachers and staff, including the custodians. (Mullen and Graves 2000, 486)

Conditioning routines for the new leaders in my study included building teams, learning how to multitask and prioritize, and, more subtly, approaching situations from different vantage points. (Chapter 11 is devoted to the team motif.) From the cultural and social to the conceptual and political to the analytical and technical, the beginning administrator can expect constant challenge in these areas of training.

A training program can literally mean a training camp or can instead take the form of conditioning routines. Regardless, the idea is that familiarity and competence are built as part of the process of acculturation and socialization itself. And challenge and growth will need to remain constant motivations.

Types of Conditioning

Cultural conditioning helps the new inductee gain proficiency and insight at both deeper and broader levels. As someone shared, "If I had the last eight months to do over again, I'd spend more time learning about the school's history and working harder to build trust and rapport." This statement fits with Bolman and Deal's (1993, 1997) practical advice for leaders, who are new to a setting, to get to know the culture by studying its history and stories, and by participating in its rituals and ceremonies. The population I studied of beginning leaders tacitly understood culture as a collection of practices for which school leadership is responsible. Consequently, cultural training was associated with skills building in areas ranging from attending parent–principal conferences to interacting with students with varying disabilities. However, this is school culture understood at a bare minimum.

Culture involves an individual interacting with the environment and the environment acting upon an individual. It is not anything that can be seen per se and its reality exceeds anything that can be neatly or discretely identified, and so our cultural experiences are like being a "fish in water," as the expression goes. If we were fish, we would not be aware of the water in which we were immersed, in much the same way we as organizational members are not aware of the culture we inhabit. Not a passive process of socialization, psychosocial forces shape the direction and quality of our work in schools (Snyder, Acker-Hocevar, and Snyder 2000), and guiding beliefs and expectations influence the way our organizations function (Hargreaves and Fullan 1998). Moreover, as Schein (1985, 1992) describes, culture is not only a pattern of assumptions discovered but also developed by a group as it acclimates, adapts, or resists the expected ways of thinking and behaving. All of these understandings of cultural conditioning are relevant to the new leadership population I studied, especially Schein's articulation.

Given this critique, it is not surprising that there were no data in my study to support a view of culture from larger comparative and global contexts. The influence of cultural variables on leadership and schooling was not addressed in the surveys or interviews. And world economic, political, and social trends and their effect on leadership at the local, state, or national level was not mentioned. (For a discussion of these understandings of culture and leadership, see Walker and Dimmock [2002]). Nor did the survey itself seek to elicit these broader cultural connections or shape the focus group sessions. It can therefore be inferred that the study itself may have had a socializing influence on the participants' thinking.

Many of the participants referred to *social conditioning*, especially with regard to interpersonal communication and conflict resolution. In their advice directed at aspiring leaders, they exclaimed, "Be flexible and personable! Also be willing to talk with parents. This helps with solving little problems that may turn into large problems!" In particular, administrative competency was prized in the area of "soft skills," which Kosseff (2003) identifies as communication, decision making, crisis management, facilitation, teaching, and group dynamics. To a lesser extent the respondents also discussed "hard skills," which I identify as cognitive

knowledge, procedural knowledge, tautological knowledge, factual information, and statistical processing.

Even learning one's school policy, for example, seemed useful for guiding the core "soft" areas: "Determining student discipline consequences
for misbehavior or rewards and supervising students after consulting the
school policy—this is how most of my day is spent." Assistant principals
responsible for school discipline will generally attest to the time this social task takes, not the learning of the procedural knowledge per se.

Conceptual conditioning requires, among other critical elements, that
the new school leader understand how procedures fit with "school policy,
state policy, district policy, and state and national legislation." Having this
information under one's belt, so to speak, will help you "be ready to lead
and make sound, well thought-out decisions." These quotes are from the
study respondents who offered insights relevant to conceptual conditioning. Together, they stressed the relative value of social awareness involving interpersonal relations over conceptual knowledge: "When I began I
thought, I don't know enough. Soon I learned you never know all you
need to know, but you must always find ways to connect with people and
treat them well." This focus is consistent with the importance Bolman and
Deal (1997) give to the human relations paradigm (social conditioning)
within the school leadership landscape. Much of this knowledge was
learned "on the job."

A type of training infrequently alluded to by the participants is *political
conditioning*. Information gathered inadvertently via telephone exchanges
with new assistant principals uncovered uncertainty and even fear, such as
when it was thought that the principal might somehow find out about the
survey: "I don't know if I should receive it from you. Will there be any
way to track my answers? I wouldn't want my principal to be privy to any
of this information." The anonymity of the study may not have been
enough of a guarantee of confidentiality for them. And, filling it out (even
receiving it!) may have meant taking an unnecessary risk, given that the
person would be specifying where his or her time was being spent and on
what jobs, a seemingly apolitical proposition that produced unexpected
reactions from a few.

It is difficult to explain this apprehensiveness. I can only speculate that
any new person who is determined to succeed might feel cautious, not
wanting to be misjudged. In at least one case, the assistant principal perceived that he and the principal lacked trust. On the one hand, the politi-

cal nature of the interpersonal relationship for principals and their apprentices was outside the bounds of this study; on the other hand, the repression of one's feelings signals cumbersome baggage and unresolved issues, and that has relevance for this study with regard to the better and worse loads that leaders carry (see chapter 6).

The more usual political tone on the telephone, however, expressed an eagerness to communicate about the conditioning obtained from one's university program. Good-natured responses included, "I've sure got lots to say about the preparation I received, so please send that survey," and, "Anytime you've got anything that deals with graduate leadership programs or being a leader, I would really like to participate. I've got tons to talk about." The new administrator will survive by learning how to map the political domain and the cultural values embedded within it, in order that decisions and actions taken will not seem naive (e.g., Bolman and Deal 1993, 1997).

Physical conditioning, the final aspect of training discussed here, was not mentioned at all in the practitioner data, yet it is essential: Consider the need to become adept at focusing on the most important aspects of the job in addition to discriminating among priorities. One could easily overreact and misjudge a situation, for example, or become distracted by the rough-and-tumble aspects of a politically charged atmosphere (see chapter 12 for an illustration). To hike these mountains, one must be vigilant. Physical conditioning is the key—it is more important than generally acknowledged.

Frances, the wellness coach who shared her story, viewed physical conditioning as a shared vision and schoolwide commitment that enhances teamwork and other goals. Health is a systemic issue, then, even though the commonplace notion in America is strictly personal, involving an individual's workout routine (e.g., yoga, meditation, jogging, swimming, sports). Such activities can offer not only athletic endurance for the long-distance hiker (Kosseff 2003) but also focus for an entire faculty, staff, or student body. Working physically can also take the more familiar community-building form of improving and maintaining a school's interior and exterior as an integral part of its public image (Mullen and Graves 2000; Mullen and Patrick, 2000).

Physical training is essential to the development of one's leadership capacities, including interpersonal, social, conceptual, political, and cultural skills. In general, "training is far and away the best bridge to becoming a leader" (Kosseff 2003, 41). By being physically fit, an individual or institution will be able to deal more effectively with emotionally taxing situations by preventing overreaction and burnout. To be able-bodied, nimble, and agile keeps pressures in perspective. As Kosseff reminds us, "leaders need to be in strong enough physical condition that they always have a reserve of strength even if their followers are exhausted" (p. 23).

Bridge through Conditioning

While gaps are inevitable in the new leader's training, conditioning will provide the opportunity to bridge theory and practice and, where possible, to apply your conceptual understandings to actual situations. Role-playing is one way to simulate practice and train for real-world settings. In my master's classes, the students assume the roles of particular characters (e.g., a principal caught in a clash between the values of faculty and parents) in the case studies we read. But first, we create our own script, based on the text, in small groups. We then draw the roles from a hat, which places demands on almost everyone's conceptual flexibility and personal values. Finally, we interact as a whole group with a member from the broader community (e.g., school counselor) who facilitates the script and critiques our performances.

LESSONS

As Sir Edmund Hillary has declared, "With practice and focus, you can extend yourself far more than you ever believed possible" (Wiesel 2003). Just as in the world of mountaineering, different kinds of conditioning—social, cultural, political, and conceptual—are all important and overlapping in school leadership. And some forms may have more value than others, depending upon your circumstances or what is demanded of your performance at any given time.

Long-distance trekker Kosseff's (2003) motto is: "Prior planning prevents poor performance" (p. 79). Producing a well-designed training program, whether it is at a school or a university, can provide the novice leader with a well-rounded perspective, set of skills, and means for satisfying goals. The perspectives on conditioning that the study respondents shared support all these training elements. From the world of backpacking, here is what the experts and their observers have to say:

Know Your Goal

Ellen Miller reached the summit of Everest for the second time in a single year—by two different routes, commenting, "I know it's easy to make a mistake on Everest; I know many things are out of my control. So my style, when I get to a mountain, is to keep my head down, stay focused, and try to reach the goal at hand—the summit." (*MountainZone.com*, 2002)

Commit to Practice

Miller, true to her character, left little to chance on her last Everest attempt: She ran near her home in Vail every day, practiced crossing ladders set up between cars in the parking lot, and frequently climbed short ice pitches to prepare for the Hillary Step. Miller said she knew her attempt could still be stopped by weather or snow conditions. But she was adamant that if there were to be a failure, it would not be her own. (*MountainZone.com*, 2002)

Expect a Bumpy Ride

She was amazing, going on to finish the last twenty kilometers with a sprained left hand, using her opposite hand to change gears in some bumpy steep sections. (*MountainZone.com*, 2002)

Prepare Diligently

I treasure the freedom that comes from having everything I need to survive resting on my back. [On the other hand] backpackers cannot carry everything they might need in case of an accident—they wouldn't be able to fit it all in their packs! (Logue 2000, xvi, 264)

BACKPACKING TIPS AND LEADER ACTIVITIES

Prepare before the Hike

- Develop leader skills before you "hit the cliffs" (Kosseff 2003, 55).
- Focus will help you to maximize your growth as an effective leader. Concentrate on the areas in which you need to build skills, using the results of the survey to guide you. Build your experience to fit your desired end. Once you have decided what type of activity and program

you are interested in leading, you can gear your reading, training, practice, and mentoring accordingly. This will extend to the type of student population you expect to be leading (e.g., at-risk youth, people with varying disabilities).

- Listen to base camp stories, old-timers' narratives about what worked for them, and inspirational journey accounts, both inside and outside (e.g., sports) the leadership and administration field.

Leadership Activities

- For trust building with teams, try blindfolding and being led (and leading) through an unfamiliar route (e.g., woods).
- Literally, become proficient with using the essential items in a first-aid kit. Learn how to improvise the equipment as well. Take a first-aid course to learn the fundamentals for promoting school health and safety. As a school leader, know what medication the students in your building might be taking, and monitor their use (Mullen and Patrick 2000). Also learn about the details involved in extended-care issues. The school leader cannot simply rely on the on-site nurse to take care of such health issues, especially in general emergencies.
- Read current federal and state legislation as well as school policies, making connections among these documents and in relation to the school situations you know. Map your own routes.

Chapter Eight

Map: Inventory Survey

No one plans on getting lost, but if you backpack long enough, chances are you will find yourself off course, wondering where you went wrong. If you know how to read a map and use a compass, you can reduce the chance of getting lost, and when you do get lost, you will be able to help get yourself back on track. The first step in prevention is to familiarize yourself with the area, and there is no better ways to do this than with maps. . . . The ability to interpret the lines, symbols, and colors will help you stay on the trail, or when the trail suddenly disappears, to find your way.

—V. S. Logue

CASE SCENARIO

"I'd like you to meet Penny, our new assistant principal," announced the principal at the first faculty meeting of the new school year. The brief applause that followed was accompanied by the teachers' knowing glances. Familiar whispers were heard:

"Here comes another inventory system."
"Time to train someone else on how to map out our needs."
"I wonder how long she'll be here."
"She'd better not get too comfortable in her new office."

This year seemed destined to be like the past ten—a new person in charge of curriculum. Out with the old, in with the new! Just when the faculty had made progress acculturating the previous assistant principal (AP) and learning that person's systems and routines, they would have to start all over again. They'd already been through this learning–training cycle nine times over the decade.

To give you a sense of the history of this school's turnover, in 1992, the Florida school district that houses what Linda Bayless (2004) calls "Mountain Valley Elementary" realigned the staffing model and administrative job responsibilities. Consequently, out of eighty elementary schools, fifty-four assistant principals assumed the curriculum leadership (AP2) role. The other twenty-six schools hired a half-time curriculum specialist to be shared with another site. Mountain Valley's reading specialist moved on to a new position, and "Sandra," one of its teachers, became the school's assistant principal of curriculum. Most of the established systems and programs remained intact since she was familiar with them, minimizing her efforts to learn the layout of the school and the staff's efforts to ascertain her leadership style. Some initiatives had to be deemphasized or dropped altogether, though, because Sandra was only at Mountain Valley twice a week.

The next few years brought a change in the school's student population, with four self-contained exceptional education classes placed on its campus. The school's boundary was also modified, moving the community's long-term residents to another zone. (A zone, an area that determines what schools children and adolescents can attend, based upon where they live, is not to be confused with the broader district/county in Florida.) These shifts changed Mountain Valley's ranking for an assistant principal. When applying the district's staffing formula (i.e., student population figure, number of buses, total exceptional education classes, and free/reduced lunch percentage and mobility rate), the school became the last in line for receiving an assistant principal. In 1994, Sandra left and "Janis" joined the staff, stepping into the AP role.

Mountain Valley's new zone includes a large number of rental properties and motels for temporary housing. The school's population thus fluctuates continuously. This affects its assistant principal ranking each semester. As a result, after just one semester, Janis left in fall 1994 and Sandra actually returned as the half-time curriculum specialist. After staying one semester, Sandra evidently tired of the roller-coaster ride, changed careers altogether and accepted a position in business. So then came "Alicia" to take her place, working for two semesters until, once again, the school qualified for an assistant principal. Then "Brenda," the new AP, came on board for the remainder of the school year.

But in 1997 Brenda was assigned to another school, and "Rita" assumed the role of assistant principal. She stayed an entire year. Things were looking promising. Maybe the school would be able to retain the same curriculum leader for more than one year! But this proved not to be the case—the attrition of curriculum leaders continued from 1998 to 1999. For the 2000–2001 school year, Mountain Valley's mandate to hire an assistant principal resulted in "Penny." So perhaps you can better see why the faculty reacted as they did on her first day.

Recently, ten days after the Full-time Teaching Equivalency (FTE) count, the district was going to pull the position. This time the school used Title I funds to keep their assistant principal. "Lack of consistency has been a major problem," confided Mountain Valley's current principal. "When I came to this school two years ago, our instructional materials were a mess. No one knew where anything was. We even had teachers using 'out of adoption' textbooks [those books the state of Florida has declared outdated] because they never knew that new texts were available." Such leaders recognize that stability in leadership is nonnegotiable for facilitating a school's operations and meeting its goals.

Mountain Valley's decade-long struggle to improve student performance naturally makes one wonder if the excessive turnover in curriculum leadership has had a significant effect on the organizational functions of the school and students' and teachers' performance. As a teacher and Title I Facilitator at "Mountain Valley" for the past fifteen years, Linda Bayless has had personal experience of the challenges that these turnovers ignite. Though she recognizes her bias, she finds it difficult to believe that these leadership changes have not adversely affected the school's goals, particularly its managerial and supervisory ones (from Bayless 2004).

REFLECTION AND DISCUSSION

Interpreting the Case

The high turnover or attrition in school leadership is a critical issue in many districts around the nation (Posise 1999), affecting what can be accomplished and the process of change itself, especially in low-performing schools (Hatch 2000; Mullen and Graves 2000). A ten-year national study of the K–8 principalship cites that the median years of tenure for principals at any one school are six (Doud and Keller 1998). The average stay in the school district that Linda Bayless studied is just five years. If these numbers are both accurate and typical, then this particular elementary school's turnover rate in leadership should be considered excessive. However, a few experienced administrators in Florida whom I have talked with about this statistic say that it is probably a conservative estimate.

Linda Bayless wrote this turnover tale as part of a case study for a master's course in educational leadership at the University of South Florida. As this Title I specialist at a disadvantaged elementary school has learned, it takes time for any new leader to build morale with staff, students, parents, and community. One teacher shared that when the new leaders already know their tenure at "Mountain Valley" will be short, emotions run deep: "We're just a stepping stone." The other teachers Linda interviewed believe that the constant turnover has affected employee morale, productivity, and probably even student learning. They may have considered themselves unimportant in the grand scheme of things. When a school has someone different at the helm every year, trust and rapport can never fully develop. Because of increased budget cuts, the principal that Linda featured feels skeptical that the school will be able to retain the new assistant principal.

Such transitions in leadership negatively influence a school's entire culture: It is not uncommon for all change efforts in progress to slip into a state of suspended animation. Those involved in the change wait, their nerves on a roller coaster of fear and hope. Frequently, good efforts at change are dismantled and a new plan constructed, only to be taken apart when the next leadership transition occurs (Wasley 1992).

Linda attests that Florida's A through F school grading system has resulted in this school's D label for three consecutive years. "Mountain Valley" competes for resources with other elementary schools in Florida, but it serves low-socioeconomic-level neighborhoods and transient families. School culture, already an unstable dynamic in such a locale, is further affected when new administrators want to implement their own agendas by changing or casting aside inherited projects.

At Mountain Valley, the staff expended energy trying to decipher each new leader's plans for achieving the school's goals. As Posise (1999) confirms, discontinuity in leadership leads to frustration and the absence of follow-through on goals and programs. At this school some staff had difficulty even remembering the names of all those who have assumed leadership in their building, let alone the vision they may have brought with them: "We do everything a different way every year," and, "We don't know where materials are because there is a new system for handling them every year. When we get our inventory lists there are things on them we've never heard of" (Bayless 2004).

In addition to the educational leadership literature (e.g., Mullen and Graves 2000), organizational psychology studies (e.g., Hom and Griffeth 1995) stress that employee turnover has a negative effect on how well an institution functions and performs. In his study of school reform, Hatch (2000) confirms that excessive turnover in leadership produces chaos: Each new leader must be trained in the school's programs and systems, and the problems are even greater in those experiencing such serious challenges as poverty, violence, or apathy. Leadership is a tool for school success—it is not an end in and of itself.

Linda Bayless's account substantiates these perspectives, for it was not only the teachers who had difficulty adjusting to the constant leadership change—the leaders themselves seemed to suffer, too. Notably, the new assistant principal whom Bayless calls "Penny" found her own transitional experience stressful beyond expectation and "very difficult to get oriented. Helping teachers with instructional materials was especially challenging. She had so much to learn and was not sure whom to consult for reliable information and help. It took time to figure out on whom she could depend" (p. 6).

Penny learned, too, about operations at the cultural and political level: After devising a "simpler plan" for "new hall duty assignments" that would reduce the number of duty days per person, her plan was met with hostility. But the school operations map had been based on a careful inventory of people and routines, so Penny was confused. She learned the hard way about the powerful role that politics and school culture would play in her future decision making. Where she had been focused on the opportunities for positive change that the organization could now reap, the faculty felt taxed. Hatch (2000) explains that this kind of schism can occur in leadership turnover situations where teachers will require recovery time and regeneration of spirit, as well as trust in the new leadership, before they can be expected to reinvest in meeting the school's goals.

When principals come and go, mapping change initiatives based on careful audits and inventories is disrupted. In this picture, Linda tells us that "teachers must spend valuable energy dealing with the management of curriculum materials instead of planning for instruction, collaborating with others, and refining instructional strategies." In addition to a superficial treatment of curriculum, "good programs that could produce results" get abandoned because when new leaders appear and disappear, different programs are implemented but then quickly dropped. The synergy that needs to exist between leaders and staff to both energize and sustain a school's improvement plans dwindles and becomes directionless. As Linda concludes, "it takes time to cultivate the trusting, productive relationships that are required for such synergy. A school with such excessive leadership turnover seems doomed to failure."

Like Mountain Valley's faculty, many school teams that work diligently to improve are in desperate need of stability and consistency in leadership. The principal in Linda's study longed for the opportunity to develop a significant partnership with an AP: "It takes time to build a strong team, and we need that to move this school forward." Research supports that co-administrative and mentoring partnership is an essential resource for schools that are committed to making progress (e.g., Crow and Matthews 1998; Mullen 2002b).

Linda's viewpoint and analysis are supported by Edmonds's (1979) school effectiveness research, which has established that "one of the most tangible and indispensable characteristics of effective schools is strong administrative leadership, without which the disparate elements of good schooling can neither be brought together nor kept together" (p. 32). Shared leadership could never happen in this unstable climate.

The way staffing formulas are implemented within school districts can have an effect on whether co-administrative partnerships will be able to thrive at the building level. From the vantage point of an insider, Linda claims that "financial constraints always play a part in how schools are staffed." Her solution is for an AP to be placed at every elementary school in the district and for districts in general "to make some effort to ensure that schools have stability in leadership positions." She believes that the strict use of a formula for determining school staffing is problematic. The districts could clearly benefit from investigating and thus mapping the effects of their policies on schools.

Mapping the Scene

The socialization of any new school leader involves learning the lay of the land beyond a basic orientation—operationally, politically, socially, and interpersonally (Bolman and Deal 1993, 1997; Schmidt 2002). Researchers place particular emphasis on the political domain. Schmidt, a former principal, recommends asking yourself decisive questions, such as who would benefit from a particular proposal and how, and who might be opposed. And she recommends, as do Bolman and Deal, that leaders develop a political sensibility: This involves, as a primary activity, mapping key constituencies and their functions and then acting on that knowledge. Examples of key constituencies include state and federal legislators, special interest groups, taxpayers, the media, private enterprise, big business, the local business community, the board of education, the superintendent, parents, school-site governance groups, teachers' union, and teachers.

Organizational mapping is a "diagnostic, analytic, planning, and implementation model" (Shapiro 2003, 225). This goes beyond the inventory or topographic and diagnostic aspects being covered in depth in this chapter. In order for a new school leader to create maps, he or she must first entertain the commonplace notion of *map*, which is to systematically arrange related elements over an aerial domain (Kealy and Webb 1995), and *to map*, as in to interpret another's representation, which can be pictorial, expository, or verbal.

The new school leader will actively create and interpret existing maps, both literally and metaphorically, to "survey the terrain" (Schmidt 2002) and thereby become oriented to a new place. A leader's acclimation to the school environment will establish the foundation for making informed, as opposed to superficial, knee-jerk decisions.

In the scenario introducing this chapter, the faculty saw their new leaders as having to "map out" the employees' needs. Further, the principals who arrived at their school were viewed as being responsible for inventory. And one teacher even equated the transitional leaders with "inventory systems," a metaphor that takes the idea of inventory to a whole new level. As we will see, mapping one's terrain and conducting inventories as part of this larger navigational process are not minor points. These are indispensable strategies for effectively leading within a new organization.

While it may be tempting for risk-takers new to mountaineering to rush up the Himalayas without any oxygen regulators, acclimation, or knowledge of what to expect, it is always smarter to carefully map out the unfamiliar area first. This also helps with keeping potentially negative reactions from coworkers in check, a strategy that could have benefited "Penny," the new AP at "Mountain View Elementary School."

The process of mapping can be understood, then, as the larger concept for which inventory management serves as the application. How is an inventory like a map, exactly? Both provide a systematic and spatial arrangement of elements for making sense of a hodgepodge of items by organizing them into piles, themes, or categories. Maps and inventories are essential tools that offer a complete and systematic picture of a place in terms of its key features or elements. If you create a map and inventory of your new school community, for example, it might include the campus, school district, and the state of Florida in regard to relevant administrative policies and mandates that affect operations, curriculum, resources, and accountability. The map you design will prove invaluable for planning and implementing decisions if you have a clear purpose in mind at the outset.

To illustrate, for this book I relied heavily on the *Florida Education Directory by FASA, 2002–2003 School Year* (2002). This critical resource provides a list of new leaders and their schools throughout Florida. The directory offers a comprehensive list of school and district personnel, not a categorization of new and experienced leaders per se. Once I had a customized listing of new school leaders, I was better oriented to my study.

But I had more mapping to do before the potential survey participants could be contacted. Knowing that my goal was to cover and thus represent the state, I consulted FASA's map of school districts. I needed to ascertain whether each county was represented by at least one beginning administrator. Comparing my personalized inventory of names to the map, it became clear that most of the school districts were indeed represented.

Why make maps? Cartographers take an inventory to map out an area, noting high/low points, roads, buildings, bodies of water, and anything else of special significance. Mountaineers do this as well. Trekkers need to know the best or most interesting trails to take, depending upon their goals, and so will locate or create maps of the area. So, too, will the new school leader get a lay of the land by carefully plotting routes as maps are followed and changed. A map enables one to organize or reorganize one's space, resources, personnel, or anything else. A map is also consequential in the way it turns out, and so, too, is an inventory (Kealy 2003). To provide a simple illustration of these ideas, if you were to do an inventory of your shoes, you would "survey" your stock. You could classify by type, function, brand, utility, age, appeal, materials, comfort level, or more, depending upon your purpose. Perhaps you wish to discern the relative state of the condition of your shoes in order to decide what needs repair and what needs to be purchased.

At this preliminary stage you would be conducting a diagnosis, not undertaking an appraisal or assessment. It is indeed important to take your time with this: Information is needed before any judgments can be made. Perhaps you will have learned that you do not own any high-quality mountaineering boots, causing you to head to a reputable athletics store. To do an appraisal, you could look at whether any of your shoes are outdated, in need of repair or polishing, and so forth.

On a far more complex scale, the school leader will refrain from making decisions that could turn out to be costly. For, just as a person might decide not to discard a really comfortable pair of unfashionable shoes, a principal would probably be acting rashly to eliminate a program that has always worked well but that falls short of today's standards. The broken-in but not broken-down pair of shoes—no longer suitable for professional contexts—might be perfect for gardening or messy chores. Similarly, an outdated program or curriculum may require that its coordinator and staff receive new training, be incorporated into a higher functioning unit, or, more severely, be allocated a less prominent space or set of resources in keeping with its diminished status.

To map out an organization by completing an inventory of its resources, ask yourself, what are the organization's current resources or assets? Do you know what needs to be surveyed or even how to go about documenting what is there in order to get the lay of the land? On the concrete, tangible level you can focus on computers and technological equipment, the budget (such as discretionary dollars), personnel (including operational and administrative), types of programs, faculty/staff specializations and educational levels, assessment scores, and so on. You can organize yourself ahead of time with key questions (that may have arisen out of your interview) or with categories that are of interest to you. In contrast, notes that have no inherent organization will be difficult to manage later and may prove futile anyway.

Recently, I had a much-needed personal experience along these lines during a time of leadership turnover in my educational leadership department at the University of South Florida. The techniques for mapping that Professor Don Orlosky used supported informed decision making at the level of team building. These strategies demonstrated interpersonal, analytical, and political approaches to gaining a picture of one's workplace. This new chair, a seasoned administrator and retired chair, led our unit in 2002–2003 for an interim phase. Taking systematic notes and organizing the process ahead of time, he interviewed every faculty member at the Tampa campus and regional campuses. He had already known the senior professors well, but others of us were new to him. Yet he favored no one's knowledge base or insights. Instead, he modeled an egalitarian, democratic process that served the interests of the collective.

Before interviewing us individually, he invited us to produce a one-page narrative for framing the session, which Don read ahead of time. He asked that we reflect on such issues as our philosophy, educational background, personal achievements, expectations of five and ten years, and the same for the department—what did we want our unit to become known for at the state and national level? After conducting the interviews, Don presented his findings at the first faculty meeting of the year. He had thematically analyzed our individual narratives and the interview commentary, using the same categories we were asked to incorporate. Don shared the philosophies we embodied as a group as well as our vision and plans for the future. The similarities and differences among us were emphasized, which allowed our differences to be respected, not homogenized. And he did not judge what he found but simply presented the results.

From the results of this qualitative data analysis, it became clear that the faculty held different views of our identity and goals as a unit. Some had felt that our main calling should be to better serve our surrounding school districts in the Tampa Bay area. Others saw a definite need to proceed with the high-profile scholarly agenda that had been set by the university in line with our recent Carnegie research status. As it turned out, departmental budgetary resources were allocated for project goals that complemented both ends—the practical and the theoretical. Faculty efforts to address the theory/practice gap in our program and the leadership field, which simultaneously fulfilled the service and research missions of the college, were valued. Consequently, this book was financially supported beyond the grant I had received for it.

From this story, we learn that map-making strategies can also be used for identifying underlying themes of an organizational unit. The goal for new leaders, then, is to get to know people and "unify the inquiry" as well as to "winnow down the insights into a few unities [key leadership goals] or factors that can be handled" (Shapiro 2003, 227). A related idea is that while an inventory involves a systematic account of items in storage or in one's possession, the items can be conceptual rather than strictly concrete. One cannot physically observe a skill, philosophy, or value.

This second idea returns us to the map-making issues exemplified by "Mountain Valley's" organizational context. A new school year will soon begin, and the district will have to again decide which sites should retain their assistant principals. This decision will impact planning and implementation at the building level. The reform efforts at Mountain Valley continue to be stymied because the leadership has not been able to get past the focus on the curriculum materials and the teachers' related needs. The new assistant principal hopes to have the opportunity to gain trust while supporting genuine instructional improvement.

Types of Inventories

To take an inventory at a comprehensive and meaningful level, school leaders can use self-assessment tests and self-study guides. The results can be discussed at a faculty meeting or analyzed by lead teachers or administration, depending upon how a school prefers to manage the results. Findings could be used as a conversation starter in a cooperative group situation or at a meeting. It makes sense to use several reliable assessments to develop a trustworthy picture of one's employees, especially if decisions will be made based on the results.

In chapter 12 we will learn about the value of journal writing as a kind of self-inventory through which personal and professional ideas take form. As a catalyst, a journal can help leaders to put thoughts and events into perspective or even to make decisions and take action.

Further, in keeping with the budgetary restrictions faced by many schools, leaders may opt for preformatted assessments that are free. For example, AdvisorTeam (2002) offers just such an online personality test called the Keirsey Temperament Sorter II Personality Instrument. According to the U.S. Department of the Interior's website, this is one of two famous tests—the other is the Myers-Briggs. At the website you must give a password and e-mail address before selecting answers on the multiple-choice test. There are seventy-five questions in all, and each question has two possible choices. An example of a question follows:

1. Are you more:
   a. routinized than whimsical
   b. whimsical than routinized

The Myers-Briggs is not offered free online. But an informal, user-friendly online personality inventory similar to the Myers-Briggs is the Humanetrics: Jung Typology Test (2003). There are no directions to follow—the test pops up and you simply click on "yes" or "no" for each prompt. There are seventy-two questions, ranging from how you work best to how you interact with people. Once you finish the test, your personality type is summarized. Here is an example of a test item:

1. You feel confident expressing yourself in a group.
   a. yes
   b. no

A third example, found at the Paladin Executive Services homepage (2003), can be retrieved via electronic mail. According to the description, this instrument can facilitate faculty placement in work groups and committees. Decisions of some magnitude can be made using this personality survey. Devised by a mother–daughter team in an attempt to operationalize Carl Jung's theories of psychology, this test is employed widely. In the 1940s during World War II, the military used this assessment to place soldiers in the appropriate division within the armed services.

Other personality style instruments feature the Gregorc Personality Style Delineator for building teams.

Many of us believe that acceptance and understanding are essential for meeting shared goals. As an inventory, this kind of diagnostic assessment helps faculty to better understand themselves and others, to appreciate the different personality types, and to steer away from hasty judgments about others' working style (Shapiro 2000, 2003). In fact, groups can be configured in such a way that all four personality types—concrete sequential, abstract random, abstract sequential, and concrete random—are represented in the development of an important program or curriculum.

Another type of assessment, as discussed in chapter 14, involves the use of self-study guides to foster the development of new skills. In order to cultivate or assess one's own or another's level of skill with standardized test data, for example, the leader could use the self-study aids provided at the Department of Education's website. When using or devising self-inventories for school faculty/staff, leaders should remain vigilant about governing principles and implicit values. As we have learned more generally in chapter 5, different cultures emphasize different values. The process of reflective practitioner mapping requires that we critique a diagnostic tool's implicit value before using it, the way we are expected to do with any educational curriculum. For example, does the inventory stress an individual over a collective approach; skills and knowledge over shared cultural values; or myopic and patriotic over diverse or global perspectives?

As described thus far, leaders will probably find it worthwhile to assess teacher behavior as well as group interaction. Along with the others who contributed to my book *New Directions in Mentoring* (Mullen and Lick 1999), I have found the "synergy audit" to be of particular value for monitoring a school team's level of cooperativeness in relation to its shared goals. This process is ideal for supporting reflective dialogue focused on group assessment, leading to clarified goals, renewed energy, and increased productivity (see Lick 1999).

Leaders can also make gains by evaluating the culture of their own organizations, which could have a significant influence on their decision-making and leader behavior at a more global level (Snyder, Acker-Hocevar, and Snyder 2000). Additionally, school climate surveys, which districts generate, offer leaders a traditional form of schoolwide assessment that takes into account perceptions of various stakeholder groups, ranging from teachers to supervisors to parents. But the results must be carefully analyzed and within the context of the school's goals if they are to yield any value (Mullen and Graves 2000).

Historically, various instruments have been developed over the decades for assessing leader behavior and producing guides to personal change. Managerial grids were popular in the 1960s and 1970s. George Kelly's psychology of personal constructs was used to assess teachers' implicit constructs and approaches to pedagogy, which others (e.g., David Hunt and Patrick Diamond) have since updated and applied to numerous organizational contexts, including self-narrative inquiries that examine issues of power and empowerment, for example (Diamond 1991; Diamond and Mullen 1999a, 1999b). In 1981, the commercial program of William Byham, educator and consultant, called Targeted Selection appeared on the market. This program led leaders (leadership aspirants and beginning administrators) to reflect not on what they would do in particular situations but rather on their perceptions of performance (Shapiro 2000). With insights gained from what they thought they had actually done in various contexts, these budding leaders were empowered to monitor their own behavior, reinforcing or modifying particular patterns.

SUMMIT DATA AND ANALYSIS

The study respondents as a whole endorsed the administrator survey as a viable mechanism for reflection and for understanding the work of new school leaders. Interestingly, support for the research instrument itself as an opportunity for personal diagnosis at the school leadership level was highlighted by several individuals: "I feel a self-inventory (similar to this) should be done by all new administrators so they know targeted areas to work on." This sharing validated the survey itself as a reflective instrument for promoting self-understanding and team building. Most participants focused more on the relative value of the core leadership areas (e.g., school organization) represented by the survey. Still others discussed how the actual activities listed reflected their own experiences: "I spent several years as an assistant principal and have learned to do all the activities listed on the survey to some degree. That experience was a great help at the beginning of this, my third year."

As directed by the instructions on the survey, all respondents used the categories and tasks as a reference point for assessing their school administrative experience: "Much of the job so far has involved working with student discipline, parent conferences, teacher evaluations, and plans for school improvement." Another replied, "Be familiar with the survey items concerning school board policies, state board rules, and district procedures." Several emphasized, in the survey's open-response section, "training in problem solving–conflict resolution skills" as an "important item" of "great significance."

School Management

This topic section on the administrator survey (see appendix C) includes the following nine tasks/items:

1. Manage budget (e.g., for instructional supplies).
2. Write and submit a grant application.
3. Review and enforce attendance/tardy policy (discipline).
4. Explore programs to improve student attendance.
5. Investigate plans for substitute (sub) coverage when teachers are absent.
6. Process student admissions/withdrawals.
7. Assess and analyze work of support personnel, paraprofessionals, and custodians.
8. Coordinate inservice training for secretaries.
9. Evaluate facilities maintenance (of buildings and grounds).

I focus on items 1 and 3 as two of the more significant skills in the core leadership area of school management.

Manage Budget (For Example, for Instructional Supplies)

Significantly, 52 percent of the respondents rated this item a "5," ascribing a priority status to this area of school management within the work of leadership. New school leaders devote a great deal of time and energy to financial management issues within their buildings, even though select duties within instructional supervision, school organization, and even community relations all "scored" higher (see table 5.3; chapter 5). Aside from personnel, the budget is the primary resource that an organization has at its disposal in order to achieve the stated mission. However, in poor schools, personnel and other nonfinancial capital (e.g., volunteers and role models) are the prime resource (Payne 1998; also see chapter 16). Basically, a school has two essential resources—money and people, and economics tends to be the gauge for determining which task receives the most attention. Budget allocations obviously become increasingly crucial and political during hard economic times.

In terms of budget-related managerial activity, the principal must constantly track the school's financial plan, resources, supplies, and inventory. For example, the school leader must know what items are being used by teachers/staff and in what quantity. Equipment, overhead projectors, computers, TVs, and so forth are usually listed within the general budget. Given increasing budgetary restrictions for public schools in Florida, all such items must be vigilantly monitored. Once monies from the district are spent for the fiscal school year, no more can be expected. Thus supplies and materials are inventoried carefully in an effort to last the entire academic year.

During graduate school, for such courses as School Finance, the preprofessional leader learns about the important role of budget in school operations and the related process of decision making: Planning, economics, and fiscal management all have an impact on solving a given problem within an organization. Of course, new administrators tend to acquire and practice these skills while working in a real-world school setting.

Review and Enforce Attendance/Tardy Policy

For this school management task, 31 percent of the administrator pool cited a "5." This response rate can be considered high, given what appears to be such a basic job. However, the feedback is not a surprise. State funding is based on the student population at any given school during the academic year. The more students that attend a particular public institution, the more monies are awarded for academic and athletic programs. Administrators are currently under great pressure to monitor teachers' attendance records. Ultimately, it is the leader's responsibility to assure that the attendance record is accurate.

The administrative task "explore programs to improve student attendance" is inextricably related to this issue of schoolwide attendance. Because this particular item received a "most important" rating from only 14 percent of the respondents, it does not "qualify" even as a tertiary entry for table 5.3. Interestingly, however, this response also suggests that attendance programs are on the horizon of school leadership, deserving mention here: These represent an emerging trend in response to increased accountability for student achievement at the state and national levels. At-tendance is what most leaders logically start with when they want to make changes to affect student learning and achievement as well as the school's grade (Mullen with Sullivan, 2002).

Largely because of accountability pressures, administrators have been focusing on their school's attendance rate. The FCAT (Florida Compre-hensive Assessment Test) school grade is partly determined by the num-ber of students that attend school regularly. Administrators are eager to have their schools receive the highest grade possible, and attendance is an area that can be impacted over time: The higher the school grade, the big-ger the yearly check from the state; also, "looking good" to the commu-nity rides upon the FCAT state rating. Formulating reward programs for good attendance is a way to improve student attendance. An example can be found in Florida's Hillsborough County, where raffles have been held for a free car, donated by a local dealership; eligibility for winning is a perfect attendance record. Building level administrators around the nation must lure the frequently absent to school. New assistant principals can be expected to participate by concocting tempting ideas.

LESSONS

One major lesson of this chapter is that the socialization of any new school leader will involve orientation—mapping and diagnosis—in at least four ways: operationally, politically, socially, and interpersonally. We also learned that schools can only implement and sustain change efforts with strong, stable administrative teams at the helm. Otherwise it is unlikely that struggling schools will ever achieve success. As the National Association of Elementary School Principals (NAESP) (2002) has outlined, standards for the principalship require that schools meet goals for supporting "stu-dent and adult learning"—and build accountability structures for doing so—by having "a full-time, qualified principal" who in turn has "adminis-trative officers" and other assistants for supporting reform practices (p. 4). However, a further and deeper problem not addressed in the NAESP doc-ument is that of leadership turnover or attrition itself: Scaffolds and re-sources are needed for producing sustainability or continuity in the princi-palship, thereby improving work conditions in school culture.

Also, the current budget situation for public schools and universities in Florida is "foreboding." One financial officer, an education dean I recently interviewed, believes that the "uncertain budget future" makes it "really hard to plan in that environment" (Mullen and Applegate 2002). The shrinking education budget for the state only serves to further complicate any leader's work with respect to decision making. Based on this economic forecast, managing a dwindling dollar may have to compete with the need to supervise instruction and keep institutions moving ahead, which depends on attracting and training competent personnel.

Another political matter involving priorities and values concerns the treatment of diverse student populations. Some practicing administrators say that school and district budgets tell you everything you need to know about the values of the organization. Even at the school building level where there is typically very little control over how the significant dollars can be spent (as in the case of preslotted personnel positions), values associated with budgetary spending are nonetheless communicated. For example, as one experienced assistant principal of curriculum in Florida shared with me, he has seen schools where the Advanced Placement (AP) (meaning gifted) classes work in relative luxury, using top-of-the-line computers and state-of-the-art software with assigned paraprofessionals on hand. In contrast, within the same school the "regular students," functioning in larger numbers within a comparable space, work at outdated computers, often in need of repair, with access only to the classroom teacher.

This contemporary picture of inequity in resource allocation may remind us of Kozol's (1991) poignant description. Moreover, as Oakes (1998) has described, if the lid of a schoolhouse were lifted off so that you could peer inside, you would see systemic tracking literally occurring. Because of their statement about values, the ways in which institutional budgets are used can be considered a social justice issue: Many U.S. public high schools still separate "vocational" from "academic" education. A disproportionate number of African Americans, Latinos, and poor students have typically been segregated in trade and industrial vocational tracks, and mostly white and Asian students in academic tracks. Notably, ability groupings differentiate students' abilities, providing different educational opportunities (Mullen with Kohan 2002; Oakes 1998).

Finally, and on another topic, this chapter has offered several self-assessment tools for new leaders. Perhaps lessons can be taken from the need to analyze the implicit values of such self-study guides, in addition to the story about my own department and how a seasoned administrator surveyed the landscape, influencing the deeper aspirations of its inhabitants. By doing so, the theory/practice split symbolized by the faculty unit and college was addressed, with a vision for integration made possible.

BACKPACKING TIPS AND LEADER ACTIVITIES

- Create a map of your organization that features key operational, political, social, and interpersonal elements in relation to a focus or goal of your own.
- Complete one or more of the self- or school-assessments discussed in this chapter and engage in dialogue with the appropriate personnel or population about the results.
- Analyze a school's current budget in terms of its major categories and specific lines: How are the monies allocated and what are the "biggest" items in terms of dollars? What does this signal about the needs and values of the institution? Next, reinterpret the budget in the context of the budgetary forecasts in education to see if you can identify what items will be affected when dollars are fewer.
- Interview an experienced financial officer (i.e., principal or college dean) to learn about the impact of budgetary issues on decision making with respect to resources and personnel in particular.

Chapter Nine

Compass: Direction Indicator

We are not blessed with an innate sense of direction. Or are we? We know that birds and many types of animals can sense which direction is which. Apparently they have some kind of a gland [that] acts like a compass. It might be possible for modern-day people to get back in touch with this long-lost skill. One way to practice is to hike along a trail, or cross-country, and try to remain aware of your direction of travel. Check your external compass every so often and see how well your internal compass is doing.

—R. Jardine

CASE SCENARIO

Watching her new principal and assistant principal (AP) at work in their elementary school in Florida, Bonita Salsman Paquette often wondered how they knew how to handle the various situations that arose at the campus. As a veteran teacher who is a leadership aspirant, she decided to interview both, asking these women administrators: "What do you think are important leadership characteristics for a school administrator? What might you have been unprepared for during your first year of administration? And what do you think colleges could do to better prepare future leaders?" Patty, a first-year assistant principal, and Vanessa, a second-year principal, are the characters in her story.

Patty. The new assistant principal, a white female in her early forties, had sixteen years' experience as a special education elementary teacher in Florida, with a master's degree in educational leadership. She joined

118

the school's staff in 2000. She described an effective leader as someone who is approachable, visible, and a good listener—characteristics she attributes to herself. When Bonita asked Patty what she might not have been ready for during her first year as an administrator, she rattled off a long list of procedural matters. Police matters and family services situations (i.e., suspected child abuse) topped her list. She also felt uncertain as to where the school's responsibility stopped and that of law enforcement began.

And the personal relationship skills required for the job could be overwhelming, Patty admitted. During her first week as a new AP, she was given the task of completing a duty roster for the second semester. During a faculty meeting, she eagerly rose to say that she had filled out a roster and that everyone had been assigned an area of duty, anticipating a positive response. However, as she began passing out the plan, the response was less than encouraging. The staff had grown accustomed to selecting their own duty posts and the weeks they would serve. Patty was unaware of that ritual. The staff rejected her new schedule: "What about our input?" one member loudly proclaimed. "Whatever happened to teacher empowerment?" another lamented. After much grumbling from the staff, she scrapped the schedule altogether in favor of soliciting feedback for a new plan. She recalls this incident with amusement, but at the time it felt as though the trust of those teachers had been lost. Patty claims that no class in college prepared her for the day-in, day-out relationship skills necessary to keep a faculty moving ahead.

When asked what colleges could do to help future administrators become more prepared, her answer was simple—a mentoring program. Patty felt that if she had been paired with a successful school administrator during her coursework, she would have had experience to complement the practical theory.

Vanessa. The new principal was a white female in her late forties and also graduated from a public university in Florida. Her experiences in education ranged from guidance counseling in elementary and secondary schools to the assistant principalship, with two years in different counties. Eager to talk about her administrative experiences, she revealed that she hoped the quality of preparation of future leaders had changed for the better since her own graduation eight years before. Vanessa revealed that an effective leader should be a good listener, a facilitator, and someone who shares the responsibilities of leadership. Such a person also knows how to set goals, motivate people, and plan effectively. She sees herself as someone that works hard in all of these areas.

The list Vanessa provided of things for which she had felt unprepared truly unsettled Bonita. During her first two years as an administrator, Vanessa had no idea how to successfully run a meeting. And she had not been taught problem-solving strategies, nor had she been trained in effective discipline techniques or given ideas for effective school improvement planning. Vanessa also admitted that budget issues were still a concern: She was unaware of how the system for ordering materials worked, or how different types of school budgets were to be managed. Such important tasks as designing and using surveys to solicit necessary information, employing effective interviewing skills, and even documenting problems with personnel had not been covered in her coursework.

When Bonita asked Vanessa what colleges of education could do to better prepare administrators, she suggested that programs focus coursework on budget management, school improvement planning, problem solving, people skills, and quality tools for use in assessment and other school contexts.

Bonita's ongoing conversations with Patty and Vanessa suggested some common problems in their preparation as administrators. For example, both expressed concerns over insufficient training in regard to conducting faculty and school meetings. Also, people skills had presented an obstacle from the outset. Finally, they strongly believed that master's programs would be much more beneficial if they offered mentoring opportunities, including shadowing experiences at school–community sites (from Paquette 2004).

REFLECTION AND DISCUSSION

Interpreting the Case

As revealed by this case scenario, some leadership aspirants seek direction from an "external compass," aligning what is learned with their own intuitive sense of direction. Bonita Salsman Paquette, an experienced elementary educator and prospective leader, attempted to point her own "internal compass" in the direction of helpful information from external sources. As two external compasses, she selected a master's program in educational leadership and the principals with whom she works in her building.

Curious about how well today's beginning school administrators are prepared for the job, Bonita undertook an inquiry for one of her master's courses taken with me in 2001. For her action research, she sought insight into the types of knowledge and skills that new leaders bring to their sites. She was also interested in detecting any gaps in practical knowledge that may characterize situations for new inductees. By learning about the major problem areas encountered by beginning leaders, she hoped to proactively address the fissures in her own socialization process before entering school administration as a career. This self-initiated strategy of personal appraisal and subsequent action has been noted by expert hikers for bringing about desirable change in one's own performance (e.g., Hobson and Clarke 1997; Jardine 2001).

After Bonita completed the interview process, she decided to find out just how generalizable or widespread her results were, so she looked into educational legislation and preparation programs across the country. Her goal was to find out if any university administrator programs offered "something beyond 'just' coursework, or theory-driven exercises, for prospective administrators." First, it was confirmed from her investigation that the problems beginning administrators experience in adjusting to their new roles are common and that this constitutes a budding area of public concern:

> Education Associations are beginning to realize that principal preparation programs need to be significantly reformed. For instance, the National Association for Elementary School Principals declared in the 1990 report *Principals for the 21st Century* that if principal preparations programs are to keep up with the accelerated pace of change, they need "major surgery." (Sherman 2000; as cited in Paquette 2004)

Second, this leadership trainee learned that progress is gradually occurring in some pockets around the nation. New programs for both aspiring and beginning school leaders, notably in California, have been formulated. Bonita was excited to read that California's state education budget allocated approximately fifteen million dollars over a three-year period for a principal training program that would establish accredited administrator programs. Additionally, this reform program would train five thousand principals and assistant principals and award each participant $4,000 for the ten days of training, with eighty hours of intensive follow-up (Association of California School Administrators 2001; as cited in Paquette 2004).

Program Reform Compass

Viable external compasses—sources that provide direction to leadership aspirants for the "real work" of schools—compel candidates like Bonita. Notably, she felt drawn to California's Leadership Development Model, in addition to other principalship training programs that have an assistant principal module. As she learned, California is also a leader in this respect: Veteran elementary teachers are paired with principals who recruit them. The novices perform a range of administrative tasks, from guiding curriculum development to assisting in fiscal management to serving as a liaison between parent groups and other organizations. (These areas have legitimacy in my own study as core leadership domains.) The new assistant principal works under the direction of an experienced principal, assisting in meeting goals from the instructional to the operational. As Bonita concludes, administrative apprenticeship programs designed to "provide assistant principals with the actual duties and responsibilities of principals" are terrific magnets.

In Bonita's school district, a principalship training program called Level Q is offered. According to her 2002 sources, in order to enroll, the assistant principal must already have had at least one year's experience. Also, the principal mentor to whom the novice is assigned cannot be the assistant principal's immediate supervisor but, rather, must be someone from outside the school. Amendments to existing programs or alternative training for seasoned teachers like Bonita, without experience requirements, would be most welcoming. Reinforcing this point, California's New Teacher Center at UC Santa Cruz offers the Beginning Teacher and Support Assessment Program at the school level to benefit future leaders who are currently educators (Paquette 2004).

Graduate Training Compass

For her preliminary study Bonita aligned the needle on her compass with north, so to speak, by asking, "Are the courses that prospective school administrators are required to take during their graduate program preparing them to be effective leaders?" Judging by the administrator interviews she conducted in Florida, practical knowledge is necessary to support the progress and growth of future leaders. In sum, given the case scenario provided at the outset, new school leaders can gain administrative direction by developing facility with the following four "cardinal points":

- Procedural knowledge (e.g., running a meeting; dealing with law enforcement and family services) (*school organization*)
- Problem-solving strategies (e.g., personal relationship skills; discipline techniques that include documenting problems with personnel) (*supervision of instruction*)
- School improvement planning (e.g., designing and using surveys; interview skills) (*school organization*; *supervision of instruction*)
- School budget (e.g., ordering materials; different types of budgets) (*school management*)

Interestingly, this list of skills (appearing in no particular order) was also included on my administrator survey (appendix C). As the results indicate, these leadership tasks received priority attention from the practicing administrators who completed it (see tables 5.2 and 5.3). The relevant core leadership area (italicized in the parentheses following each of the tasks/items) clarifies the correspondence between those pivotal skills identified by the newly practicing leaders in Bonita's study and my own. Accordingly, the results with respect to the core leadership areas and the survey itself can be used as external compasses for graduate program designers, professors, and researchers.

As discussed in other chapters, the graduate training compass needs serious adjustment in Florida and elsewhere. Many leadership researchers (e.g., Murphy and Forsyth 1999) have articulated this perspective, with personal disclosures supported from Bonita's case study. Recommendations based upon Bonita's practitioner interviews and research reinforce the call for program reform of principalship training. To this end, mentoring programs that include shadowing experiences (Malone 2001; Mullen and Cairns 2001) and action research (Mullen 2002b) have been strongly advocated in addition to relevant simulations of real-world activity.

When professional training and development include on-site mentorship from qualified administrators, aspiring and newly practicing leaders have a far greater chance of gaining a level of efficacy for sustaining themselves and their schools during difficult decision making and shifting paradigms in education (Bolman and Deal 1993; Clement and Vandenberghe 2001). With the opportunity for effective mentor–mentee pairing during their coursework, aspirants believe that the concepts they are learning will be better applied to address the theory/practice gap. They want to be able to place their feet on the leadership trails they will soon follow and have the opportunity to gain wisdom from an experienced Sherpa guide.

Success will need to be developed in both technical and human areas for aspiring and new leaders. The administrators Bonita talked to felt ill-equipped to deal with people on many levels, lacking a political skill all leaders need for coping with and transcending serious obstacles (e.g., McDaniel 1999; Schmidt 2002). Malone (2001) believes that mentoring, which can be built into courses, internships, or practica, is mandatory for preparing all future administrators. Aspiring leaders gain breadth and depth from putting their internal compass to good use early, developing a network of peers at the level of school/district/state administration while learning intensively from mentor principals and effective teachers. (For more ideas about graduate program development, see in particular chapters 15, 16, and 17.)

SUMMIT DATA AND ANALYSIS

Taking a Broader View

In this section, several administrator items/tasks will be discussed for their relevance to the metaphor of the compass as a tool for new leaders: "review curriculum documents"; "attend faculty meetings selectively"; "serve on a school committee; and attend principal/assistant principal meetings."

Valuing Administrative Experience

Review Curriculum Documents

Out of the respondent pool, 36 percent cited this school organization item (leadership task) as being "most important." The phrase "curriculum documents" is understandably vague and implies a multitude of educational resources. It can refer to an instructor's daily lesson plans, for example, or the curriculum guide for a particular grade and subject area. Regardless of its exact meaning, "review curriculum documents" carries an implicit meaning for the administrator. As stated in other chapters, leaders must be aware of what is occurring in the classrooms within their building. A regular inspection of curricular material sends a strong message to teachers: The leadership team is concerned with classroom learning and student achievement, in particular, which is of utmost importance. Novice leaders can reinforce their position on student learning and teacher accountability by keeping a close eye on curricular documents of all sorts.

Attend Faculty Meetings Selectively

Also within school organization, "attend faculty meetings selectively" was given a solid rating. In fact, 53 percent assessed it as a "5." Administrators are busy from the first bell until the last bus leaves the parking lot. They cannot attend every meeting, even though many in their building may expect them to, and still finish the day's tasks. Leaders must selectively choose which meetings are most relevant to their role at the school and which can be safely assigned to representatives or even ignored. The new leaders obviously consider this a vital skill, which implies that those who "work smart" avoid burnout by both discriminating among priorities and delegating responsibilities.

Serve on a School Committee

Thirty (33 percent) of the respondents rated the item "serve on a school committee" a "5." An individual school may have as many as twelve committees actively working to improve the condition of some facet of its operations. From a reading improvement committee to a grant-writing group, teachers chair these committees and facilitate the meetings. Accreditation meetings can consume an entire building, with multiple committees formed around a single purpose. Each has a discrete objective for mobilizing the school improvement planning, such as formulating the school's profile, monitoring research instruments and results, and creating an action plan for implementing the new goals (Mullen with Stover and Corley 2001).

Attend Principal/Assistant Principal Meetings

Of greater significance, 44 percent of the administrator respondents re-garded this survey item as "most important." Each week or less fre-quently, the principal of a school can be expected to call a meeting of the administrative staff. Here, budget concerns, instructional problems, and personnel issues are usually placed on the table for open discussion. The proceedings from the school committees may be shared in this context. This time is allotted for identifying and resolving problems, as well as ad-dressing ambiguities in school policy. New administrators know these ses-sions are a requirement of their position, and they typically come ready to fully participate and receive counsel.

LESSONS

In the real world of summit climbing, a compass and map are essential for providing direction and hence circumventing circular routes. Many trekkers "take for granted that they know how to use these simple tools, but some find out the hard way that they actually don't. To understand the proper use of a map and compass, you must first know how compasses work" (Farley 2003). The lesson here is that you or those you guide may need to learn how to find their way by first becoming proficient with us-ing a compass and map, metaphorically speaking.

In school leadership contexts, a compass can be an instrument (e.g., testing guide), a person (e.g., peer coach), a document (e.g., how-to guide), or even a process (e.g., informal support system) or program (e.g., graduate preparation). Compasses can be both internal and external; these direction indicators can be powerfully aligned to improve the quality and effect of one's journey. The empowered leadership aspirant will not wait idly for the external compasses (i.e., programs and people) in their lives to point them in the direction for their trek. They will take the initiative to address the gaps they have sensed or learned about through such mecha-nisms as self-reflection, dialogue with leaders, and results from inquiry.

Generally, educational leadership preparation programs are in need of high-power external compasses. Californian legislators may have shown some mountaineering wisdom through the vigorous reform agenda they funded in support of mentoring future principals across the state. Not all external compasses are viewed as valid or even as necessarily sound, however. While some strongly endorse the Interstate School Leaders Licensure Consortium (ISLLC) and National Council of Accreditation for Teacher Education/Educational Leadership Constituent Council (NCATE/ELCC) standards as a legitimate compass for guiding the field (e.g., ELCC chair and coordinator Richard Flanary and Honor Fede, respectively [Fede and Flanary 2003]), others, notably Fenwick English, critique these as "cookie-cutter" solutions to complex issues that necessitate wide variances in graduate program designs and goals.

Specifically, Fede and Flanary (2003) argue that the standards are the outgrowth of a peer-reviewed, rigorous process, similar to the assessments of educational leadership programs that are being executed. Further, they believe this reform model has been responsible for significantly improving the quality of these programs. An objective of the NCATE/ELCC standards committee has been to reduce the gap between university preparation and the readiness of new leaders, in line with the expectations of school districts. English (2003c) counters that the premise of these standards is "managementspeak," a "rational-technical apparatus" that harnesses the field instead of a "foundational epistemology" that would guide it (pp. vii, 127, 129).

Further, the "policing muscle" of these national administrative associations that is being flexed in educational leadership programs has been recently associated with the "Russian tradition of mystical authoritarianism," exalting the standards as good and professors who are theory-bound as bad. English (2003d) views this "anti-change doctrine" as severely detrimental to professional preparation, largely because of its colonizing, specifically managerial and theological, assumptions of "prediction and control." This normalizing, pseudoscientific practice has consequences for marginalizing the work of the professoriate that falls outside the standards. School leadership and the superintendency also do not escape unscarred, because they are expected to communicate "a shared vision of learning" with *all* stakeholder groups. Unattainable goals steeped in godlike perfection and profound knowledge are evident as undercurrents running throughout the standards. Many dark sides of the standards are revealed in this essay: Among other things, they establish a "hierarchical arrangement" between school leader and the stakeholder group (e.g., parent) whereby the former must market and sell the vision of the facility rather than engaging the latter in a process involving equals. This clearly smacks of coercion.

Also, and as directly relevant to my own study, educational leadership programs that adhere to the NCATE/ELCC standards will give significant weight to the role of the administrator as manager of school operations. Of course this emphasis would squeeze out any room for the change agent who seeks to recreate the traditional model of instructional supervision through shared governance and egalitarianism, as well as peer learning and mentorship in one's daily work. The value of diversity would struggle to thrive and grow in a hierarchical, standards-driven environment, whether at the university or school level. The repercussions are unlimited insofar as constitutional rights and human freedom issues are concerned.

The direction any compass affords must be mindfully interrogated, not simply followed.

All such external compasses will have to be carefully weighed by those invested in preparing school leaders instead of simply adopted as gospel. And, of course, such scrutiny would also need to be guided by one's internal compass—vision and intuitive understanding. This sensibility can be applied to the "cardinal points"—core leadership areas and accompanying tasks—that my research supports to foster improved thinking and systems.

BACKPACKING TIPS AND LEADER ACTIVITIES

- Practice using a compass and map properly. Consider having your faculty or a group of graduate students simulate this activity. They can then interpret its value in the context of a staff improvement reform, shared leadership program, new accountability initiative, or anything else. As Farley's (2003) outdoors field guide indicates, compasses "do *not* point to the north pole or 'true north.' They point to magnetic fields near the Hudson Bay in Canada. Knowing this is the first key to understanding how to use one in conjunction with a map."
- Use your compass with a map, or guide others to do this. Decide what direction you want to travel in relation to true north. You can do this precisely by "plac[ing] a map protractor on point A to come up with a direction to point B" (Farley 2003).

Chapter Ten

Swiss Army Knife:
Basic Know-How

This may seem elementary, but looking back at my early forays into outdoor leadership I realize how ignorant I was about the things I didn't know. Any new skill—paddling a kayak, lighting a stove, recognizing hypothermia, or working to reach consensus in a group—will seem uncomfortable at first. Practice, especially with feedback on your performance, will allow you to overcome the discomfort and move into competence. Mastery of skills is important not only for leadership, but also for teaching.

— A. Kosseff

CASE SCENARIO

As a beginning teacher, Ashley Sullivan feels compelled to experiment with different approaches to learning and communication. When something new is offered to educators, she makes certain that she is introduced to it. However, the goal of staying abreast of technology, such as voice recognition software, faster modems, e-mail programs, homework websites, and online grade books, seems to fall short of being a major priority in many schools. Notably, the results obtained from her survey indicated that only 11 percent of the teacher respondents were willing to learn how to use new technology. In contrast, many of the youngsters at the school are technology literate.

The middle school in Florida that Ashley investigated is well equipped with technology. The building has a computer lab with thirty workstations. Each teacher/counselor/administrator has at least one computer for

personal access. A technology coordinator also offers on-site training. The
school district has an intranet and e-mail capabilities, and technology use
is expected of all personnel: The handbook advises staff members to
check their e-mail at least once a day. However, the survey participants
typically commented, "I don't have time to check our e-mail server—this
is useless—why use it when you have runners and aides?"

According to the data that Ashley obtained from educators, students,
and parents at the site, only 75 percent of the teachers knew their intranet
(district) e-mail address, and 12 percent had *never* checked it. After con-
firming these facts with the technology trainer, she learned that this picture was, unfortunately, accurate. In addition, only a few school officials
had taken advantage of the trainings, and only 53 percent had even heard
of FIRN, Florida's Information Resource Network that provides valuable
governmental statistics. Deciding to test what appeared to be a situation
involving inadequate technology use and related knowledge, Ashley
e-mailed 105 teaching and administrative staff during the workweek.
Only forty-seven people had read her message, and most after three days.

At this school, only a handful of teachers have implemented new technology to improve their communications with staff, students, and parents.
These teachers also, coincidentally, happen to be "popular" with the students and parents. They have their homework guidelines available online,
sometimes at least two weeks in advance. Students and parents access
their grades and overall averages via a secure website. As noted in the case
scenario, one technology-savvy teacher's class web page gives visitors access to homework links for all subjects. Users also surf this website to
e-mail "Sharon" comments or questions. It is not hard to see why the students value these teachers in contrast with those they criticized for not
having computer literacy, commenting that "the teachers need to give our
grades online often and not only at mid-term," and "all teachers need to
have their homework online."

Sharon receives electronic messages daily from students regarding assignments, extra credit, and progress reports. Many parents also turn to
these technologically attuned educators for guidance on their child's behavior, other family issues, and computer problems. Students often request to be placed in their classes. So what makes these teachers stand
out? Their reputations have been shaped by the desire for effective and
prompt communication with stakeholders—anyone connected to the

child's welfare. Parents have produced commendation letters for these teachers while their peers with seniority lag behind.

After analyzing the survey data, Ashley was startled to see the contrast between the number of students and parents who expect personnel to use e-mail and the teachers and administrators who are not so inclined. The majority of students and parents pleaded for more communication from their school in any form, especially technological. However, most of the staff believed it takes time and resources, beyond what they have, to be technology partners.

Given the increased expectations for schools today, why would some personnel opt not to use computers for facilitating faster and better communication and stronger relationships? With every new invention come great accolades. Ashley recognizes that she is something of a zealot when it comes to technology for improving schools; some might even consider her overemphasis on the positive as a limitation. This is not to say that she believes technology is the answer to all school issues, but electronic systems are bound to be at the forefront of communication in society (from Sullivan 2004).

REFLECTION AND DISCUSSION

Interpreting the Case

At least one curious leadership aspirant wants to know, "Are school personnel and administrative staff using the available technology to effectively communicate with community members?" Ashley Sullivan, a middle school teacher in Florida and graduate of a master's program in educational leadership, wrote this scenario as part of a case study in one of my courses. The study itself is an outgrowth of her desire to educate future teachers and leaders about effectively incorporating technology into the school community. This early career educator believes computer technology use to be a basic skill, insofar as it involves such functions as electronic mail, online grading, Web posting, and Internet surfing. About this issue, one focus group participant who is a teacher-administrator remarked that "major corporations could not survive in today's world without technology. How can educators?"

One would naturally expect the daily performance of all school personnel and administrative staff to adhere to the changing standards of technology. Policy and training requirements for educators and administrators
alike in both school and university contexts cover technology use. Those
who lag behind are sometimes criticized for not fully participating within
their domains or modeling expectations for others. Those of us who teach
in nontechnology disciplines—such as math and English at the school
level, and educational leadership and higher education at the university
level—have suddenly found ourselves accountable for this new realm of
professionalism. As another focus group member shared, "We can easily
incorporate technology into most disciplines if we worked at it."

Despite any concerns or even mixed reviews that some may have, the
educational climate supports moving ahead and problem solving one's
way to solutions as a matter of course. Just as no one wants to be viewed
as a Luddite—rioters who fought the displacement of factory workers by
machinery in the eighteenth century (*New Webster's Dictionary and Thesaurus of the English Language* 1993)—we should be wary of "jumping
onto the band wagon" of every form of technology that comes our way,
without reflection and assessment (Mullen 2002e).

Ashley tenaciously holds the position that technology is here to stay, for
better or worse, and that has itself rapidly become a basic tenet for anyone who works in education. This teacher is passionate about the role of
communications technology in particular, and within the context of the
performance and accountability of both teachers and administrators. Staying in contact becomes a breeze! In an effort to improve the educational
culture for all school–community members, including students and parents, and even beginning teachers like Ashley, she strongly advocates the
widespread implementation of computer-based technology within classrooms and across schools and districts. After researching a middle school
site and reading the relevant literature, she explains her point of view:

> The most obvious problem blocking [progress] at the school I studied in-
> volves insufficient training, coupled with an entrenched mindset. Those ed-
> ucators and administrators who have not grown up in the age of computers
> may not understand the opportunities that are being offered to them. Real-
> ity has changed: Email, websites, and listservs are the mainstay of commu-
> nications, even for schools.

She offers an open critique of the survey results as opposed to an unbiased presentation of them.

From an on-site investigation using a survey of her own making, Ashley's suspicions that electronic mail is not a "a regular and collective form of communication within all of our school systems" were confirmed. It is her impression from having widely polled teachers, administrators, parents, and students that those adults who "can no longer blame poor communications on a lack of computer access, instead complain about the time needed for training and implementing the new technology." Usually, technology trainings are offered after school and on the weekends. For these practitioners, the inclination is to protect one's time, at the cost of meeting the expectations of students and parents for technology communications. In the context of this finding, Ashley wants these reluctant practitioners to know that "it takes only a few minutes to learn how to input information on most grade book or homework websites" or to "post and update new information" for one's school and community groups.

Swiss Army Knife: Basic Know-How

Ashley's persistent message can be easily translated into mountaineering language. For this purpose, the Swiss army knife serves as an exemplar for basic proficiency. Trekkers and others involved in outdoor sports find this specialized multitool indispensable, as do professionals in their everyday work settings. Swiss Knives Express (2003, online) describes the tool's altitude and temperature display, as well as the following attachments:

- Compass/clock
- Knife
- Pliers
- Screwdriver
- Wire cutter
- Bottle opener
- Chisel/scraper
- Wire bender
- Can opener
- Scissors
- Toothpick

- Saw
- Tweezers
- Nail file
- Pen
- Ruler

In her case study, Ashley identified a similar set of basic items that, collectively, form a fundamental structure for the teacher's day, and, where applicable, the administrator's as well. The respondents in her study made some of these suggestions for improving the quality of their work lives. In order to perform well as school-based communicators who serve in an "efficient and prompt" manner, particular items will need to be included in the practitioner's Swiss army knife, with adjustments for the individual's particular role and function:

- A working e-mail address that is checked on a regular basis and available to parents and other stakeholder groups.
- Updated computers, installed with applications that benefit one's subject matter and professional interests.
- Homework and grades posted routinely and securely online, with hyperlinked text connected to web pages and additional resources.
- A functioning, up-to-date classroom and school website that anyone (e.g., parent, student, prospective member) can visit, with relevant online forms.
- School–home partnerships, facilitated through such means as electronic newsletters and subject-specific websites that contain grades, homework, resources, and more.
- User-friendly design of the school's technology systems, including instructions and training, for personnel and others new to computers.
- Knowledge of people's rights and those of institutions and states, as e-mail can be mistakenly sent, intercepted, or accessed.
- The practice of "netiquette": Knowing what to say and how to say it is a learned social skill that technology training should address. (Sullivan 2004)

These appear to be a sold base of "tools" from which to work.

Veteran hikers (e.g., Jardine 2001; Kosseff 2003) share that the task-specific items performed by master teachers seem very elementary to them. But if you were to look back on your own technological or any other growth, you will more readily see how any new skill could feel awkward and perhaps unsettling to a newcomer or even an experienced practitioner who is undergoing retooling. In the world of outdoor leadership, "paddling a kayak" or "working to reach consensus in a group" are challenging tasks to those who lack the basic skills or who have not been oriented. If we recall our ignorance at the start of our own journeys, we can better empathize with the struggle others may exhibit in an area that is new to them—a mentoring capacity that is not only critical for technology trainers but also seasoned principals socializing new administrators. In the context of technology, some persons send e-mail messages, convert file formats, and other computer-based tasks in an automatic and almost "natural" manner. For others, even a simple process like attaching a file to an electronic message is a demanding task. However, school districts do provide training in these areas if one wants it.

Obviously, the issue of basic know-how is far broader than the domain of computer technology and related communications for schools. For example, basic tasks involving the development of duty rosters, facilitation of staff meetings, and the use of problem-solving strategies, discipline techniques, and school improvement planning all require know-how and effective implementation. And knowing how different types of school budgets are to be managed is not a challenge to be underestimated; even learning how the system works for ordering materials can pose a stumbling block for those new to the job. Other important tasks of a more basic but nonetheless initially troublesome nature include designing and using surveys, developing interviewing skills, and even learning how to document personnel problems (Llewellyn 2004; Paquette 2004). But even these tasks that administrators do revolve around computer technology.

Even straightforward tasks and procedural issues, some of which have been mentioned here, are culturally and organizationally embedded and will require decoding by the newcomer. Partly for this reason, concept is a far more empowering tool than technical skills mastery. According to O'Neil (1995), technology should no longer be used to simply augment traditional processes of communication and teaching, learning, and administering. To have an impact, technology will be used to bridge the school, home, and community. This implies that the most basic uses of technology have a vital function beyond their apparent application, a message that

Ashley has clearly sent. Further, this means that conceptual adaptability, not procedural knowledge, is the overriding capacity needed to flourish as a leader and school.

Just When We Thought She Was Expecting Too Much

Just when we may have thought that Ashley Sullivan and other avid supporters of technology like herself have unreasonable standards for their school communities, we learn that such expectations are embedded in the new standards for cultural reform. Administrators are now required to not only learn new technologies for their jobs but also to model state-of-the-art practices (Mullen et al. 2002; Mullen 2002e). Recent educational policies, such as the *Technology Standards for School Administrators (TSSA)*, mandate that (1) aspiring leaders have the opportunity to use learning technologies so they can better lead change in their future jobs, and (2) current administrators adapt to the new expectations for high-power performance and leadership (National Policy Board for Educational Administers for the Educational Leadership Constituent Council 1995). These technology standards may be a significant impetus for change within school systems, with implications for graduate preparation program delivery.

In fact, the TSSA Collaborative has gained ground in leading this reculturing movement to change public school education across the country and at all levels. This national consortium, which is engineered by significant stakeholders, has focused on the effective implementation of technology standards at the level of school administration, with attention to the principal, district program director, and superintendent. TSSA's stakeholders include the National Association of Elementary School Principals (NAESP) and the National Association of Secondary School Principals (NASSP).

Importantly, the collaborative describes its mission as leading "the initiative to develop and document a national consensus on what PK–12 administrators should know about and be able to do to optimize benefits of technology use in schools" (2003, TSSA Collaborative, http://cnet.iste .org/tssa) . The vision of this association is to comprehensively and effectively implement technology as a "large-scale systemic reform" project and that school leadership is the linchpin for "enhancing learning and school operations through the use of technology." The TSSA standards that govern technology for schools cover these six domains, which some aspiring leaders in my master's classes believe provide a solid beginning point for the direction of reform:

1. Leadership and vision
2. Learning and teaching
3. Productivity and professional practice
4. Support, management, and operations
5. Assessment and evaluation
6. Social, legal, and ethical values

Further, practicing administrators and other educational leaders are expected to apply these standards to many different contexts in order to keep pace with school improvement via technology infusion:

- Administrator preparation and professional development program design
- Assessment and evaluation
- Role definition and job descriptions
- Individual and system accountability
- Accreditation of schools and administrator preparation programs
- Certification (credentialing) of administrators
- Self-assessment and goal setting
- Design of technology tools for school administrators

The Technology Summit: Caveats

The benefits of technology notwithstanding, caveats are in order here: The technology summit I have been describing has some uncertain, slippery slopes. For example, many naturalists and environmentalists strongly believe that society has become a slave to technology and that we as humans are turning into a "technology" ourselves, inseparable from the computer screen and separable from the deeper wonderment of life, which compromises our capacity to live more fully. Another slippery trail involves the technology literature and related educational standards: These seem colored by a positive, even strongly advocating, tone. As Hargreaves, Earl, and Schmidt (2002) attest, "the underlying assumption in a technological perspective is that everyone shares a common interest in advancing the innovation. The only issue is how best to implement it" (p. 73). This advocacy probably underlies even assessment models for technological effectiveness.

An overridingly favorable bias poses challenges for the novice technology user striving to understand the pedagogical value of such trends: Critical perspectives on distance education are underrepresented, as are critical frameworks for evaluating technology-infused learning (Mullen 2002e). Bowers (1998), for one, argues that the discourse in this field is "dominated by advocates who now control the direction of educational reform" (p. 76). Technology, which has been ascribed status apart from its pedagogical function, is reified as "a transformer" (Mendis 2001) or ideal summit to climb. Such attribution potentially detracts from the teaching/learning focus, which is cause for concern (Mullen 2002e).

SUMMIT DATA AND ANALYSIS

The results from my own study for this book indicate that basic skills can be mapped onto entire administrative positions at the school level. In other words, the assistant principal who is in charge of student affairs at the building level is functioning within an entry-level administrative position. These individuals are in charge of student discipline in particular, but bus duty, locker assignments, lunchroom monitoring, nonacademic complaints, and paperwork all round out their daily tasks. As viewed by administrators, this is "the lowest" position in the hierarchy of school leadership. Many aspirants start here and work their way up.

In other words, an individual in any job can fulfill basic skills, but a position in administration can also signify a basic level of operations. Assistant principal, level 1 (AP1), is the "can opener" position held by deans of discipline in Florida, in charge of the duties previously listed. On an implied level, this person deals with the status quo of the school and maintaining it. The assistant principal, level 2 (AP2), is a higher-level administrator position with responsibility for developing curriculum and well-rounded student programs of study. Also implicitly understood, this individual charts the school toward the future, and thereby has a greater role to play as a Sherpa guide.

In this personnel context, the AP1 position fulfills basic tasks that my survey respondents described in a range of ways: Most direct and perhaps illuminating among these was, "Beginning experiences are very basic, 'grunt' type tasks, but they are a necessary foundation for success with more abstract assignments." (Such job descriptions, ranked accordingly, are available in the personnel files of Florida schools. The focus group participants, who are beginning administrators and experienced teachers, shared the implications of the distinctions between the AP1 and AP2 levels.)

The "technical side of the job" for administration more generally covers such elements as budgetary systems, Full-time Teaching Equivalency (FTE), curriculum, policies, school board rules, and discipline. One person said that the experience ran a gamut that included "review of school discipline plan and procedures and review of district student code and conduct policies." Of course the actual list of jobs of this nature is much longer than what is depicted here.

School Organization

An analysis of the "school organization" section of the survey data yielded noteworthy results. The administrative tasks most highly rated were as follows: "design master schedule, including specials"; "plan staff orientation/school opening activities"; review curriculum documents"; "attend faculty meetings selectively"; and "serve on a school committee."

Design Master Schedule, Including Specials

This area of school organization was rated a "5," or "most important" on the Likert scale, by 42 percent of the respondents. Designing a master schedule is one of the most important tasks an administrator can assume at a school site. The schedule lists the subjects (e.g., math) being taught and by whom and in which classroom during a specified time of the day. *Specials* is the jargon used in public schools, especially at the elementary level, referring to classes that are attended once or twice a week as opposed to every day. These include such subjects as art or physical education.

The formation of a master schedule is a meticulous job; it must be assumed by a competent administrator in order for the institution to run efficiently and without faculty complaint. Usually an experienced assistant principal in the elementary and middle school levels performs this scheduling task. In high school, the AP2 completes the master schedule each year. In order to achieve the elevated status and attain the pay raise afforded this level of the principalship, the ability to design a master schedule should already be integral to an assistant principal's repertoire. In fact, achieving this higher level of assistant principalship most often depends upon it.

Plan Staff Orientation/School-Opening Activities

Thirty-seven (41 percent) of the participants marked the survey item "plan staff orientation/school-opening activities" a "5." Staff orientation, which occurs before students return for the new school year, is referred to as "preplanning" or "preschool." At this time teachers are encouraged to ready their classrooms and prepare lesson plans. Another component of this staff orientation is school-opening activities. This is the point at which school administrators plan activities that will help create a positive climate at the institution. The activities are also designed to augment the cohesion that has hopefully already formed among faculty members. Approximately two days of preplanning are reserved for these administrator-led group exercises. New administrators are expected to help organize and plan these days. The learning curve of administration is usually rapidly activated while performing this duty.

Community Relations

The last topic section covered on the survey was community relations. The ninety-one respondents rated the following items with a great number of "5" responses: "plan open house," "newsletter (student/staff accomplishments)," and "participate in PTSA/SAC involvement." The first two administrative leader tasks are described here.

Plan Open House

Forty percent (40 percent) cited "plan open house" as "most important." To commence each academic year, the staff of every school in districts across Florida invite parents to tour the school and meet the teachers at open house. This is usually the first vital step in establishing communication between home and school. Administrators are in control of the planning and coordination of this public relations event. The new leaders realize that an early connection can result in many benefits. If an administrator has discipline problems with a student during the year, he or she will feel more comfortable calling a parent already met at open house. New and seasoned leaders realize the value of strong home–school relationships. This is obviously where technology communications enters the picture.

Newsletter (Student/Staff Accomplishments)

Thirty-eight percent of the new administrators marked "newsletter" as a "5." In most schools, a newsletter is sent home regularly, detailing upcoming school activities and events. This is also a community forum for teachers, administrators, and students to broadcast "points of pride" about the school, teacher awards, student achievements, and administrative accomplishments, and so forth. Usually an administrator organizes the information for the monthly bulletin and support personnel format it. The principal performs or delegates a final appraisal of the newsletter before it is mailed.

As a new leader, assistant principals may also find themselves responsible for gathering the information for the newsletter each month and overseeing this project. The expectation that this administrative function will be performed by newcomers is apparent, given the high rating it received. The use of technology for developing and distributing newsletters and other informational and promotional materials is invaluable.

LESSONS

While technology use and other sorts of basic know-how can be equated with a "can opener," almost any simple function is embedded within a more complex cultural framework of teaching, learning, and administering. It is important that principals who mentor others and technology trainers alike keep this lesson in mind as they retool their sites for increased efficiency and enhanced outcomes.

The bigger picture here is that school leaders must thrive in progressively complex environments if they are to lead successfully, and that new skills and knowledge are consequently required of them. What is considered an advanced skill today will, for many of us, become a basic one tomorrow.

Higher expectations for accountability in teaching and learning at the K–12 level and shared responsibility for quality education by multiple stakeholders (e.g., teachers and school administrators) are major goals of school reform (Jossey-Bass Publishers 2000; Mullen et al. 2002). Technology is rapidly reshaping how we teach, learn, research, and evaluate at all levels of the academy and the nation's schools. Contexts for such study include high poverty with high minority ratios (Lanahan 2002), student learning and achievement aimed at school improvement (McNabb, Hawkes, and Rouk 1999), and university innovations that promote forays into institutional and global partnership (Boyer 2003).

Finally, *technology* is more than a word today—it is a powerful force that is revolutionizing education, with the expectation that the twenty-first-century school and academy will be significantly different. Similar to mountaineering, "technology is a lifeline, one needed for guiding the work of every school and for creating much needed, family–school partnerships. The actual use of technology by school personnel should be a priority" (Sullivan 2004, 8). In other words, the technology compass is a new standard for providing direction to our educational institutions. Administration has a key role to play in this scenario as a cultural transformer, and constant learning will be required to achieve this climb.

BACKPACKING TIPS AND LEADER ACTIVITIES

The TSSA standards specify that administrators should comprehensively apply technology standards within their schools and, to lead this mission, not rely on others to act as their technology crutch. This challenge provides an opportunity to actively learn: With your school team or university colleagues, discuss the standards and the contexts in which these are to be applied. Seek an understanding that fits with your own setting, vision, and resources, as well as grade level. Devise a set of scenarios for illustrating the standards and applications, and use these as a basis for problem solving and socializing others. Cooperative learning contexts are terrific mechanisms for kindling the spirit and producing mastery.

Ashley Sullivan (2004) encourages teachers and administrators to explore the more than nine thousand school websites, including the following excellent resources:

- SchoolSpace is a software package that enables administrators to manage information and teachers, parents, and students to communicate. It offers a streamlined approach to report analysis, grading, attendance, and information organization and storage. Also, IT software provides different online modules for administrators, guidance counselors, and teachers to record and store information.
- Schoolnotes.com allows teachers to store homework assignments online for free, so students and parents can easily locate their school assignments.
- MyGradeBook.com is another website that allows teachers to calculate and securely post grades online. There is a minimal yearly access fee required, but Ashley Sullivan says it is "worth gold" and that parents even offer to pay the fee so they can have instant access to their children's grades. Parents and students can access their accounts using individualized passwords.
- Cancellations.com is another noteworthy website, which allows districts to post school closings online and send e-mail alerts to parents who are registered.
- Another helpful website, bigchalk.com, allows teachers space to maintain a calendar, publish a homepage, post images and student artwork, and access research databases.
- Finally, "Yahoo! Geocities," a website that can be reached via geocities .com, provides free online storage space for creating homepages for a class or school.

Chapter Eleven

Rope: Mentoring Scaffolds

A three-person team is best for most climbs. The most experienced climber leads; the weakest or least experienced takes the middle place. For a one-day climb, the team should pick a clear day and start early to allow plenty of time for both ascent and descent. If a rope is used to connect the climbers, it should be kept taut to provide immediate support for any person who slips. The pace should be steady but not hurried and the intervals between rest breaks timed to allow for the sharpness of ascent and the altitude.

—*Compton's Reference Collection* 1995

CASE SCENARIO

In 1995, Thomas "Tom" Graves became the principal of a low-performing middle school in rural Florida at risk of being placed on academic caution status. Tom realized he had assumed leadership within a culture that seemed apathetic on the surface but that desperately yearned for strong leadership and positive change. By launching a whole-school reform program, Tom made the staff responsible for a series of innovations. Democratic practice in his school meant that accountability "targets" for improvement would be addressed through a team-building philosophy. School goals focused on increased expectations, shared leadership, enhanced communication and interdependence, leadership by example, and student responsibility.

The strategy of increased expectations had as its core value personal accountability (discipline, responsibility, and hard work). As principal, Tom

144

Figure 11.1. The Scaffolds of Nepal Bridge
Source: Marc Shapiro

knew the cooperation of the community, staff, and students would need to be enlisted, so he worked with Jerry, the assistant principal, to win their support. Tom also used the democratic concepts of team building and shared leadership to foster a group effort in school improvement, so cooperative teamwork structures were developed for empowering stakeholders. Recognizing that communication was essential to the reforms, the administrative staff formed the Teacher Leadership Council (TLC), which functioned democratically as the "teacher voice," and synergistically in deciding accountability issues. This opportunity to cocreate policy, share concerns, and stay informed helped the teachers feel included.

Increased communication and interdependence were team-building strategies focused on including all teachers and staff. Whole-school involvement occurred through the TLC, grade-level subcommittees, and "Rambo Day," an outdoors event that modeled the value of teamwork. The new assistant principal and Tom created a co-administrative relationship that structurally included the TLC. To forge their competence, Tom focused on vision, teamwork, and school operations, and his partner monitored school progress by collecting and analyzing data. But they also worked together across all of the school's programs—strategies that proved invaluable for expediting change and coordinating operations.

A principal can practice democratic accountability by modeling personal accountability. Tom modeled high expectations *every day* by arriving at 4:30 A.M., picking up trash with custodial staff, and making weekly visits to the fifty-six classrooms, where he observed and participated in activities. Also, he substitute taught twice a month and showed team spirit by serving lunches in the cafeteria.

To promote student responsibility, new programs were implemented with the faculty team's assistance: the No-Tolerance Schoolwide Discipline Plan; the No-Tolerance Tardy Policy; Opportunity (Saturday) School; and the Student Mediation Program. The student body contributed to the new accountability standards. Because some had felt apprehensive about harassment and safety at school, the no-tolerance discipline policy was developed and enforced. And others wanted to be able to make up work not completed in class, which led to the establishment of after-school options.

Finally, parents and other stakeholders formally evaluated and supported the administration and the approaches taken to effect change. The school's leadership style was characterized as "firm, fair, and consistent management," embedded within "an incredibly intense work ethic" and "an optimistic outlook." (from Mullen and Graves 2000, "The Principal's Story," 484–89)

REFLECTION AND DISCUSSION

Interpreting the Case

"Constructing comentoring partnerships" is "a walkway we must travel" literally and figuratively as leaders in education (Mullen 2000). It is hard to empower by giving power over to all in a democratic fashion and, as we will learn, this requires accountability from leaders and their teams. Anyone who meets Tom Graves, whose story launches this chapter, is struck by his charismatic, energetic presence and "can-do" attitude. He is intensely committed to bettering education, particularly by team building and shared leadership. These values inevitably permeate any space he occupies, inspiring others to rise to the occasion and leaving no one behind.

The doctoral courses he took with me during my tenure at Auburn University, Alabama, were no exception. From 1998 to 2000, I tapped into Tom's incredible capacity to convert a room of strangers into a committed, synergistic team with shared goals. In an activity he voluntarily coordinated, the members led one another, taking turns being blindfolded and untangling themselves from a long rope, relying on one another's guidance as they gingerly moved under and over until they were free. Such strategies, particularly those inviting the kinesthetic movement of all group members, proved invaluable for preparing isolated hikers to function as a team ready to take on the challenges of any trail—in this case, collaborative action research by teachers on organizational and mentoring issues.

As an outgrowth of the synergy we shared as practitioners and scholars, Tom and I conducted action research, publishing an article that featured his story of change as a beginning principal (Mullen and Graves 2000). This case study specifically examined effective ways to reform schools through optimistic leadership and democratic accountability. The construct of democratic accountability resulted from our "eureka" that principals must find creative ways to bridge democracy and accountability, seemingly opposing political ideologies in theory but not necessarily in practice. For Tom's school, these poles coexisted, each undergirding the other and reinforcing the school's restructuring efforts through various opportunities for teacher leadership (e.g., Teacher Leadership Council) and student development (e.g., Student Mediation Program).

Instead of relying solely on Tom's account, we collected anonymous information from interviews and surveys with seventeen representative school stakeholders at all levels. We also used school climate surveys to scrutinize others' perceptions of the changes. We traveled back in time to do this, as he had moved and become a full-time doctoral student in educational leadership in Alabama by then. Through this process, Tom's metamorphosis story of the "wild west," as one Florida teacher called it, was thoroughly validated. Although Tom was already convinced by the success of the transformations during his tenure at the school, I retained a healthy skepticism, not having personally lived the changes. As our action research got underway, and after the data were collected and analyzed, the value of Tom's leadership and capacity building of the low-performing middle school became overwhelmingly apparent—more so than is revealed by his story. Even the district superintendent commented, "I would have never thought this school could be turned around so quickly" (1995 school climate survey data).

Building Mentoring Scaffolds

Roped Together

Being roped together symbolizes a close and highly functioning relationship developed out of the sheer need for survival in any setting, including school leadership. Tom and Jerry, the assistant principal, succeeded at becoming a "comentoring team" partly by learning about one another's strengths (and weaknesses) and putting that to good use. Two (or more) heads are better than one. After the interview process, Tom followed up with a self-assessment inventory—simply a list of broad leadership duties (e.g., instructional supervision and school management). After the participants rated themselves, an open conversation about the results ensued: They discussed ways to develop a viable administrative partnership based on individual specializations and shared roles, forging an understanding in the context of the school's goals and programs.

A "synergy audit" that features the rating of common goals can also be used to monitor a comentoring relationship or process to further improve effectiveness and productivity (Lick 1999). Tom's synergistic, roped-together relationship with Jerry reminds me of Braque's account of his relationship with Picasso: "The things [we] said to one another during those years will never be said again, and even if they were, no one would understand them anymore. It was like being roped together on a mountain" (as cited in Johnston, Johnston, and Holubec 1993, 8).

Before getting started on the journey of school leadership with a potential partner, this kind of discourse is ideal. Knowing the destination is essential: "Success will require that both of you have that internal fire, the lofty dream and the unwavering focus on the distant goal" (Jardine 2001, 443). Otherwise, the first set of hardships could interfere with the dream and even jeopardize your relationship. It is important that others' voices, including those of your administrative partners and assistants, as well as faculty, students, and parents, not be ignored or subverted: Administration should not be perceived as a clique. Even though there are leaders who think they have symbiotic relationships with their staff, some believe or project that they are "superior in terms of understanding issues, problems, and courses of action, and in intellectual leadership" (Sarason 1990, 66). Hierarchical authority relations and structures unfortunately "breed" such top-down attitudes, which slows down the momentum of synergy and change.

As Diamond and Mullen (1999b) caution, leaders can use their power, authority, and privileges—symbolically the rope—either to support or restrain others. In the world of trekking, "a length of rope, at least ten feet long and approximately three-sixteenths of an inch in diameter, is absolutely necessary. As a matter of fact, it would be wise to carry several lengths of rope ranging from a few feet to twenty feet in length. Rope will definitely prove its usefulness on a hike down any trail" (Logue 2000, 180). The rope is a metaphor for climbing cooperatively with others, for connecting those moving along slippery passages or rocks, and for providing immediate support for any person who slips. Principals like Tom Graves who seek interpersonal and communal synergy to strengthen the organization find many ways to supportively use the rope while strengthening their own leadership capacity, similar to Bloom and Krovetz's (2001) picture of effective leadership: "Principals who invest in building the capacity of their subordinates increase their own effectiveness as they build the strength of their teams" (p. 12). Principals must talk the talk *and* walk the walk in terms of democratic leadership.

Not everyone who starts out in the world of school administration finds an appropriate partner. If you don't find one, do not dismay. As Jardine (2001) reassures us, based on his own trekking excursions, "the chances of meeting other hikers in the same predicament, once you have begun, are quite good—at least along the more popular trails. Many lasting partnerships have formed in this way. So do not be reluctant to start out on your own. Action is an excellent catalyst" (p. 442).

But to trek alone for long distances as a new leader is potentially dangerous. Consider the lesson in Hemingway's (1987) story about snow-covered Kilimanjaro, "said to be the highest mountain in Africa. Its western summit is called the House of God . . . where there is the dried and frozen carcass of a leopard. No one has explained what the leopard was seeking at that altitude" (p. 39). An animal making a long, difficult journey by itself would have problems surviving for an extended period of time. Hemingway's story signifies the dangers of trying to reach the summit alone. In the context of my book, the message is not about hindering your self-initiative and independence but rather about learning to integrate this capacity with a strong value for teamwork.

Being roped together as partners, groups, or units can take healthy or destructive forms in educational relationships (Diamond and Mullen 1999b) and school cultures. In an administration context, one new principal's reflection on her apprenticeship offers rich insights: Sometimes she had received "explicit directions" regarding her "responsibilities as a site administrator," whereas at other times she learned implicitly from watching the former principal's "interactions with others and her approaches to creating new solutions." She and the principal had also "spent time debriefing and reflecting" on their work together, which proved "invaluable" for nurturing "habits of mind" for the school leader (Bloom and Krovetz 2001, 12).

A rope can prove indispensable to a newcomer's socialization, in this case taking the form of clear instructions and observational learning. When climbing, the rope that attaches us to a more experienced climber can keep us moving toward our goal while protecting us from danger, and it can instill in us ways of thinking and behaving—blueprints—that guide our future leadership. A rope can be used to support or strangle the burgeoning initiative of new leaders.

Surviving Everest's high altitudes takes vision, strong willpower, dedication, and the capacity to endure fatigue and discomfort. Picture seasoned climbers Sir Edmund and Tenzing encountering a slope—a forty-foot icy rock, to be exact—just before reaching the summit. Imagine their excruciating decision-making moments as they assessed their ability to climb it. In those days there was no actual rope lodged in the earth to turn to for assistance, so the courageous imagineers hacked steps in the ice and climbed over twenty-nine thousand feet. Sir Edmund reflected on the summit ordeal in 2003, at age eighty-three, saying that not having had ropes available meant that he and his climbing partner had to tackle the problems as they arose, overcoming them one at a time (National Public Radio [NPR] 2003).

Since that famous climb, a rope has been affixed to that ice step—a life-line for future hikers. In the same way, educational leaders can create steps, or mentoring scaffolds, for newcomers to the profession. Ropes, stories, and exemplary practices all help newcomers develop their craft and ultimately build their own leadership legacies. As former school principal Schmidt (2002) says, "[Good mentors] are big-picture people who can see farther down the road than you ever dreamed of going, and pinpoint the skills you need to get there" (p. 149).

This story of the summit climb powerfully captures the spirit of teamwork as a *synergistic comentoring relationship*. Lick (1999) describes this process as embodying "willingness—common goals and interdependence" and "ability—empowerment and participative involvement" (p. 38). Moreover, my own contribution to this construct emphasizes the potential for a synergistic comentoring relationship to function as a "proactive force in personal and social change" that "enables organizational cultures to be reworked" and "leadership and teacher development" to be reshaped more powerfully as socialization processes (Mullen 1999, 52). Interestingly, the successful climb to the highest point on Earth has since motivated hundreds of people not only to attempt the ascent themselves but also to use this outdoor challenge as an incentive for leadership development and personal change (e.g., Amatt 2000). Even Sir Edmund Hillary's commitment to humanity deepened; he used the unexpected riches gained from his summit success to have schools built in Nepal, improving the lives of generations (Jones 2003).

School Teams

Teamwork and team building are also essential values in the development of students (Mullen and Graves 2000). How are students to work together cooperatively if they see no models of cooperation? Cooperative learning is an important ability students will need to learn. Social development for boys and girls will need to encompass both the relational and the competitive skills needed for full participation in westernized societies. Each gender will be shortchanged if girls are socialized only to be cooperative, and boys, solely competitive (Bailey 1996; Sills 1994). The idea of a leader as somehow separate from or above the group that follows his or her charge is outdated (Banks 2000). Leaders cannot survive and build alone, and yet, paradoxically, such "an individual [can be] named as the prime mover of major changes" (Goodson and Anstead, 1998, 68).

It is expected that educational leaders will possess group and systems learning skills and demonstrate these to their faculties and student bodies. Marsh (2000) identifies collaboration (development of high-performing work teams and learning communities) and systems building (creation of an infrastructure that supports learning, performance, and partnership) as core skills areas. Practitioners can model or learn these skills by becoming involved in as many different forms of supportive teaming as possible, ranging from co-administrative governance councils (Mullen and Graves 2000) to curriculum restructuring committees (Mullen with Sullivan 2002) to action research partnership groups (Mullen and Lick 1999).

In one case study of a secondary school in Florida, the value of teamwork was recognized as a critical element in the maturation and leadership development of adolescent students (Mullen with Tuten, 2004). In fact, all of the teachers we interviewed used cooperative group learning as a key strategy for fostering student leadership and citizenry. This is a particular form of teamwork that has been documented as the preferred learning style, particularly for females.

Additionally, Elizabeth Tuten, who is a secondary teacher, and I surveyed segments of the student population at this school. We learned that boys are increasingly experiencing learning and leading as a relational, cooperative enterprise, and that girls have had multiple opportunities for leadership and teamwork. These results suggested that contemporary socialization was occurring in the school, which is a far cry from the traditional valuing of the individual (not the group) and competition (not cooperation) in American society. These emerging forms of adolescent socialization could be interpreted as the "light" of change that one can only hope to see everywhere as new leaders begin their climbs.

SUMMIT DATA AND ANALYSIS

People who are roped together need each other to survive and succeed, whether in a hiking or principalship experience. A leader cannot "cut" the rope and hope to succeed in the long run. While an individual can climb some distances without a rope, spectacular rock climbing must involve a line and at least one other person. One assistant principal, a focus group member, supported this observation with a powerful insight:

> As I sat there it struck me how I was a participant in a gestalt experiment that worked—the whole being greater than the sum of its parts [synergy]. Individually, we could not have reached the same intellectual heights, using your Himalayas metaphor, as we did by working collectively and feeding off each other's reflections and energy while tackling the meanings we gave to the data. (Workshop evaluation form, April 2003)

In the survey data collected for this study, mentoring scaffolds were thematically defined as essential strategies for socialization that take different forms. For some new school leaders, the issue of "ongoing staff and professional development" was viewed as crucial. Mentoring scaffolds require that ongoing support be provided to the "newbie" leader: "My first few months as an AP have been successful because of the high level of support I have from my principal and co-administrators." This is key: Because the need for mentors was underscored beyond formal training, the rope must be further extended once novice leaders have assumed their new positions: "Training is not adequate; one needs more mentors in addition to on-the-job training." Beginning school leaders will in turn need to seek the security of a rope, as their role will not only entail administrating, mentoring, and leading, but also active learning: "The day flies by. I am always busy. I am constantly learning from students and staff."

Another message is that the principalship staff at one's school should "support the faculty whenever possible." But the quality of and approach taken to teamwork is important. Belief must be followed by action. For example, one person's belief is that "new APs must understand the *professional* relationship they have with their staff—it should not be a *personal* relationship." Of course, the issue of values shines through in such a statement, a point of view not expressed by other respondents.

Teamwork also means "some duties I do—some I do not," as a few individuals put it. But this seems reductionistic—just half of the picture that synergists like Tom Graves have created of the leader who specializes but also assumes responsibility for the whole (core leadership duties) in relation to the part (preferred tasks). In fact, many participants viewed focus and teamwork as interdependent leadership strategies: "Assistant principals

have too many duties for one person to do. Teamwork is an essential because it [makes] the job more workable." Also, an indispensable part of
teamwork, they concurred, is communication, which was described as "the
key to providing an educational setting that is productive," as in the case of
"ongoing and positive communication with parents and staff."

Supervision of Instruction

Assist Teachers with Instructional Plans

For this survey item on the administrator survey, 47 percent of the beginning leaders cited teacher assistance as most important ("5"). New and
struggling teachers as well as those retooling will need guidance in outlining a basic curricular plan for the academic year. Part of an administrator's job is to see that each and every educator has daily lesson plans. This
type of organizational activity is required, in most of Florida's districts,
for contracted educators. If problems occur or questions are raised concerning the material in a certain discipline or at a specific grade level, administrators must be prepared to help shape instruction and mold subject
matter. The high response rate may be explained by the fact that instructional assistance to teachers is listed as a job description for most administrators in Florida school handbooks (e.g., Pasco, Hillsborough, and
Pinellas Counties).

Advise Teachers Regarding Classroom Management

In all, 52 percent of the respondents gave this survey item a rating of
"most important." Classroom management is often viewed as synonymous with classroom discipline. Students behaving inappropriately within
an academic setting can rarely learn. It is the teacher's role to keep the instructional process flowing smoothly. However, at some point, a teacher
may not be able to follow this plan without help. Here the administrator
must step in and advise teachers on how to ensure a disruption-free, productive classroom.

Based on the high response rate, the feedback received on the survey
underscores that administrators are required to know appropriate classroom management skills and have the ability to impart this knowledge to

teachers. Sometimes an AP2 (assistant principal of curriculum) may be judged exclusively on this topic. If he or she were an effective classroom manager, this individual would be seen as one who can discipline students sent to the dean's office. With regard to the current influx of new educators, leaders are expected to mentor these individuals. As Florida's population of school-age youngsters grows, new teachers will be required to meet the increased demands placed upon instructional personnel.

Observe Teacher–Student Interaction

This survey item elicited a rating of "5" from 52 percent of the new administrators. The job description of any administrator from assistant principal to principal includes the observation of teachers, which is more intense or frequent for those untenured. It is in the classroom where the leader can best determine the quality of teaching and patterns of learning, as well as the nature of teacher–student interaction. Student and teacher interactions are not always nurturing and instructive. Any inappropriate behavior that may be occurring with the whole group or with individual students, from neglect to derogatory name-calling to racist and sexual misconduct, will need to be documented. Not only is the administrator expected to know the particulars of negative situations but also to rectify any such situations immediately. If not, public reprimand or a lawsuit could follow. As the survey results suggest, the new administrator seems to recognize the importance of this responsibility. As a key function of their day-to-day role, observations of classrooms must be held as a high priority.

Communicate That Every School Employee Supports Instruction

For this survey item, 52 percent of the new leaders assigned a rating of "5." Consider that in order for a school to function effectively for teachers and students alike, the institution must impart to all employees their roles in creating an efficient, organized educational site that is supportive of others. Every person matters to the success of the school, a message that effective administrations endorse (see Mullen and Graves 2000). This trend is relatively recent. At one time, administrators and teachers were seen as the key factors of organizational success. Support personnel are now rightly recognized. As is evident, this tenet is easier stated than implemented. This leadership task (survey item) supports the concept of school culture and the important part each individual plays in creating a positive environment (Hay 1995; Mullen et al. 2002; Schechter 2000; Snyder, Acker-Hocevar, and Snyder 2000).

During most graduate programs in educational leadership, each and every instructor instills in the aspiring leadership body the importance of a positive culture for an effective school. Without this, most administrative initiatives will falter or even fail. Knowledgeable professionals who teach leadership development courses or lead training sessions often reiterate this precept.

Assist in Interviewing and Hiring Potential Faculty and Staff

Within the topic section entitled Supervision of Instruction, "assist in interviewing and hiring potential faculty and staff" elicited a rating of "5" from 63 percent of the new administrators. The attention this item received on the survey resulted in its being allocated a high place within the primary administrative tasks selected; instructional supervision, a core leadership area that encompasses this task, was also given significance in relation to a number of administrative duties (see tables 5.2 and 5.3, or chapter 5, for more details).

All members of an administrative team are expected to interview prospective faculty members. From the cafeteria manager to the science department head, leaders must competently assess whether a potential employee would fit a certain role in his or her school. The learning curve will occur on the job, and novice administrators must quickly acquire effective interviewing skills and learn the procedures. Interviewing for new faculty positions occurs annually, roughly from May until early August, and non-instructional personnel are hired year round.

LESSONS

A significant lesson of this chapter involves teamwork and team building at the level of partnerships, groups, and organizations. The focus has been on administration, with an eye toward "units" of responsibility, particularly students, but also teachers. This value can be summed up in the famous words of American anthropologist Margaret Mead: "Never doubt that a small group of thoughtful, committed citizens can change the world. Indeed, it's the only thing that ever has." Other memorable quotes from various cultural icons that new leaders can use to help build synergy within their schools are:

- "If I have seen further it is by standing on the shoulders of giants." —Isaac Newton
- "By working together, pooling our resources and building on our strengths, we can accomplish great things."—Ronald Reagan
- "Alone we can do so little, together we can do so much."—Helen Keller

A related focus in this section was on the necessity of hiking with a partner when tackling the awesome task of transforming a school into a high-performing educational center. This team-building advice could be extended to any school, especially large and challenging establishments. It is important to keep in mind that no synergistic leader, even one such as Tom Graves, could have accomplished anything without the support of the people in the school, the stakeholder groups, and the community (Mullen and Graves 2000). The leader's enthusiasm, energy, and tireless devotion can be the sparks that reignite staff, teachers, and students, but it will be their labor and willingness to change that makes the envisioned structures work. One side of the school cannot be successful without the synergistic support of the other. That is mentoring. And that is also team-building—the willing participation and ownership of many to make a system work.

Finally, we learned that a variety of tools are needed to be an effective leader, ready for all crises. And this includes the rope: The creation of mentoring scaffolds within a school system requires that people become roped together in particular ways and that the synergistic mentoring that is generated through co-administrative relationships will model the values for future leaders.

BACKPACKING TIPS AND LEADER ACTIVITIES

- Try some of the classic trust-building activities for groups, such as blindfolding in pairs and rope entanglement, or try more adventuresome team-building activities, such as wilderness trekking, mountaineering, or rock climbing.

- Collect your favorite quotes about team building or another topic and share them with your school. Use the sources of inspiration as an ice-breaker at beginning-of-the-year events and school and faculty meetings. Build the quotes into your revised mission statement.

- Do a self-assessment inventory exercise, either with administrative staff or the faculty/staff, and discuss the results. Arrive at a shared understanding of one another's strengths and areas of responsibility, and develop teams that support these deeper, more explicit processes. (Chapter 8 provides examples of inventory surveys.)

- Construct a picture of an administration's effectiveness through action research. Use various sources such as school climate surveys, school board records, standardized test scores, and communication from parents and community members. Share the results to provide supportive critique and new directions for improvement.

Chapter Twelve

Journal: Emotional Expression

When you journey into the backcountry your senses will expand, and you will start to notice more detail. Recording those bits of wisdom, the observations, and the many interesting details of your hike may not seem important beforehand, or even at the moment, especially when you are tired. But months and months later you will probably [reminisce and relive] your experiences through your trail journals.

—R. Jardine

CASE SCENARIO

Saiid Abdul was an eleventh grader at Bayview High School whose Middle Eastern ethnicity was evident, not just by his name but also by his physical appearance. His family had moved to the United States from Bahrain three years ago. Quiet and well mannered, he had made a few friends at school, but they soon began to distance themselves from him after September 11. With the nation focused on the threat of terrorism, some students began viewing Saiid with suspicion. Rumors quickly spread that Saiid had terrorists for relatives and that he was himself a menace to the school's safety. Saiid tried to ignore the rumors but then erupted when a student angrily accused him of being a terrorist. The teacher who stopped the argument took no further action.

One clique in particular targeted Saiid, calling him names, spreading rumors, and outright bullying him. Teachers occasionally reprimanded these students but rarely followed up with disciplinary action. Twice he was asked to empty the contents of his locker for inspection purposes. Saiid's father was furious about the discrimination against his son. After intense words were exchanged with administrators, he was overheard saying, "My son and family will not sit by and tolerate such bigotry!" Students and teachers alike reported this pronouncement to the principal and school resource officer.

Things started to settle down until the Friday of that week, before classes started. At 7:20 A.M. a teacher on hall duty witnessed a folded piece of paper fall from a student's locker, releasing white powder. Four other students also had contents spill on them in this manner. A teacher quickly cleared the area and ordered a student talking on her cell phone to call the main office. (Talking on a cell phone during instructional hours is against most school policies.) Administrators heard reports of the incidents. The principal, after contacting the district office, immediately announced that all students and staff were to keep their lockers closed and report to the fire-drill stations outside the building.

The commotion grew instantly, and so the principal, deciding to treat the situation like a fire drill, triggered the alarm. Administrators, joined by staff members, moved throughout the campus, shepherding students away from their lockers and toward their stations. Radioing the school crisis management team, the principal convened the members. She reviewed responsibilities for dealing with media personnel and parents and communicating internally with the staff. The school team started to regain a sense of control and, once the district crisis management team arrived, the situation seemed to improve.

When the fire safety officers arrived, the principal explained that anthrax may be on school grounds, and that those who had been exposed were taken to the hospital after being isolated. In the meantime, student witnesses gossiped—judgments quickly flew about who the culprit must be. Students got on their cell phones, and parents responded by showing up. (This sequence of events happens in times of crisis, but the stellar administrator will stop as much of it as possible, as such activity is, once again, against school policy.) When police arrived, the principal divulged that some of her staff suspected Saiid was behind the attack. The boy was quickly pulled aside, questioned, and detained.

Despite the best efforts of Bayview High School and the district, the story hit the news and was being labeled an anthrax attack with possible terrorist origins. Over the course of the day, some order was regained when tests revealed that the white powder was in fact baking powder, not anthrax. The following week, investigators found that Saiid was not responsible—it had been a hoax carried out by the group of students targeting him, in hopes of verifying their scandalous lies. All of this subterfuge was gradually uncovered.

Further, the school and district review team found that, according to Florida Emergency Planning Standards, problems had ensued from the way the situation had been handled. Despite the availability of emergency management procedures, the new principal had had difficulty determining which to use given the unique nature of the problem. In years past the potential threat to schools could be clearly defined and addressed. Most drills occurred during class when the environment was relatively orderly, not during transitions. Life has changed—a greater variety of crises now affects schools. While it is difficult to prepare for such a wide range of contingencies with individualized plans, better management and greater sensitivity are necessary. (from Bouleris et al. 2003, 3–5)

REFLECTION AND DISCUSSION

Interpreting the Case

During one of my master's courses in 2003, K–12 teachers Sue Bouleris, Collett De Ette, Mike Mauntler, and Shirley Ray created this fictitious scenario, complete with crisis response training guidelines. Their case study highlighted the emotional dimension of school crisis: Racial profiling was the core issue presented in relationship to school leadership, safety, and liberty. This approach to crisis management contrasts with the cognitive and technical treatment on which school teams in general traditionally focus when developing and implementing crisis emergency plans. This chapter deals with the role of emotional expression in schools and society relative to racial diversity and the invaluable strategies of consciousness raising, reflection, and modeling for effecting change.

The authors gave this story a national scope: Prior to the anthrax scare, when Bayview High School's new principal arrived, she "arranged for preservice training of the entire school staff on crisis preparedness. The

National Security Level continued to fluctuate between High and Elevated due to continued tensions in the Middle East, so the training seemed appropriate" (Bouleris et al. 2003, 3). A sheriff, in conjunction with a school district director, presented the emergency management plan for the school. Procedures were covered for severe weather conditions, lockdown, bomb threats, fire, trespassers, weapons, accidents (e.g., hazardous material), hostage situations, and unmanageable persons.

As the story goes, the general consensus was a feeling of preparedness. The administrators and personnel all felt comfortable knowing they could count on practice drills. They liked the security of a quick reference flip chart and a school resource officer on the premises. These designated police officers can arrest students and keep the peace and are considered an invaluable resource at rough urban schools.

However, while the school had focused on emergency procedures for protecting its citizens, one critical thing remained missing in its organizational planning—diversity awareness and antiracial training for the staff and multicultural curriculum for the students. Specific issues involving how to identify and handle bigotry and racial targeting at all levels of the school's operations were therefore bypassed. Yet this is the very issue that soon erupted at the school, rendering its coordination planning incomplete, at the very least. We can expect that the racial tensions will remain acute in such an unsettled atmosphere, unless the emotion stirred up from the incident involving the falsely accused, bullied youngster becomes the catalyst for making social justice a guiding principle in its reculturing process.

The case authors also provide a list of anthrax precautions that any school could adopt as guidelines. Relevant to my own reflection on supporting new school leaders is one key point they include: "List all people who were in the area when the suspicious package was recognized. Give a copy of this list to both the local public health authorities and law enforcement officials for follow-up investigation and advice" (Bouleris et al. 2003, 6). If the new principal they featured had handled the situation in this way instead of identifying the Middle Eastern boy to the local authorities as the probable culprit, they could have described a better outcome. As is, a lawsuit could definitely result in real life. An equitable and rational way to handle this kind of situation involves providing authorities with a list of names in the manner described, thereby avoiding the trap of assigning guilt where there is no evidence and falling prey to assumptions that create subsequent liability.

This fictitious scenario implies that schools in the new millennium will need to do a better job of protecting American civil liberties. By engaging in consciousness raising and conducting nondiscriminatory actions in support of guaranteed constitutional rights for all, schools can become safer places of learning. The teacher researchers disclose some of the confounding factors that contribute to how a person's civil liberties can be compromised, if not violated. In addition to the teachers' apathy when official reports of student conflict should have been made, student and staff behaviors involved racial targeting, finger-pointing, suspicion, abandonment, blame, and bullying. These actions are associated with strong, unresolved racial emotions, notably fear, anger, and hostility, as demonstrated by how the Middle Eastern boy was victimized in the school community.

Several key concepts undergird this chapter. *Terrorism* means to repress or domineer by means of panic and fear, and *bioterrorism* is "the intentional use of infectious biological agents, or germs, to cause illness" (Connecticut Department of Public Health 2003, para. 2). *Diversity awareness* reflects social justice goals to build inclusive communities and eliminate "systemic racism" through critique (Skrla et al. 2001). *Rationalized racism* involves the escalated stereotyping or scapegoating of ethnic and racial groups as security tightens. Similarly, *racial profiling* is pervasive, denying particular groups the right to equal treatment in all public spheres, including schools, and ranging from employment to law enforcement contexts (Hoover 2003).

Security Regimes

It is not as though systemic racism thrives within our educational institutions only in wartime. American-born persons of color have historically experienced forms of segregation and discrimination, particularly within Euro-American schools and colleges (Mullen and Kohan 2002; Webb-Johnson 2000). Institutional racism silences individuals and entire cultures that do not fit the "standards of status quo mores" (Webb-Johnson 2002, 3).

History teaches that great threats to liberty often come in times of urgency, when constitutional rights seem too extravagant to endure. Famous

Supreme Court Justice Thurgood Marshall said in 1972 that the American people must be reassured that constitutional guarantees will apply in times of crisis and tranquility alike (Romero 2001). Perhaps this crucial lesson could be used as a "teachable moment" for students in almost any age category, if brought up in an appropriate classroom setting. As my master's students Neale, Saltzgaver, and Sutton (2003) warn, "Ethnicity alone is not enough. If ethnic profiling of Middle Eastern men is enough to warrant disparate treatment, we accept that all or most Middle Eastern men have a proclivity for terrorism, just as during WWII all resident Japanese had a proclivity for espionage" (p. 5). These aspiring leaders exhibit the level of consciousness that schools need today.

Given that the nation's security concerns have changed so dramatically since the tragedy of 9/11 in 2001 and the war with Iraq in 2003, schools are being called upon to think and act differently. At a time when one might expect civil liberties to become entrenched for Americans, many describe what they see as a "new security regime" coming to life, one that is "dangerous" and goes beyond the attempt to protect U.S. citizens in order to promote "a new political order" (e.g., Rizvi 2003, 26).

The vigilant activity of the FBI has apparently "increased at colleges and universities since the September 11 attacks and the passage of the USA Patriot Act in 2001" (Arnone 2003, A14). This act gives the FBI and other national and state authorities the freedom to conduct surveillance and intelligence work without hindrance, in effect suspending the civil rights of students and faculty at school and college campuses (Arnone 2003). International students and faculty have been targeted during such campaigns, some experiencing detainment and imprisonment, particularly where terrorist connections have been alleged.

Consider the story of a Middle Eastern university student, for example, who experienced blatant mistreatment by national authorities. Handcuffed and detained after he registered, as required, by the U.S. Immigration and Naturalization Service (INS) for having aroused suspicion, it was later discovered that he had been "guilty" only of taking less than a full course load that semester, even though his advisor had approved the change (Hoover 2003).

Recent surveys indicate that 66 percent of whites and 71 percent of African Americans support the ethnic profiling of people who look to be of Middle Eastern descent (Neale, Saltzgaver, and Sutton 2003; Nowicki 2002)—"roughly 6.5 million Muslims in the United States and 3.5 million Arab Americans," not counting the numbers of "groups across the political, religious, ethnic and racial spectrums" (Romero 2001, 17). Constructions of "the enemy" continue to proliferate based on race (e.g., Romero). Assuming this picture is accurate, what does this say about us as a nation?

It appears that even when communities of color access what Berry (2002) refers to as "institutionalized sites of whiteness," "signs of racial superiority and cultural hegemony" remain hidden, obscuring "the violence of power and privilege" (p. 89). Once triggered, incidents involving racially motivated assaults in the guise of security, protection, and patriotism can arise. It becomes obvious, then, why emergency procedures should not be developed and enforced without consideration of a school's diversity mission and conduct, which may run counter to the national climate but is in keeping with the U.S. Constitution.

Bullying Prevention

Beyond the fact that the compliance procedures for emergency situations were poorly managed by the principal of Bayview High School, of greater concern is the fact that "the standard of providing a supportive climate for diversity and the prevention of bullying was not upheld" (Bouleris et al., 7). This leads the authors to conclude "in this case that deficiency led directly to a direr schoolwide crisis" (p. 8).

During the 107th Congress from 2001 to 2002, a U.S. Senate bill entitled Racial Profiling Education and Awareness Act of 2002 was presented to eliminate racial profiling (see http://www.theorator.com/bills107/s2114.html). Case writers Bouleris and coauthors selected a key statement from the bill that communicates a core value regarding civil liberty for all citizens: "Using race, ethnicity, or national origin as a proxy for criminal suspicion violates the constitutional requirement that police and other government officials accord to all citizens the equal protection of the law" (U.S. Senate 2002, para. 4). Although laws have been developed to eliminate racial profiling, this form of prejudice is still alive in our educational institutions, as evidenced by the need for an Awareness Act.

The teacher researchers in the case scenario bring attention to how "Saiid was a victim in an environment that should have been inclusive" (p. 5) by drawing upon definitions of victimization. The National Association of School Psychologists (NASP) explains that "a victim is any child who has directly or indirectly suffered as the result of isolated or repeated confrontations or personal violations by another child. Primary victims suffer the physical and affective consequences of direct assaults. Secondary victims experience indirect affective reactions as a result of witnessing or hearing about a victimization incident" (as cited in Bouleris et al., p. 5).

In the context of the case scenario provided, Saiid Abdul was a "primary victim" who suffered physical and emotional consequences, and possibly others as well. There were also a host of secondary victims who witnessed the situation and the authorities' reactions. Leaders can bring meaning to any such incidents within their schools by using credible research that "maps onto" people's actions. The hypothetical case of Saiid Abdul establishes what a "victim" is and distinguishes between primary and secondary types. Such illuminating notions can be directly built into staff emergency planning and coordination training.

Today's educational environment in general holds the challenge of becoming a community that accepts cultural diversity while experiencing new demographic trends in America. Schools that are exemplary centers of inclusion have great potential to become "cohesive, integrated, family-like villages in which each student has a place, and a sense of mutuality and regard. Until this occurs [for every school], all efforts to reduce violence, including bullying, will at best, be stopgap measures" (Hoover and Oliver, 1996, *Bullying Prevention Handbook*, as cited in Bouleris et al., 7).

Channeling Emotion

Cultural Change

Continuing to delve deeply into diversity initiatives, we now turn to an evaluative case study. Laura Meadows's (2003) paper represents a real "flesh and blood" example of action research in contrast with the earlier "imagineering" case by Bouleris and coauthors. Laura, a seasoned teacher, assessed a diversity committee process at a Florida school for one of my master's courses in 2003. The politics behind a staff development process where cultural diversity is a goal of school improvement can elicit strong emotions and bring buried tensions to the surface. Staff development within this context can also prove to be dysfunctional and polarized, even divisive, where racial tensions are activated, resulting in fragmentation at the deeper level of community.

According to Laura, Florida Comprehensive Assessment Test (FCAT) scores for the site revealed a gap among black, white, and Hispanic students: "Since accountability matters and school scores matter, it was in the school's best interest to see why those gaps exist. The principal at the magnet middle school had organized a diversity committee to help meet the needs of the school community" (Meadows 2003, 4). Laura looked at whether the school's change process was just a "Band-Aid" or in fact a "miracle cure" for addressing diversity issues: "The creation of this committee was the first step in trying to pull together a program that would ensure that all students from a variety of cultures and socioeconomic backgrounds could have their academic needs met" (p. 2).

The survey Laura developed collected data from staff, teachers, and administrators to determine if the plan proposed by the committee was meeting its goals. The questions ranged from defining cultural responsiveness to assessing whether the plan was working. Regarding the definition of cultural responsiveness, most respondents indicated that "it was about being sensitive to other cultures, while only a few related it directly to lesson planning and curriculum adjustments" (p. 3). Laura interpreted these results, providing this direction for change: "More training is probably needed for teachers to understand that educators are held to a high standard of cultural sensitivity. It must be about how we approach teaching our diverse student population, not just that we recognize students' cultural differences" (p. 5).

The diversity committee at the school opted to review Laura's survey results. After careful discussion, it was decided that the plan needed to be changed to incorporate staff development options. "It came to light during that discussion that there was a lot of racial tension in the school" between teacher groups and in relation to the administrator. While some cultural groups among the faculty had been given permission to initiate different cultural events, others were blocked, which was sending "mixed messages" to the teachers: "The African American teachers are angry," Laura shared, adding, "Who could blame them?" (p. 7). She continues,

> The diversity committee at this school then asked for all teachers to come together and join the chorus teacher in producing a Black History Concert that would be meaningful. Finally, some did cooperate and the concert came

and went. Some who have been hurt in the past participated and the healing process appears to be underway. The diversity committee saw the wounds and sought to address them openly and honestly. The members agreed to prepare a Black History Month celebration every year, as well as seek new ways to bring diverse issues before the teachers in the manner of staff development opportunities in the future. (p. 9)

Often, a school's attempt to create a more culturally responsive community will start with a plan that was in fact that "Band-Aid" that Nieto (2000) cautions us to avoid. It was the diversity committee's dedication, vision, and ongoing work that made the difference. Laura believes that the wounds would not have had the chance to heal at all without this deeper commitment: "This committee will be about going deeper into the change process for as long as it is allowed to function within this school's environment" (Meadows 2003, 10). The diversity committee's first steps taken to resolving any administrative problem can be applied more generally.

Curricular Change

Commitments to change that deal with racial tension at the systemic level, such as the one just described, take courage, but they have the potential to heal and transform a school's culture over the long haul. Complementary types of curricula that help children and adolescents understand racially sensitive issues have begun to emerge. With a focus on terrorism, these programs explore "wrongful attribution," as well as powerful feelings of fear, hatred, and anger (Jolly, Malloy, and Felt 2001).

Innovative programs for school administrators include, for example, the Texas School Safety Center. This training focuses on crisis intervention and terrorism awareness but also addresses the need for cultural sensitivity in developing more secure school environments. Given the current climate, school leaders should not deemphasize or subordinate cultural issues in the development of safer schools. Diversity awareness building can be carried out simultaneously with emergency preparedness to reinforce their interrelatedness. Indeed, an understanding of this change process beyond sketchy programmatic descriptions has yet to be illuminated in the literature.

Figure 12.1.   Journaling as a Meditative Key to Decision Making
Source: Nova Development Corporation

Documenting Change

The mountaineering image of the journal represents meditation, reflection, and emotion as well as a tool for empowering decision making. Each night, when Sir Edmund Hillary went to bed, he would let his mind "dwell on the likely things that might happen the next day, and think out carefully the sorts of decisions that might be necessary to make" (Wiesel 2003). Of course, as intimated thus far, not all content to be recorded in a leadership journal is about pleasant experiences, just as not all human emotions are rational and centered, equitable and unbiased. Even Jardine's (2001) concept of the "trail journal" encourages backpackers to go beyond making simple observations when recording entries. He sees this as a workspace for describing lessons, philosophizing beyond situations, expressing feelings, and problem solving, all in an effort to develop one's reflective capacity and share "wisdom" with other trekkers.

Principals and other administrators are "trekkers" in the educational leadership realm. Those who journal as a regular practice can influence and justify their own decisions. Expert backpackers (e.g., Kosseff 2001; Logue 2003) claim this is an important habit of mind to develop before you "hit the trails" each day. Such habits can be developed through graduate leadership programs and other training venues. The importance of this practice is clear when we consider the decision-making process that one school leader inadvertently revealed:

> A principal of a secondary school described to us how being an educational leader these days was like living in an endless present—always responding to immediate and insistent pressures, with no time to think ahead or to reflect on how things had gone already. Reflex reactions are superficial reactions. (Hargreaves and Fullan 1998, 20–21)

We witnessed just such a reflex reaction in the case of "Bayview High School's" new principal, to whom the scenario writers gave a whirlwind environment. But she needed to find a calm center, a place for reflection. For not only did she publicly target a student on the basis of staff suspicion, but she also "overlooked" incorporating diversity awareness and antiracial profiling into the school's emergency planning. Laura Meadows believes that some of the responses received from her real-life practitioners were similarly superficial, and even negative and resistant to change.

Journal writing is widely established as a means of reflecting on the development of experiences—relationship, ideas, events, and issues—in progress. There are at least two types of journals that administration can use: self-reflective and dialogue. So far we have been discussing the first type; the second type involves interactive writing, or at least sharing reflections with others.

As Diamond and Mullen (1999b) learned, a dialogue journal extends the use of a self-reflective journal to include mutual reflection and sharing. Fishman and Raver (1989) even used a dialogue journal between a teacher mentor and teacher candidate to further the exchange of their views and document the progress of the latter. As a professor, Oberg (1990) found self-reflective journaling a helpful tool for graduate students to record and share their daily practice and reflection. Using response journaling, Oberg acted as their co-inquirer and as her own. They found that more is learned about events and ideas by writing and talking about them with others than keeping ideas strictly to oneself. As writers develop trust and self-acceptance, they become more open and questioning of their experience, thus knowledge arises from such dialogue between a mentor and protégé.

The idea of the interactive journal applies naturally to the principalship where internship assignments, such as portfolio development, are common. Administrators or other key players can keep a joint journal or write individually and share accounts, and even record meta-analyses in a third journal. Within administration, the dialogue journal could help keep open lines of communication between new and experienced leaders while serving to nurture an equalitarian relationship. To my knowledge, there is no literature that suggests such a process in administrative socialization. This innovative idea was sparked from my own participation in teacher education and higher education circles.

In addition to growth, accountability is monitored for any professional when we take the time to write and share our thoughts. School leaders can revisit decisions and look for better, more informed options. Events will be more accurately tracked, and our ability to recall critical details will improve. If your documentation is used at any point to clarify or resolve difficult situations, you will be relieved to have had it on hand. I realize that finding the time to journal may be difficult, but can it can be found, with commitment and time management.

SUMMIT DATA AND ANALYSIS

Emotional expression was defined contextually in my administrator survey data as an expression of stress or challenge as a new administrator. The language used by participants was personal, direct, and emotional but not necessarily completely revealing or deeply reflective. It was not unlike the quality of language one might expect to appear in a personal journal when it has been edited for others to see.

A state of feeling overwhelmed was common. A major adjustment was required, as though every day involved another summit climb: "The job is very overwhelming—never stops," said a new principal, and, for an assistant principal of a few years, "This year has been a challenge because the need to strive for perfection in every area is overwhelming." Someone else portrayed the first day on the job as a flurry of activity: "My first day I was shocked at how busy I was and how little time I had to make decisions. I dealt with a variety of duties from Buses, Hall, Lunch, to Bus Duty again, and then, in between, I also dealt with discipline issues and teacher concerns." This individual's strong language—"shocked"—and his use of capital letters to suggest the weight of his duties convey considerable emotional charge. The sheer number of hours required within the workweek helped account for the learning curve described in other chapters: "Adjusting to sixty-to-seventy-hour weeks has been a major change in my life."

While a minority chose to describe it as "rewarding," most of the early careerists saw the job of leadership as "challenging." These two words connote different emotions; the former implies a more gratifying experience, whereas the latter suggests difficulty in the process of socialization. The challenging aspects that were described emphasized the workload and the interpersonal dimensions—communications and conflicts—involving parents, teachers, and students.

Political aspects that illuminate socializing elements of the job were seldom divulged. But when they were, these were powerful sentiments, as in: "As an AP, you're at the 'mercy' of your principal," and, "Being a new AP is like being thrown in the deep end of a pool. I arrived and the principal left, and the new principal never had been a principal." Subservience in one instance, drowning in another—both striking emotions.

The importance of the principal as a socializing, mentoring, and stabilizing force for the assistant principal can be easily inferred from such statements, with solid support from the literature (e.g., Bayless 2004; Mullen and Cairns 2001). Issues of power and domination are suggested in the first respondent's quote, whereas a situation involving premature leadership without any modeling is connoted in the second. Both use emotional language to describe a situation for which they were apparently not ready. Other such disclosures did appear in the data, constituting a sporadic phenomenon, though not a prevalent pattern.

Some respondents also communicated emotion in the form of relief. They felt released from the type of managerial work that was once required as a teacher, "Now I am free of all the ESE paperwork!" A few others were glad to have the grading of papers behind them.

Positive, glowing emotion was rare but nonetheless noteworthy. Feelings of centeredness, fortitude, and even happiness seemed evident for at least two individuals: "I hope that the kind of fulfillment I get as AP continues long beyond my retirement," and "Quite simply, I love what I do and want to keep going."

Identifying Vital Administration Skills

Review and Enforce School Safety Program

In all, 47 percent of the participants deemed school safety program management to be a "most important" area of their work. Throughout Florida, each leadership team formulates a safety program for its school. This includes the actions teachers and students should take during a bomb or terrorist threat or any other emergency. Since the 9/11 tragedy, such a plan is not only advisable but necessary (Mullen 2004). The administrative team at each school in Florida documents the procedures in the institution's handbook and instructs educators on how to follow them. New administrators, once again, are not taught this component of leadership in graduate school. The skill is acquired while "on site."

Attend Parent–Principal Conferences

This survey item received a "5" or "most important" rating from 52 percent of the respondents, ascribing considerable weight to this leadership task. Parent–principal conferences are also attended by a teacher, usually the major player present, who discusses the child's academics, behavior, adjustment, or even remediation. The parent is present to hear the problem and perhaps begin to take steps to correct the issue. When a parent requests a conference with a teacher, an administrator is expected to be present and in a mediation role. This is a well-established practice across most school districts that functions as a safety precaution for the teacher, should a parent become verbally or even physically abusive. An administrator must be prepared to control the situation when actions or words get "out of hand." A better solution would be for an administrator to foresee and forestall or defuse such problems. Beginning administrative leaders who responded to this survey recognized, and rightly so, the importance of such a skill.

LESSONS

School leaders can learn to deal productively with what may superficially appear to be a contradiction between emergency prevention and diversity awareness. This requires more than sensitivity to the complex issues involved, perhaps even the recognition of a new leadership disposition—an attitude that fosters safety, tolerance, and inclusion while vigilantly monitoring racial incidents. A new ethic is expected to emerge with respect to diversity–terrorism emergency planning for schools, affirming the rights of ethnic groups and foreign internationals as well as equitable treatment in all public spheres (Mullen 2004).

Schools, like the imaginary one that opened this chapter, should establish guidelines for evaluating emergency plans and actions that would affect basic civil liberties. As Romero (2001) notes in regard to this democratic issue, "any proposals to restrict liberty should be examined and debated in public; they should be proven effective in increasing safety and security; and they should be fairly applied in a nondiscriminatory manner" (para. 21). While schools prepare for the threat of terrorism and bioterrorism, racism can become rampant and profoundly rationalized. Inclusive, schoolwide consciousness-raising efforts could support a climate where violence prevention and humanitarian values go hand-in-hand. The contradictions embedded in homeland securities that forsake human freedoms for protection offer lessons for learning and leadership. The outcomes of this administration study support the use of crisis planning to explore tensions in democratic vision.

BACKPACKING TIPS AND LEADER ACTIVITIES

- Role-play test grade issues (or another topic) with key personnel at a faculty meeting or in the lunchroom. Assume the roles of administrator, teacher, parent, student, journalist, and so forth, in order to gain as many different points of view as possible. Ask an expert to be on hand to observe the behaviors. Deconstruct what happened. Discuss individual and collective emotional responses. Use the insights elicited for becoming better informed as a professional group. Consider organizing a school-community forum that focuses on the issue selected.

- Engage in a reflective activity initiated by a journaling process. Outdoor educator Jardine (2001) writes about three pages a day and designs his own lightweight journal. You can adapt this practice as a school leader. Write freely or use categories that are meaningful to you for eliciting and organizing your thoughts. Analyze your journal for themes as you develop material; write an overview of what you have learned. You may wish to share the summary with your administrative staff and/or others or begin a dialogue journal process.

- Develop a curriculum or slide show based on lessons of the government's 1941 internment of Japanese Americans and other racially motivated episodes of repression in American society. Adapt the information for contexts ranging from diversity training to classroom activity. Invite others (e.g., teachers and staff) to reflect on current behaviors and emotions in light of the evolving societal picture: What similarities do they see between then and now, and what are unique issues for contemporary times?

- University educators of educational leadership programs and crisis emergency training coordinators can ask the question, "What challenges, omissions, and tensions in crisis planning exist in preparing teachers for their future roles as school leaders?" A course assignment (e.g., case study complete with a training module) can be developed that enables emergency preparation and diversity awareness to be co-examined for school improvement purposes.

- To learn more about diversity awareness, school leaders and personnel can become a trainer of trainers. Laura Meadows recommends Ruby Payne's (1998) workshop and book, *A Framework for Understanding Poverty*.

Chapter Thirteen

First-Aid Kit: Coping Skills

Keeping in mind the fact that it is next to impossible to create a perfect first-aid kit, [some items are particularly helpful in making up] a close-to-perfect kit. . . .

Unless you have a special need or problem, do not carry too many specific items in your first-aid kit. Also, remember to repack your first-aid kit seasonally or yearly. Your first-aid kit should reflect your personal needs as well as the season and geographic area through which you're hiking. Most importantly, do not carry anything in your kit that you do not know how to use.

—V. S. Logue

CASE SCENARIO

Sweltering, muggy heat had taken over in May. The teachers at Unity Elementary dreaded going outside, but they had to. "A Code 2 evacuation will take effect immediately," the intercom blurted out. Within seconds, Mrs. Carter had grabbed the class emergency list, lined up the students, and announced, "Carry all your personal items." She led the children out to the field to the usual spot while they complained of the heat. To everyone's relief, they were soon instructed to return inside.

All seemed normal at first, until a child complained of a headache. Mrs. Carter applied a wet paper towel to her forehead, but then others claimed to have headaches as well as chills. The teacher attributed the symptoms to hunger and the excessive heat. After taking the class to lunch, she informed Nurse Miller of the situation.

As the day progressed, the nurse learned of other classes that had developed similar symptoms. The numbers mysteriously increased. Principal Hogerty, concerned, consulted the county's crisis management plan and contacted the district office's Security Services Department. The ill students were dismissed at the regular time, but the symptoms worsened that night.

The next morning the affected students stayed home. Unity Elementary had the highest absentee rate in its history. Principal Hogerty called a crisis management team meeting, and Mr. Saffer, the district crisis management director, arrived to guide the process. A plan would have to be set up to determine commonalities in the students' symptoms and to identify the cause. Because Principal Hogerty also started feeling ill, he had to force himself to work with the district crisis management team while relying almost completely on his assistant principal's know-how. In compliance with the emergency plan, the school was already in lockdown mode. As the principal wiped his forehead, he learned that Mrs. Carter had passed out. Crisis Director Saffer immediately called 911.

After Mrs. Carter was taken away in an ambulance, Nurse Miller was overwhelmed with the students showing up at the clinic in droves, including parents demanding an explanation. With all of the commotion, Principal Hogerty simply couldn't think straight. Assistant Principal Knowles stepped up to the plate again—this time to help the district officials deal with the parents. The county spokesperson contacted the Center for Disease Control (CDC), and the school was immediately put under quarantine.

In the meantime, the hospital called with the diagnosis—Mrs. Carter had been infected with the Ebola virus. The telephone dropped from Mr. Hogerty's hand—the nurse, moving him into a chair, applied a cold compress to his forehead. While this was occurring, the doctor advised the assistant principal how to brief the school on the process of quarantine. Crisis Director Saffer had the police block anyone from entering the school, and the fire department surrounded its perimeter.

The hospital informed the CDC that in order for Mrs. Carter to contract the Ebola virus, she must have come in contact with the virus itself. A doctor explained that Mrs. Carter had to have touched someone or something that was still in the school (American Red Cross 2002). The Center for Disease Control was notified that the origination point had yet to be discovered and took the next decisive step in the investigation—the classroom with the first identified carrier would undergo a thorough examination that same day. (from Buntin, Rovellada Gutierrez, and Spires 2003, 2–5)

REFLECTION AND DISCUSSION

Interpreting the Case

In this roller coaster of a disaster story, many more details flash before the reader, communicating the importance of coping as a critical capacity for any school or leader. Toward this end, crisis management planning was treated as an integral part of the elementary school's preparedness training. Jeanette Buntin, Carrie Rovellada Gutierrez, and Carisa Spires—teachers from Florida schools—wrote this fictitious scenario as part of their crisis management report for Case Studies in School Administration, a master's course I taught in the summer of 2003.

In their paper, the actions taken by all key personnel in the building, particularly the school leaders, were the focus. School disasters can quickly become a whole-community effort that the principal must coordinate, drawing heavily upon the expertise of all personnel, the appropriate school district specialists, and public service agencies. In the high-alert situation described, a biological terrorism attack affected personnel and eventually the entire building. Ebola Fever, discovered to be the source of the problem, is "a powerful, highly contagious hemorrhagic fever caused by a strain of virus. This disease has devastating symptoms, followed by death. There is no known effective treatment, and the means of contagious transmission is not fully understood" (Information Resources 2003). For a school that knew only how to evacuate in the case of a bomb threat, this level of danger was nowhere on the radar screen of preparedness, either on paper or in the minds of the leaders (Mullen 2004).

Racism, and particularly racial profiling, and diversity training were integral developments in the longer version of this crisis story. The students and families identified as probable assailants were internationals of color, innocent of the crime. The principal had fallen into the trap of making wrongful accusations, which led to the school board calling for the "mandatory training of all county employees on the topic of racial profiling" in concert with "bioterrorism procedures." Because the interrelated issues of diversity and terrorism have already been featured in chapter 12, the focus herein is on coping skills—a "first-aid kit" in action—more generally, with allusions to the diversity–terrorism dialectic as it relates to the case scenario.

Coping Skills

Coping skills are whatever an individual should be able to do in order to deal with a difficult situation or an unexpected problem. Leaders can use or adapt initiatives for their own purposes, but the focus is on prevention, planning, information gathering, expert consultation, community building, early detection, counseling, and self-care.

Mandatory Measures

Schools in Florida and elsewhere in the United States are now required to implement preventive emergency measures and ready-made systems to deal with crises (Buntin, Rovellada Gutierrez, and Spires 2003; Neale, Saltzgaver, and Sutton 2003). The expectation for schools is to be proactive, not reactive. An indispensable strategy for coping is the development of school crisis management plans, to be coordinated among all building-level and school-district personnel. Every school in Florida is also expected to create crisis emergency plans for virtually every type of catastrophe imaginable, as well as regularly practice evacuations; teachers and even students need to know exact procedures for different types of attacks.

However, the teachers in my master's classes who have been faced with these challenges generally seem unaware of the status of the emergency plans in their own schools and district. For this reason, some of my student groups interviewed knowledgeable leaders in their districts and the state (e.g., county director of transportation) and reported their results to the class. From this encounter, they learned from an individual who chose to remain anonymous that "All schools in our Florida county have evacuation plans for inclement weather, bomb threats, etc., but no official plans to specifically address terrorism." Some schools in Florida are beginning to make these changes, but it is a slow process at this time.

The American Red Cross (2003) has alerted our institutions and businesses to prepare for the unthinkable. The U.S. Office of Homeland

Security's code orange (high security) dictates that school leaders become "alert to suspicious activity and report it to proper authorities" and "review emergency plans," as well as "discuss children's fears concerning possible terrorist attacks." As Buntin and coauthors (2003) have learned, a crisis prevention plan focuses on coordination training to accommodate different types of disasters and situations. Every person in the school would have a critical role in meeting the plan's objectives, starting with a detailed vulnerability assessment to prioritize deficiencies and establish policies, procedures, and regulations. Other steps could include holding security council meetings and reviewing crisis preparedness guidelines. The core crisis committees would function most effectively with primary and alternate team members.

School Safety Resources

Articles and news updates pertaining to security and terrorism precautions, accessible via the Internet (e.g., National School Safety and Security Services 2001), emphasize the value of particular interventions. Among the most popular elements are student-run, antiviolence organizations; ongoing communication with local experts in emergency operating systems; partnerships with mental health services, emergency personnel, and other agencies; regular whole-school drills that extend beyond bomb threats; security improvement through surveillance measures and increased awareness; and student–staff assemblies that focus on resolving conflict and identifying violent behavior (Della-Giustina, Kerr, and Georgevich 2000).

Another literature base emphasizes that emergency plans must be developed on-site by administrators, teachers, and other partners. Context supersedes the value of adapting templates developed by others (Fullan 1999), as "no single strategy" or set of change strategies fits all schools. However, school teams may find others' templates useful starting points for creating and enforcing their own security plans.

Locating the necessary resources is essential for helping schools to cope and build resilience. Such knowledgeable publications are provided in my classes to enhance school security (e.g., Federal Emergency Management Agency's [n.d.] *Emergency Management Guide for Business and Industry* and the U.S. Department of Justice's [2001] *OVC Handbook for Coping after Terrorism*). My master's students view expert advice, clear procedures, reports, and school funding as indispensable resources for emergency planning. They recommend that funding from the state and federal government be obtained for expert consultation and to cover the costs of staff training related to crisis management (Mullen 2004).

Ongoing research is also encouraged for local emergency and other officials. The need to update school emergency policies and expertise is essential. Llewellyn (2004) emphasizes that the capability of readily accessing the necessary information at one's school requires that educators themselves take action, if necessary. My master's groups even believe that one critical resource, which is easy to overlook, is the memorization of procedures for every conceivable emergency, and even the names and phone numbers of key agencies.

Partnering with External Agencies

In my master's students' reports from 2002 to 2003, partnership development has been recognized as a solution for resolving the relative isolation, complacency, and even deficiencies of schools. In one such case study, the role of the local emergency ward of a hospital became an avenue for immediate treatment and the basis of an ongoing relationship. Better relations with one's own school district personnel and board members were also generally perceived as valuable. It was maintained that any specialist at the school, district, or community level involved in crisis management should become an immediate ally in the development and implementation of emergency plans at the building level.

My classes have also emphasized the necessity of creating and sustaining new unions with existing agencies. These included law enforcement and public health as well as disease, poison control, and bioterrorism alert centers. Local agencies and state experts such as FBI agents and county sheriffs can provide, for example, surveillance tips (e.g., maintaining highly visible, well-lit school buildings so that intruders and objects cannot be concealed), and even school weather stations could play a role. Schools across the nation could help save lives in the event of a chemical or biological attack by participating in a national weather monitoring network (*eSchool News staff and Wire Service Reports* 2003).

These results fit with the National Public Health Leadership Institute's (2003) recommendation that critical relationships be built and reinforced at the school level, beyond skills-based training that prepares leaders for emergencies and terrorism, particularly bioterrorism. A partnership between local authorities and school officials is the only way schools can afford to be up-to-date in emergency preparation. As one empirical case study (Mullen and Kochan 2000) has illustrated, the development of "multi-institutional partnerships" that link schools, universities, and businesses, particularly in impoverished and vulnerable areas of the country, can bring strength and power to each school entity.

Trauma Counseling

One serious effect of crisis is posttraumatic stress disorder. Diagnostic criteria include recurrent and distressing recollections or dreams of the event, difficulty concentrating, hypervigilance, and startled responses. If it lasts three months or more, the individual is thought to be in a chronic state of distress (Internet Mental Health 2003). Various agencies (e.g., American Red Cross, the International Society for Traumatic Stress Studies, the Florida Department of Public Health) offer assistance to schools facing such trauma.

In my own classes, the theme of coping has been included as an integral part of coordination plans. The development of strong bonds with students, families, faculty, government workers, and community agencies is emphasized. Emotional management is also an integral part of school preparation that involves the ongoing training of staff at all educational levels. Florida's Pinellas County, for example, has its own department at the district office to deal with coping-related issues; qualified experts visit schools and counsel students who have experienced trauma.

Early Detection

As a result of constant media exposure to worldwide terrorism, some children have already been experiencing fear and anxiety (Aidelbaum et al. 2003). Teachers need to recognize the warning signs of emotional distress and be prepared to support the affected students. Aidelbaum and coauthors, who teach in the elementary and middle school grades, indicate that "children react to trauma in various ways. Some may show signs of stress soon after an event, while others may show signs weeks or months later. Knowing the most common signs at different ages can help parents and teachers to recognize disconcerting behaviors, and respond appropriately" (p. 6).

Grounding their suggestions in the research conducted by the National Mental Health Information Center (2002), Aidelbaum et al. provide information about the signs students may exhibit and relate this to their own situations. For example, young children age one to five find it very difficult to adjust to change and loss. They have not yet developed coping skills, so they must depend on parents, family members, and teachers to help them through difficult times. One sign is exaggerated or repetitive storytelling about the traumatic event. Adolescents twelve to fourteen may experiment with high-risk behaviors, such as drinking or drug abuse. Similarly, older teens show symptoms by denying the extent of their emotional reactions to the traumatic event, withdrawing, and rejecting opportunities for emotional contact.

Reassurance is the key to helping children through a traumatic time. Very young children need to be physically held and verbally supported, for instance. Additionally, it is recommended that adults answer questions honestly but not dwell on frightening details or allow the subject to dominate family or classroom time. It is also important for administrators to understand the cultural differences that affect students in their buildings (National Mental Health Information Center 2002). Just as American students may consider different cultural behaviors and responses strange, ethnic and non-Anglophone groups from outside the United States may similarly find certain American conduct odd or even improper.

In the classroom, providing students an opportunity to express their emotions through guidance and role-playing could help them handle any potentially disarming situation, ranging from divorce to death to terrorism. Mental health counselors should also be called upon as needed, perhaps using the diagnostic criteria for students and adults for early detection. According to the American Red Cross (2003), when the country has been placed on code red (severe) alert status, qualified counselors *must* be available onsite.

Supply Kit

As school practitioners Neale, Salzgaver, and Sutton (2003) declare, "Preparation is the key. An emergency can happen at any time, so it is best to stock supplies in advance and have everything that you need stored in the shelter" (p. 3). They suggest having two types of disaster supply kits, one for each classroom and one for the whole school:

> Each classroom disaster kit should contain emergency phone numbers for all students and for emergency personnel, flashlight and extra batteries, whistle, moist towelettes, garbage bags, facial masks, one gallon of water, paper cups, minimal first aid supplies (gloves, Band-Aids, disinfectant), map of area in case of evacuation, duct tape, and plastic sheeting. The school disaster kit should contain, aside from items normally found at a site, a large quantity of water, facial masks, extra gloves, comprehensive first aid kit, battery powered radio, nonperishable foods, and staff members' phone numbers. (p. 3)

Using the instructions provided by the Centers for Disease Control and Prevention (2001, 2003), Neale and her colleagues further instruct that the supplies in the school's shelter should be checked every six months. Stale and expired items, including water, should be replaced to keep everything fresh. (Experienced trekkers recommend the same procedure.) In many schools, this course of action would be challenging to operationalize; it would have to be an assigned duty of a specific person(s) in order to get the job done. The supply kits should also be adapted to ready a school for a terrorist or biological attack. Basic information about various biochemical warfare agents (e.g., anthrax) and contagious diseases (e.g., smallpox), especially the symptoms and treatments, could prove life saving.

Self-Care

As Kosseff (2003) rightly declares, "Amid all of the responsibilities of leadership, awareness of your own needs can seem selfish or overly time consuming." He adds that "leaders who respect their own needs are generally able to function at a higher level than those who don't. This is particularly important to remember during a crisis, when it's easy to ignore your own needs" (pp. 72–73). The school leader who understands self-care will not try to be present at all times, dealing with (or controlling) every issue. Others can fill the leader's shoes from time to time. Again, shared leadership is essential. In the crisis story at the outset of this chapter, the principal who became ill had to rely on the nurse's assistance and let go of trying to manage the situation; the assistant principal stepped up to the plate.

Inside any first-aid or supply kit you should find batteries, which turn chemicals into energy. Similarly, principals need as many personal sources of energy as possible. Besides collaboration and teaming, there is a range of ways to recharge one's battery—celebrations, retreats, workshops, nature walks, hiking, gardening, motivational tapes, exercise, and healthy diet, to name a few. Anyone who cares about your well-being and from whom you seek advice and confidentiality can be an energizer, too. In the case of one new principal, the outright resistance experienced from faculty to his leadership style was offset by cathartic conversations, shared with a veteran principal-confidant, over meals (Bolman and Deal 1993). Energizers also come in such forms as meditation, yoga, prayer, napping, art, cultural events, meals with colleagues, and courses. One participant in my study actually equated university learning with a personal energizer that positively affected his professional performance: "Each graduate class expands my horizons and what I bring to the job. I am energized and able to convey new ideas to my principal and the faculty. I'm still in the process of taking classes, and I hope each course continues to enhance my performance."

Whether climbing the summit of school leadership or the real Himalayas, you will need to find ways to "recharge" your personal and professional battery every day and to help others do the same. School leaders who have rituals, such as award recognition parties, can use these as refueling opportunities to help people cope with problems and transitions and symbolically mark beginnings and endings. Relatively minor efforts can go a long way toward promoting a healthy work culture that can endure the hard times (Bolman and Deal 1993, 1997). Combining work and play is how I keep my own intense schedule, and by using good humor as a "quick fix" for refueling in the moment.

SUMMIT DATA AND ANALYSIS

Solving an administrative problem or making the optimal decision in a crisis is what this study has defined as *coping skills*. Because adaptation and challenge were so prominent for the group of developing school leaders in

Florida, a few mentioned that the pace of events affects one's ability to cope. Also, what may seem trivial to an experienced leader could actually prove daunting for someone newly practicing: "Becoming a school principal has been a challenge. If I were to start the year over again, I'd take a slower approach to addressing even the most mundane of changes—location of soda machines for example."

In order to cope better, many of the beginning school leaders felt that they needed knowledge and experience in areas that currently represent deficiencies for them. Such areas range from curriculum skills—"I need to work on gaining more experience in the curriculum area to improve my instructional leadership role"—to interpersonal skills—"communication skills and active listening are the glue that allows me as an administrator to assist in reaching goals and resolving conflicts." These are examples of skills and capacities that really must be developed through experiential learning. It was also believed that the leader must have a foundational interest in and "a strong commitment to student achievement within a safe learning environment."

Having a lucid philosophical foundation that is reinforced on a daily basis within the school system is critical for maintaining safety and helping people to better cope. Lynne Patrick, a third-year principal of a K–6 low-performing school within a gang neighborhood in Alabama, operationalized the belief that student achievement is inextricably linked to safety. Her philosophy of child advocacy recently awakened a school where most of the children had experienced trauma and neglect and about 40 percent exhibited problems related to the effects of chemical abuse. The strategies Lynne used for developing the school's capacities were simultaneously effective at the human level. Alongside the social services coordinator, Lynne applied Maslow's "hierarchy of needs" model to the daily work, convinced that "children cannot learn, or be taught, until their basic needs are met" and that "curricular and instructional improvements" matter only when such needs are satisfied (Mullen and Patrick 2000, 245).

Convincing community stakeholders of their responsibility to make a difference, Lynne persuaded donors throughout the state to rescue the school by providing the necessary aid. Children without appropriate school clothes suddenly had access to a clothing store on the school's premises, and many were placed in after-school and summer programs, in addition to having computer access in their classes. The values reorientation on the children's welfare provided the backbone the leadership and faculty needed to pull itself out of a historic slump and onto the local news as the most improved at-risk school in the state (Mullen and Patrick 2000). (See chapter 16 for a development of the Lynne Patrick story within the context of applied knowing and the theory-practice gap.)

LESSONS

Coping initiatives that leaders can adapt for their own purposes can generate constructive power at personal, professional, human, and systemic levels. Strategies for accomplishing such capacity building include:

- *Mandatory measures*—prevention and coordination planning (identify high-risk, (bio)terrorist targets within schools (e.g., water systems) as well as markers surrounding them (e.g., airstrips).
- *School safety resources*—information gathering, expert advice/consultation, and research-based documents and guidelines should all be used for developing terrorism prevention plans; school district plans should be tailored to individual sites.
- *Partnering with external agencies*—community building and support systems (e.g., terrorism alert centers) provide information and resources and help relieve the relative isolation of schools.
- *Early detection*—knowing the signs, applying diagnosis criteria, age-related and progressive symptoms of trauma and stress.
- *Counseling*—posttraumatic stress disorder, mandatory service in high-alert state.
- *Supply (first-aid) kit*—for the classroom and school, tailored to different emergencies.
- *Self-care*—personal and professional needs, sources of refueling.

On the topic of supply (first-aid) kits, we have once again drawn lessons for schools from the wisdom of expert backpackers. They caution us not to carry items that we have either not practiced using or would not know how to apply in a serious situation (such as suture tools and prescription medicines). This vital message reinforces that training and conditioning involve preparation, skill building, and practical knowing, all of which promote a successful, healthy hike.

First aid is an aspect of leadership training that should be extended to schools and maybe even graduate preparation programs. Every outdoor leader needs some first-aid training, as we can find ourselves leading activities when emergency medical care is not within reach. Wilderness first-aid courses teach you how to improvise equipment and deal with extended care. Traditional first-aid courses only clarify what to do during the brief interval before help arrives (Kosseff 2003; Logue 2000). Conversely, coping techniques must be practiced and refined over time.

Consider the value of these ideas for the scenario that launched this chapter. The principal's capacity to cope was limited, if not highly problematic, for a number of reasons. Administrative assistants and school personnel who know emergency care and can maneuver through a crisis, including those with a capacity for coping and healing, are invaluable resources for any principalship team. Learn to "condition" your "nerve endings" to "the notion that a crisis is an opportunity for creativity—and sometimes greatness" (Schmidt 2002, 183).

BACKPACKING TIPS AND LEADER ACTIVITIES

- List "tips for refueling" on an electronic message or handout and encourage others to add to it. Plan retreats, luncheons, or anything else that adds to the goals of team building and a spirit of renewal.
- Start a book club that focuses on learning about vision, strategizing, and courage from a field other than education. How do great leaders cope, and what skills do they demonstrate in the face of danger? Outdoor leadership accounts (e.g., Kosseff 2003) are one type of "survivor autobiography" (Schmidt 2002) that you might find inspiring.
- Design a classroom and school supply kit or revisit those on your premises and update the contents. This activity can be integrated into a school or university context, and the contents can be real or virtual.

Chapter Fourteen

Ax: Accountability Climate

Hillary and Tenzing climbed steadily and confidently, but before getting to the top [of Mt. Everest in May 1953], they encountered a ridge 40 feet high. Using an ice ax to pull himself up, Hillary somehow led the way over this jagged, icy obstacle. So famous is the ridge and Hillary's effort that today the final hurdle is known as the "Hillary Step."

—T. Jones

CASE SCENARIO

Maryann Lippek is a teacher who studied one Florida elementary school to find out if students' learning improves as a result of the FCAT (Florida Comprehensive Assessment Test). In her interview of a school faculty in 2003, one teacher reflected, "In some cases teachers are more focused on adhering to the broader expectations for content; however the FCAT test has limited our teachers' breadth of topics within some subjects. At the same time, students learn the topics in less depth in order that all the expectations be covered before testing."

One example of such curriculum condensing occurs in the county math calendar, which is designed so all five math topics are taught in the first three to nine weeks of school. The final nine weeks are used to accelerate students who have mastered the content and remediate those in need of more help. Perhaps this explains why the teachers viewed standardized tests as an inadequate measure of student success. Stiggins (2002) agrees, stating that too often assessments are designed to measure student performance without any real plan for improving learning.

Teachers shared that students can be prone to test anxiety because of the pressure on their performance. In *The Hurried Child*, Elkind (2001) declares that children have been forced into the role of victim due to "overwhelming stress." Teachers feel similar pressure to ensure that their students perform well on this high-stakes test: "A parent initiated a conference with me this year as FCAT drew near because her son had insomnia. There is something seriously wrong when a ten-year-old can't sleep because he fears he will fail." On a larger scale, "overstressed children and struggling learners may not meet the high expectations" when "state tests instill the fear of failure and reduce learning" (Stiggins 2002, 8).

An overwhelming majority of the teachers who participated in Maryann's study—93 percent—say the FCAT has decreased their sense of job satisfaction. They also disagreed with the perception that FCAT motivates educators to teach better. Many resent that the standardized scores determine whether they can be deemed quality teachers. They say job satisfaction is not derived from high-stakes tests but, rather, from daily interaction with students and witnessing their achievements. Although FCAT is based on the Sunshine State Standards, it only amounts to one day's performance, in contrast with "alternative assessments that produce greater insight into the students' abilities."

In short, assessment reforms have left many practitioners frustrated and concerned. Although many of the teachers with whom Maryann spoke were uncertain of any benefits of the FCAT, most cherish contact and communication with their students: "It is easy to be hopeful when things are rosy. It is essential to be hopeful when they are not," and "Teaching is about hope, and every student is one teacher's hope for the future" (Hargreaves and Fullan 1998, 57). We all need to foster hope so students can succeed and grow as healthy people (Lippek 2003, 3–6).

REFLECTION AND DISCUSSION

Interpreting the Case

Maryann Lippek, an elementary teacher, completed this investigation within Administrative Analysis and Change, a master's course I taught at the University of South Florida in spring 2003. Her paper addressed the current reality of assessment in education and its effect on teacher pedagogy and school culture. For this purpose, she surveyed and interviewed thirty elementary teachers with respect to legislative policy, testing, and its impact on instructional delivery. Her school survey covered teacher perceptions of the FCAT, job satisfaction with high-stakes testing, and changes in instructional delivery in regard to test preparation.

Maryann learned much more than the case scenario itself describes, particularly the larger point that "there is massive incongruity between what teachers believe are legitimate classroom practices and cultures and what legislative and business elites are demanding" (Barksdale-Ladd and Thomas 2000, 3). Noneducational "stakeholders" are controlling outcomes. The current accountability craze has affected many school faculties and leaders, as well as states and nations, having converted this pathway of change into a narrow, slippery climb:

> We are a nation obsessed with the belief that the path to school improvement is paved with better, more frequent, and more intense standardized testing. The problem is that such tests developed to "leave no student behind," are, in fact, causing major segments of our student population to be left behind because the tests are the basis as to why many give up in hopelessness—just the opposite effect from that which politicians intended. (Stiggins 2002, 2)

This process of performance-based accountability appears to be a distortion of a continuous improvement perspective. Fullan (2003), for example, has asserted that accountability systems that enforce measures of student performance are necessary but inept without the working conditions that make it possible for teachers to meet standards and improve.

Background Topographic Issues

Through Maryann's Eyes

The 1983 publication of *A Nation at Risk* has been the catalyst of high-stakes testing and accountability throughout the United States (National Commission on Excellence in Education, online). Currently, forty-nine of the fifty states implement a form of high-stakes testing. According to the

National Center for Fair and Open Testing (2003), tests are considered "high-stakes" when the results are used to inform major decisions about students' educational progress.

The Florida Department of Education (DOE) has designed the Sunshine State Standards to recount knowledge and skills requisites from kindergarten through high school. The FCAT, a criterion-referenced, performance-based assessment, was implemented to measure mastery of the Sunshine State Standards (see DOE online). Policymakers often attach the promise of merit for schools that produce high scores and sanctions for those that do not (Stiggins 2002). Under Florida's system of School Improvement and Accountability, grades are directly linked to these accountability restrictions and rewards (see DOE online). For the teachers, leaders, students, and parents in Florida's education system, the meaning seems clear: If they are to "enjoy" the earned privileges of promotion and graduation, funding, and resources, constant attention must be given to improving results on the standardized tests (Finn 1999).

The Florida Department of Education's (http://www.fldoe.org, 2002) stance is that students are increasingly expected to display high levels of learning and perform complex problem solving in order to compete in the job market. Unresolved questions come to mind: Does high-stakes testing ensure that students will be able to compete in the global workforce? Do "high stakes" help school personnel become more reflective of their practices while remaining optimistic about their job in relation to young people's lives? (Hargreaves and Fullan 1998; Lippek 2003).

Through My Own Eyes

In response to this question, according to the teachers and administrators in my master's classes, high-stakes accountability causes stress and a greater discrepancy between the educational "haves" and the "have-nots" of the world.

Given that the data for this book were collected in and across Florida, it makes sense to briefly provide more contextual information about the situations of the participants. As you know, the lives of these beginning school leaders are shaped in large part around the controversial FCAT, which tests student progress in reading, writing, math, and, as of 2003, science. A social science portion is also forthcoming. Additionally, since

1999 Florida's A-Plus Program—"a school accountability system with teeth"—has annually assigned a grade, ranging from A to F, to schools based primarily on student performance on the FCAT (DOE, 2001, online). (To clarify, the A to F grading system in Florida translates into "good" [A] to "unsatisfactory" [F] in at least one state—South Carolina [Parkay and Stanford 2004]). Economic rewards are provided to school sites showing progress. However, schools considered low-performing in the context of standardized testing, which are typically high-minority and high-poverty, are left frustrated, out in the cold, despite improvement in student learning (e.g., Acker-Hocevar and Touchton 2002; Waite, Boone, and McGhee 2001).

Achievement assessment never aimed to subject students to unattainable academic goals. High-stakes testing has grown out of the drive for school improvement and particularly increased student achievement, nationally and worldwide. The intent was to improve educational programs and curriculum in order to ensure that all learners would receive a quality education, enabling them to compete in the global market (Hargreaves and Fullan 1998). While the motives behind high-stakes testing were good, it does not work in practice. Consistent with this picture, the teachers Maryann studied believed, as many do, that assessment *should* be used to improve the learning of all students, based on study of individual performance over time.

Principal leadership is the key to dealing with and resolving the biases evident in schooling with regard to testing and other situations, such as discipline. Although the high-stakes reforms are "focused on eliminating social injustice, with the hopes of increasing the academic achievement of all children," they "fail to identify the dilemmas that are created by models and notions of leadership that are grounded in power-over conceptions" (Brunner 2002, 705). As Burrell (2002), a practicing middle school teacher in Florida, further reflects, "Principals must take the leadership in modeling key components of equity to staff and staff must model them to students. Equity ensures that each student receives what he or she needs to be successful. Everyday interaction should reflect access, instruction, attitudes, and interaction" (p. 7).

Brandi Burrell provided a positive leadership strategy that resulted from her action research conducted in one of my master's classes. The example, which is nonprogrammatic and also nonmeasurable, is powerful for the effect it promises to have on the culture of a middle school she investigated. This involves a situation wherein a "principal addressed the achievement gap between minority and white students" with his entire faculty at the beginning of the school year. The minority teacher she interviewed elaborated, saying that "despite the fact we had earned an A grade, our principal conveyed his disappointment and made us aware that the achievement gap was an area our school needed to improve in. He suggested that we embrace the theory that every student can learn, regardless of ethnicity or socioeconomic status. As a minority teacher, I really felt his concern was genuine" (Burrell 2002, 7). Such accountability messages delivered at the whole-school interpersonal level can make a difference for strengthening the resolve of each and every educator to reduce racial bias within his or her own educational place.

Similarly, the ax, a tool sometimes used in mountaineering, is not intended to be a danger to anyone. To the contrary, it helps trekkers progress, cutting through icy patches and negotiating difficult passages. But the accountability ax has become just a blunt instrument for some K–12 schools instead of a handy device for making and measuring student progress and institutional goals. Specifically, the prevailing high-stakes accountability system of rewards and punishment determines the fate of schools in the United States, England, and, more recently, those countries that follow the lead of Anglophone trend-setting nations, such as Australia and New Zealand (Scott and Dinham 2002).

The repercussions of what can be construed as a weapon are felt in many ways and places. Humanitarian goals for education have been turned into mandates governing the expectation of higher academic achievement for *all* students and schools (Stiggins 2002), regardless of the variances among sites at the same level and despite the significant nonacademic challenges faced daily within those that are economically disadvantaged (Mullen and Patrick 2000).

Rewards and punishments can accrue in many forms. For example, testing scores are publicized, enabling parents who value performance indicators as measures of quality and reputation to use as a guide for selecting schools. Also, funding allocations are made for individual sites based on their test scores, shutting them down in the most radical of instances (Scott and Dinham 2002). These are grave consequences that can affect school survival, as well as professional and emotional well-being.

Professional accountability for schools has largely been reduced to out-comes-based performance indicators—measurable progress on students' test scores. Consequently, school culture, including morale, reputation, reward structure, and graduation rates, has been significantly altered. School culture itself may become less rich and multifaceted, if testing is the primary educational goal, excluding all others. Florida is just one of seventeen states in the United States that make the high school diploma contingent on an exit test (or final course exams) (Parkay and Stanford 2004). Increasingly, schools, states, and entire nations live under the rule of national auditing agencies, notoriously epitomized by the British Office for Standards in English (OFSTED) and its vigilant inspections (Scott and Dinham 2002). Importantly, in general, students from low socioeconomic family situations, and those who contend with language barriers or learning disabilities, have been the most severely affected. Where scores are deemed unacceptable, progress has been impeded and retention inevitable (Mullen and Patrick 2000; Mullen 2002a; Mullen 2002b; Scott and Dinham 2002).

Teaching to the Test

Student achievement and "teaching to the test" have become almost synonymous in this age of educational reform. The higher the stakes of a test, the greater the intensity a teacher may bring to test preparation. This, unfortunately, has increased the likelihood of teaching to the test, to the detriment of other crucial aspects of teaching and learning (Lippek 2003; Scott and Dinham 2002; Waite, Boone, and McGhee 2001). According to the Florida Department of Education (http://www.fldoe.org, 2003), teaching to the test means educators are to use the Sunshine State Standards for guiding and delivering instruction rather than teaching students how to take the test.

However, it is widely known that some teachers have students work on test preparation materials in lieu of subject matter content. In one Florida-based case study, teachers are described as turning worksheets into "test format"—anxious that their school could end up with an F grade and be, euphemistically speaking, "reconstituted." Interestingly, school officials actually even closed an elementary school in Pensacola, Florida, for receiving an F (Parkay and Stanford 2004). Importantly, the issue of ethics is correlative in this context, something readers will struggle with as they view school personnel succumbing to the pressures, fearful of the punitive measures for schools that fail to make the grade when it comes to normative academic standards (Bruner and Livingston 2002).

Danielson (2002) distinguishes between teaching to the curriculum and teaching to the test, claiming that teachers should teach to the curriculum because it is aligned with state and district standards. However, the pressures associated with high-stakes testing lead teachers to focus on material that will be covered by the test and exclude other content and experiences, such as the arts and even recess at the elementary level.

Lippek's study (2003) shows that teachers generally felt that "curriculum and instruction [have] not changed for the better [as a result of] the FCAT." State testing has forced them to focus on content and on test preparation materials themselves. Additionally, she reports, these teachers experienced "pressure from administration to conduct test-prep practice as the FCAT test approaches." Lippek concluded that "students' 'love of learning'" is probably affected when high-stakes testing interferes with school curriculum and teachers' pedagogical focus.

Melting the "Ice" in "Ice Ax"

Human consequences relative to this high-stakes accountability movement cannot be ignored. Over the past decade, researchers have empirically and anecdotally produced sociocultural critiques of decreased job satisfaction for teachers; diminished motivation of fully qualified graduates to enter administration; and reduced emotional well-being of the student and teacher (e.g., Elkind 2001; Kincheloe and Weil 2001; Mullen 2002b, 2002c; Scott and Dinham 2002; Waite, Boone, and McGhee 2001; Weil and Kincheloe 2003). The pressure to achieve high scores has had detrimental effects on teaching, causing many K–12 teachers around the nation to feel anxiety, shame, loss of esteem, and alienation (Barksdale-Ladd and Thomas 2000). Some even end up questioning the good of the education profession itself in a climate where, as Scott and Dinham (2002) dramatically put it, "the beatings will continue until quality improves." Where is John Dewey when we need him?

When state policymakers develop standards and assessments, teachers serve as token members of committees whose voices are often not heard (Barksdale-Ladd and Thomas 2000; Mullen 2002a). Educators' efficacy and activism are controlled and thereby greatly limited in a system of top-down, strict accountability (Mullen 2002a, 2002b; Scott and Dinham

2002). Metaphorically speaking, the "ice" in "ice ax" may also be the state mandates that freeze administrative creativity in an attempt to provide the best services for both teachers and students.

SUMMIT DATA AND ANALYSIS

Taking a Broader View

The pervasive drive to do well on high-stakes standardized tests is a new way of understanding professional accountability within schools, one that jeopardizes the exercise of teacher and administrator autonomy (Kincheloe and Weil 2001). In the context of the data provided by beginning leaders for my study, accountability is associated with professional and academic standards that focus predominantly on two core leadership areas: supervision of instruction and student services (see table 5.3). Holding faculty accountable for students' attainment of state-mandated educational standards was one emphatic area, but in relation to the responsibility of leaders to interpret test results for teachers.

New leaders should keep in mind a perennial challenge embedded in their role, that "principals do not provide sufficient leadership in many areas of instruction and management" (Parkay and Stanford 2004, 441). On the other hand, new leaders will also need to learn how to delegate, because no one person can perform all complex tasks equally well. According to one focus group participant, "Unfortunately, new leaders are expected to be well versed in all aspects of FCAT testing, as it is a required component of their job." It is essential that a climate be developed whereby administrators and teachers engage in collaborative decision making regarding teaching, learning, and student services (Mullen and Graves 2000; Parkay and Stanford 2004).

The term *accountability* has a much more powerful, if not radical, meaning in the leadership literature than is revealed in the survey data. For example, Waite and coauthors (2001) believe that accountability is the contested site of polarized groups engaged in a modern "culture war." These researchers say it has become a "cultural iconic metaphor" similar to the "American flag, Democracy, and motherhood." They attribute this regression to the "maneuvering" of "conservative forces" that have managed to successfully infiltrate high-stakes accountability systems across the nation's schools and deep within our psyches.

In the survey data for my study, the stages of the principalship were characterized as differing levels of responsibility. As one participant noted about the increase in the responsibilities of the school leader, "The change in the level of accountability from AP to principal is tremendous. I love the job, but some days are overwhelming!" Principals and assistant principals alike underscored that one should really have previous "experience organizing and conducting state-mandated testing." They stressed that this is a "*huge* job" and recommended a heavy emphasis on "monitoring inservice and professional development for teachers." Increasingly, professional development for teachers is related to issues of accountability and testing, not to the broader or deeper quest of school improvement and learning.

The beginning principals also suggested that the grading of Florida schools has changed the nature of and expectations for their role: "Being a first time principal in a school rated 'F' before I took over, I'm finding that I have to give much assistance in roles, whereas at other schools this wouldn't be necessary." This principal's transitional experience is not surprising, given that the implementation of high-stakes standardized testing has only served to impair students and schools most at risk of failure (e.g., Scott and Dinham 2002). The stress to both students and teachers must be unbelievable—the students feel the anxiety of the teachers, who experience it in the form of pressure from their leaders. The leaders in this study who are stationed at disadvantaged schools find that dealing with negative public perceptions, keeping up teacher and student morale, and managing academic standards while coping with family issues, including poverty, require much extra effort. Research supports these experiences as generally characteristic of school leaders' experiences in challenging, stymied, or disadvantaged schools (see, e.g., Mullen and Graves 2000; Mullen and Patrick 2000; Mullen with Sullivan 2001).

Identifying Vital Administration Skills

Interpret Standardized Test Results with/for Teachers

For this task, within the core leadership area known as supervision of instruction, 49 percent of the surveyed administrators marked a "5." Knowing how to interpret various sources of data (e.g., test scores, student demographics, attendance rates, graduation rates, employment statistics) is indispensable for new administrative leaders. Otherwise, schools will lack an overall picture of where they stand (relative to other schools at the same level), their progress, and areas for improvement.

A pressing focus concerns not only analyzing but also using standardized test results. Administrators are responsible for interpreting school and student data and also for "reporting their results to stakeholders and legislative bodies, and for making informed program and restructuring decisions based on their interpretive processes." Besides analyzing data that they may have generated or been forwarded, they must know how "to use their findings to make informed judgments" and "how to work with others to discuss the data" (Mullen 2002c, 86; see also Lortie 1998).

National and state-level test scores should be closely audited, internally, as part of a larger focus of statistical management. When a school is undergoing a major restructuring effort—as in the case of principal Elaine Sullivan's secondary site in Florida that changed from a traditional institution to a career academy—data monitoring efforts will prove essential. In Elaine's school, a close watch was kept on the Sanford Achievement Test, Ninth Edition (SAT–9), for example. Her student population doubled within the same few years that the conversion of buildings and programs occurred. Anchors were sought in the form of data analysis, to ensure that students' progress was not overlooked while the school was changing (Mullen with Sullivan 2001).

The FCAT is required for fourth, eighth, and tenth graders in Florida every academic year. They prepare for it the other years. As previously mentioned, the results are used for placement into accelerated or remedial classes and will determine graduation. Not only are the scores on this instrument important for the welfare of the student, they are also highly influential for the school. Funds are awarded based on the scores of individual institutions—the better the score, the more monies received from the state coffers. It is in the best interest of the school for administrators to fully explain the meaning of the scores to their faculty, in addition to the implications of these results for the future. Administrators, considered the "experts" on this subject at the building level, would lose integrity if they could not elucidate to teachers the importance of the FCAT and other standardized tests.

Administrators have been advised to take inservice classes to learn how to interpret standardized test results, and many do. Florida counties offer courses on gathering, managing, and interpreting standardized test data. Even the DOE's website provides such self-study aids as "Data in a Day," which outlines how to collect and analyze data using basic action research steps (online). Further, recently developed test accommodations for students with disabilities should be studied and implemented at the building level (see DOE online).

Explore Programs to Improve Student Attendance

Based on the results of the administrator survey, 14 percent of the participants rated improving student attendance a "5." Developing attendance programs falls within the leadership category of school management. Because of the consuming emphasis schools place on high-stakes testing, student attendance could also be viewed as a subset of instructional supervision (the category previously discussed). Attendance is the starting point for most leaders when they want to affect student learning and achievement and the school's grade (Mullen with Sullivan 2002).

Largely because of accountability pressures, administrators have become more concerned with their school's attendance rate. Entire committees are formed to think up incentives for students to attend school regularly. The FCAT school grade is partly determined by the number of students who regularly attend school. Administrators are eager to receive the highest possible grade, and attendance can be impacted over time. Formulating reward programs for good attendance is one way to improve student attendance. An example appears in one Florida county where raffles have been held for a free car, donated by a local dealership; eligibility to win is a perfect attendance record.

LESSONS

One lesson of this chapter is that school leaders can turn the tide of high-stakes accountability to their advantage, thereby melting the "ice" in "ice ax," or turning the ax itself into a constructive image. New leaders should identify teacher leaders, curriculum specialists, and others to help their culture become "assessment literate" about the role of accountability and data in informed decision making. As Hargreaves and Fullan (1998) illustrate, schools that expand their "assessment repertoire" will be able to explain to parents, communities, and evaluators ("critical consumers") how student performance, preestablished outcomes in learning, and changes in curriculum and teaching strategies are meaningfully connected.

Administrators and teachers alike can be proactive in many different ways, ranging from professional development and action research to legislative networking and protest marches. Behind such movements are increasingly powerful strategies for "emerging from our cocoons to take action" to promote "social consciousness development in education" (Mullen 2002a, 11). Wider and deeper systemic changes will imbue the accountability ax metaphor with new meaning when schools' visions, rooted in student learning, can be fashioned in educational policy reform. Further, it should be empowering to realize that, at least potentially, "taking control of your own data means taking charge of how the argument about standards and accountability is conducted" (Hargreaves and Fullan 1998, 99). When invested as an administrator, you can use the ax (e.g., well-developed arguments supported with evidence) to your advantage as you campaign for more funding and resources for your school or district.

The accountability ax metaphor initially has an unpleasant if not outright severe connotation, but it also has a productive meaning in the context of this book. This construct can have a positive outlook where desirable change and professional well-being are empowered. Brunner (2002) adds that conceptions and experiences of power can be changed from top-down to "with/to." One major way the basis of power can shift and the directions for change make more sense for schools is when states involve representative personnel in common goals aimed at student learning (Mullen 2002a, 2002c, 2002d). However, "in a complacent society, teachers, administrators, and supervisors are not expected to take an active role," acknowledges a former school superintendent (Shapiro 2000, 89).

The current climate of school leadership seems to signal "a stark retreat of teacher activism in primary schools across Westernized countries" that must be "buffered with an emphasis on teacher voice and role" (Mullen 2002a, 11). A serious flaw in policymaking processes that persists as standards-led reforms are developed in Anglophone nations is that "practitioners are rarely consulted when changes are being formulated, but rather these solutions are at least partially composed of a variety of 'carrots' and 'sticks,' designed to entice or bully compliance" (Scott and Dinham, 15). School leaders need to somehow "get to the table" when such decisions about their own lives and those within their care are being made. School administrators continue to be underrepresented in the governance aspects of their own sites and districts.

BACKPACKING TIPS AND LEADER ACTIVITIES

- Give examples of the accountability ax at work in your own school or life and discuss solutions for transforming it into a positive, constructive force.
- Write a list of some of the concrete ways new leaders and teacher mentors, as well as entire school communities, can become "assessment literate."
- Talk confidentially to teachers, administrators, parents, students, and any other stakeholders in regard to their views on high-stakes accountability. Or rely on an observation record that can be kept over time. As part of this action research process, analyze the data, search for themes, and present the results, complete with quotes, in various forms (e.g., narrative, exposition, matrix display). Integrate relevant literature (e.g., published research, school reports, educational policy), as well as steps to be taken at the local and state level.
- Contact the local legislative representative who is responsible for educational interests and find out how you can have your concerns heard. Share your action research report, complete with potential steps within the policy-making arena.

Chapter Fifteen

Tarp: Real-World Experience

Tarps are not like tents where the tendency is to pitch them rain or shine, and the perceived security draws a person in and compels him or her to shut out the world. Where possible we slept in the open, and this was a marvelous experience for everyone. With the starry canopy overhead and the earth's gentle embrace beneath, we found that our simple, low-tech style allowed us more profound interaction with the natural world.

—R. Jardine

CASE SCENARIO

"It's 4:30 A.M. on your FM dial. We're looking at another stormy, muggy day, folks! Be sure to take the necessary emergency precautions—we're still under a tornado watch. Expect a high of 93 degrees with a 'feel like' temperature of 103. Next up, an oldie by the Carpenters—'Rainy Days and Mondays.'" Singing along to the Carpenters' tune, you gear up for meeting with the principal. Taking a good long look at yourself in the new blue suit, you feel pleased that you've finally arrived. A school administrator, imagine! All those years of hard work as a graduate student and a teacher have paid off. Adrenalin pumping, palms sweaty, you check the time once again and leave for the school, ready to enter a new world of exciting challenges.

You arrive early at your new job at Holiday Elementary School. Feeling nervous about the impending meeting, you head straight for the principal's office: "Dr. Benson will be out until about noon—family emergency!"

sputters the new secretary. She directs you to the conference room, advising you to keep an eye on the weather forecast. With the TV on, you glance at a brochure outlining the newly revised tornado drill procedures established by the school district. You feel distracted by the banging sounds of the workers but flip through another brochure that describes your new "home" as a large, urban public school with over thirteen hundred students. The first and second graders are housed outside in the portables because the main building was overcrowded—but the pamphlet does not say this. Dr. Benson had shared this reality during the interview. She had given up on trying to move the fourth and fifth graders to the portables, exclaiming, "Those kids are just too darn big. There's no way anyone could move around in there with them!"

The noise of workers becomes even louder. They're busy fixing the intercom between the portables and the main building. As you close the door, the familiar "beep, beep, beep" signal from the TV overpowers the racket. A broadcaster proclaims that *this area* is now under a tornado warning!

At that very moment the skies look glum as never before. A funnel cloud has formed, and it's moving this way. Your mind is racing—the intercoms are broken, so you can't contact the teachers in the portables. Those kids will need to be herded inside the school for protection, pronto! And because the tornado drill procedures have just been changed, most of the staff will probably be confused. Their eyes will fall on you, the second in command, for leadership. But you don't have any idea what to do!

Not knowing how to handle this emergency, fumbling and distraught, you feel overwhelmed: What should you do right now, and what next? What are all of the steps that need to be taken, and in what sequence, to ensure the safety of the school and its occupants?" Your mind reels, and panic sets in. (from Mullen and Cairns 2001, 126–27)

REFLECTION AND DISCUSSION

Interpreting the Case

Sonja Cairns, a veteran of eighteen years as an educator, wrote "Unforeseen School Emergencies Hail Risks," a story about an unprepared, newly hired school leader. Her account became the basis of an action research project carried out in Case Studies in School Administration, a master's course I taught in 2000. Sonja's and my joint efforts turned into a full-blown study on the efficacy of graduate school training in relation to the "real world" of school administration (Mullen and Cairns 2001). While the emergency school scenario depicted is fictionalized, to construct it Sonja drew on her own observations and experiences as both an elementary teacher and master's student in Florida, including three bomb threats in a single year.

Exposing Gaps in Formal Preparation

This school emergency story illustrates a pivotal point: Despite her wealth of leadership experiences and credits accumulated in educational administration, Sonja would neither feel comfortable nor confident currently assuming an assistant principalship. This may seem surprising, especially considering that Sonja has had more teaching experience than many school administrators. Besides, she has always been able to ensure the safety of the children in her care in addition to mentoring teachers and interns. However, this seasoned professional lacks the real-world procedural knowledge of how to "weather" an emergency. Like the character she portrays, Sonja is uncertain how to safeguard students and school personnel; she is also unsure how to operate the necessary equipment. Issues of protection and shelter in the principal's jurisdiction have simply not been covered in any of her administration courses, readings, or trainings.

Left to her own devices, she has asked countless questions about how to handle a weather-related school emergency, including:

- Who would the administrator typically need to contact on a walkie-talkie, and with what information and directives?
- Where should "portable" students be relocated, or should they even be evacuated during severe weather?
- Who needs to assist during emergencies?
- What tasks should be allocated and to whom?
- What is to be done with electrical devices in the building?
- What school officials and community agencies are to be contacted during and after a weather emergency?

- What is to be done if an injury occurs, and what precautions should be taken to prevent injuries?
- And, how can the leader be certain that everyone is accounted for?

Of course Sonja also wonders about different kinds of crises of even greater magnitude, especially since the tragic events of September 11, 2001, and consequently seeks concrete step-by-step information that could prove vital, if not life saving.

Sonja is not alone in feeling anxious about entering a profession for which she lacks the practical knowledge required for success. The question remains, how do we prepare future administrators? Consider that, in the world of mountain climbing, veteran trekkers prepare for the altitude change by taking time to acclimate on their way *into* base camp and *at* base camp. An experienced mountaineer may spend two months at any one time on Mount Everest devoting much more time to acclimating than climbing (National Public Radio [NPR] 1997). In contrast, amateur hikers (often tourists) do not properly prepare, frequently rushing to ascend the slopes without prior conditioning. Consequently, they may end up enduring mountain sickness from the altitude changes, symptoms that progress from headache, nausea, and insomnia to severe lung congestion and worse (NPR 1997).

Similarly, the time needed for adjusting to the challenges ahead of the aspiring administrator should not be rushed. Directly put, professional transition and socialization take time and the administrator has to be willing to adhere to this reality. But these new experiences can be better supported, and the learning itself scaffolded and escalated. In order for this to happen, sufficient and ongoing training at graduate school (base camp) and on the way into base camp are required. In a very real sense, the school is potentially a base camp from which to progressively acclimate to the principalship.

Sonja's success as a future school leader would obviously depend upon some kind of game plan that does not amount to a meaningless academic exercise. If only she had been exposed to an internship or even a series of simulations (e.g., role plays) staging the decision making involved in emergency situations, such vicarious learning could have demonstrated the necessary procedural steps, resulting in increased confidence. Toward this end, Sonja took it upon herself to conduct interviews with newly practicing assistant principals in the Tampa Bay area. Through this process, not only were some of her questions answered but also her newfound ability in collecting and assessing complex data was discovered.

Unfortunately, the story Sonja relays about the assistant principal's first day on the job may not be much of an exaggeration, either in terms of the events or the deep fear of the unknown depicted. As we know, the assumption at hiring is that the graduate is ready to assume the mantle of administrative headship—regardless of a "storm" that may be brewing. Florida's schools have recently taken a proactive stance to adapt to changing societal and global conditions through crisis preparedness planning. Rehearsals involving mock bomb threats are common, although the equivalent training in terrorism and bioterrorism in Florida still in the distance, despite the warnings from national authorities (Mullen 2004).

Filling the Gaps through Inquiry

Pamela Llewellyn, another master's student/veteran teacher, has also reflected on the issue of administrative preparation as related to school emergencies. In fact, she conducted action research in one of my courses. As Pamela acknowledges, "Florida school law requires district school boards to establish emergency procedures for weapon-use, hostage situations, exposure resulting from a man-made emergency and other life-threatening emergencies" (*Legislative Update* 2000, as cited in Llewellyn 2004). As this educator attests, teachers can contact their county district to see if a plan for school crisis prevention and emergency procedures exists. If such a plan is available, it will no doubt need to be updated as well as modified to fit one's own context.

Should no emergency plan exist at the school or district level, the practitioner can contact other educational sites to compare plans at the same level (e.g., elementary). By doing so, this individual can then select the best ideas and procedures and adapt these to his or her own setting, thereby creating a solid base at the level of administration for others to improve upon. As an extension of these actions, Pamela also advises that a brief report be written and submitted to the relevant school district in an effort to stimulate the generation of a uniform plan. Based on her own investigations, this teacher researcher recommends including "steps for administrators to follow during different types of emergencies, such as hazardous spills, tornado alerts, weapons on campus, as well as lockdown procedures" (Llewellyn 2004). Also, the plan should aim to "help schools maximize their ability to keep all children safe and protect the district from future liability issues. It is important that all components of a crisis plan be aligned so no component contradicts another."

Although each approached the gaps in her graduate preparation differently, both Sonja and Pamela discovered the value of action research for gaining practical knowledge and real-world experience. While these educators believe that "the best way to learn to become an outdoor leader is experience in the field" (Kosseff 2003, 53), they also realized the power of real-world simulated learning through an engaging, active type of research. In the world of backpacking, leading is *always* learning: Increasingly experienced trekkers select which personal or collective gaps in knowledge and skill are most in need of improvement. And then they tailor their hikes to advance in these areas (Jardine 2001; Kosseff 2003).

SUMMIT DATA AND ANALYSIS

Taking a Broader View

Thus far we have identified school emergency preparation as one facet of the administrator's role in schools. Before returning to this topic, we will take a broader view of this issue of real-world experience, which emerged as a significant construct in the beginning leaders' responses. Contextually defined in relation to the survey data that were collected and analyzed, real-work experience is associated with hands-on, practical experiences during and prior to administrative duty. Moreover, the participants perceived on-site school experiences to be of greater import or need than college administrative theory. This reinforces my point, threaded throughout the book, that theory and practice are separated in some practitioners' minds.

Learning curve also emerged as a major thematic pattern in its own right—a "competitor" of real-world experience in one sense, and a "cousin" in another. The learning curve is a defining aspect of the new leader's socialization where learning, performance, and accountability concurrently exist, adding to the feeling of overload. Where real-world experience has not been accessed through one's university preparation programs, the learning curve is steeper; conversely, exposure to real-world experiences reduces the overload of learning.

The beginning leaders I studied displayed a preference for preparation through a series of "wilderness trainings" or "accumulated outings," as the trekkers say. Solutions they suggested for closing this theory/practice gap highlight internship, practicum, mentoring, and various university classroom simulations. The high value placed on real-world experience seems obvious enough. A richer meaning is the relationship implied between real-world experience and the learning curve: Greater and more persistent forms of apprenticeship learning would have better acclimated the new administrators, taking "the edge off." Momentous challenges in learning distract from leading. This message was clearly signaled in the data.

Valuing Administrative Experience

The participants also considered previous administrative experience particularly indispensable: "My years spent as a Title 1 Facilitator were invaluable. Coming right from the classroom to AP [assistant principal] I would have been lost!" It is rare for a teacher in a Florida high school to directly become a vice principal. Usually, the individual does an extended internship not connected with a university graduate program. This type of work would instead constitute a "deal" worked out with the principal wherein experience would be gained without pay. The department chair of an academic discipline and specialists within the school are also used as a transitional role to the principalship. Certain opportunities aligned with the core leadership areas (e.g., student services) also provided helpful fodder to the assistant principalship: "I worked as a varying exceptionalities specialist for eight years. My role was similar to an AP's role." Another, referring to herself as a "dean of students," apparently "learned a lot dealing with the administration aspect of the school." Such experiences were considered invaluable.

These practicing leaders recommend that one should "be involved in every aspect of school management on every level, with previous experience being the basis of adjustment" to succeed in administration. And the more opportunities seized upon for learning the various administrator tasks prior to assuming the role of school leader, the better. Along these lines, some expressed that the experiences they had had as an assistant principal proved invaluable for entering the next career stage: "My previous experiences as a vice principal prepared me well for my principalship." However, for others, the idea that a linear route to the principalship exists is a myth: "There is no clear and distinct path from school administrator to principal because the jobs can be quite separate and the requirements will need to be learned on the job."

Specifically, "on-the-job training" in a range of administrative roles and forms best served the respondents, especially when combined with "hands-on internship experiences." Some even emphasized the value of on-site learning by contrasting this experience at base camp with the university preparation they received: "Most of my training was on the job. My master's degree provided little practical knowledge." However, a number of others did not expect a perfect fit between their preparation and real-world leadership experiences and consequently expressed a perhaps dissimilar and more tolerant view: "Just like in teaching, the theory taught doesn't always mirror the real-life experience. You can't always teach the good judgment needed in crisis situations and everyday problem solving." For the minority, the base camps of university and school were qualitatively different training grounds that could not be expected to function in harmony.

Identifying Vital Administration Skills

Educational researchers have identified school safety and violence prevention as a significant responsibility that falls within student services (Mullen and Cairns 2001). In the context of my administrator survey, the core leadership area of student services subsumes fifteen items. While all of these tasks or skills are discussed within the scope of this book, for the purposes of this chapter, three in particular proved relevant: "Supervise and assess evacuations, fire, and tornado drills"; "review and enforce the school safety program"; and "relate to students with disabilities." Each task category received a high rating of "most important" (i.e., "5") but not exclusively among the fifteen items.

Supervise and Assess Evacuations, Fire, and Tornado Drills

Fifty-one percent of the new administrators say this task is a major responsibility. Every month, according to Florida district's safety guidelines, public and private schools are expected to perform a fire and/or tornado drill, checking for efficacy of evacuation procedures. The role of the principal and/or assistant principal is integral to the success of such a drill. The moment the alarm bell rings, administrators are expected to guide students to the designated evacuation point and give clear verbal directions over the intercom. A beginning administrator must quickly learn these techniques while on the job.

These safety guidelines constitute a confidential local school document, however; no official source is published online or distributed to teaching faculty, as only administrators can access it (personal communications, Pinellas County principal, May 2003). The cultural separation of faculty from administration is intended to better protect a school should a crisis occur, yet this practice gives weight to Sonja and Pamela's concerns. One question that arises is how might future leaders prepare for this crucial area of the principalship when they are not permitted to know certain procedural aspects pertaining to the operation of their own school and district?

Review and Enforce the School Safety Program

In all, 47 percent of the participants deemed school safety program management to be a "most important" area of their work. Throughout Florida, each leadership team formulates a safety program for its school. This includes actions teachers and students should take during a bomb or terrorist threat, or any other emergency. Since the 9/11 tragedy, the formulation of such a plan of action is not just advisable, but necessary (Mullen 2004). The administrators at each Florida school document the procedures in the institution's handbook and instruct educators accordingly. New administrators, once again, are not taught this component of the leadership position while in graduate school, but rather on site.

Relate to Students with Disabilities

For this item, 41 percent marked a "5," signaling its important status. Typically, any school within a given district has students with special needs and varying disabilities. Some require help with academic tasks and may also be physically impaired. Students with varying exceptionalities also require more paperwork and some, special accommodations.

Each child has an Individualized Education Program (IEP) aimed at satisfying personal academic goals. A school leader is expected to work with the special education teacher to form an appropriate IEP for each student—a very challenging, time-consuming activity. To clarify, the typical classification of disabilities generally encompasses three types of student cases—attention deficit disorder (ADD), learning disabilities (e.g., speech and hearing impediments), and health conditions (e.g., HIV, AIDS, lupus, and multiple sclerosis) (Mullen 2001).

An effective administrator must learn to effectively interact with these students and their teachers, paraprofessionals, and especially parents. Those with disabilities should be treated like any other student. One study that I conducted several years ago in Alabama narrated the powerful teachings of a student disabilities specialist with a severe congenital disability (Mullen 2001). Lisa helped my preservice groups see, from her own perspective and those she represents, the value of an inclusive education for students with varying exceptionalities. Aspiring teachers and leaders were advised to treat students with disabilities just as they treat "regular" students, despite the pressures from internal and external groups alike to segregate them.

There may be an additional reason my study respondents identified relating to students with disabilities as an essential leadership skill. Youngsters labeled "varying exceptionalities" tend to be more "valuable" in a particular sense to an individual school site. In the Full-time Teaching Equivalency (FTE) count taken every year at public K–12 institutions, a special education student receives more funding than a regular education pupil. The assumption is that it takes more financial support to educate this type of learner. This additional funding can serve as an added boost to many extracurricular programs and other academically related services that would not otherwise be funded. Perhaps this set of dynamics helps explain the thinking behind the student disabilities specialist from Alabama who shared that some student disabilities, ADD in particular, can be overdiagnosed within the educational community (Mullen 2001).

LESSONS

Why the Tarp, Not the Tent

We may all need to learn how to better harmonize security with risk in our professional lives. Obviously, a feeling of personal security comes from supportive relationships and predictable routines—even where learning is

Figure 15.1.   Taking Nature's Risky Path Lets You Connect
Source: Marc Shapiro

overshadowed to guarantee prediction and certainty. However, this picture does not represent reality (Hargreaves and Fullan 1998), despite attempts by individuals, programs, and institutions to conform to it. No amount of learning can prepare the aspirant for what is to come. Some of the respondents sent a resounding epistemological message to this effect. Even mountaineering Sherpas must improvise and contend with the unexpected elements as they lead others along trails they themselves have traveled before. They rely on their ingenuity so progress can be made and safety assured to the deepest extent possible, despite the narrow, slippery paths erected over colossal drops (NPR1997).

Metaphorically, the Sherpa mind-set is a balance of risk and security best symbolized by the tarp, not the tent. In the outdoors, the tarp is a piece of canvas equipment for harmonizing security with risk, whereas the tent blocks the natural elements, providing a false sense of comfort. Too much security is not a good thing, veteran trekkers agree. The tarp, a permeable shelter, enables you to "remain more a part of the landscape," which "facilitates connection with nature greatly—even while in bed" (Jardine 2001, 34).

Connection potentially allows for a profound awakening, ranging from meditation to reflection to revelation. In this context, the tarp is used to filter experience to one's advantage. Interestingly, a tarp is also stronger than a lightweight tent and paradoxically "allows for fresh air and wonderful ventilation, and reduces the condensation in clothing" (p. 34). Besides keeping one drier, if the wind picks up, the tarp can be easily reconfigured—in this case, pitched sideways and lower to the ground for protection. You can also move more freely with a tarp should danger be near, and it can be worn as shelter if conditions become harsh. For Sonja and Pamela, the tarp might be represented by a cue card with briefly annotated emergency school procedures and crisis phone numbers, as opposed to a manual of school procedures—a "tent" that would take time to consult, may not be found when needed, and is heavy to carry.

The analogy to school leadership is that the more secure one's tent, the less apt one will be to welcome profound experiences, deeper reflection, and positive change. It is ironic that if you overinflate your means for shelter, say in the form of towering, secure buildings with metal detectors, that you might inadvertently become complacent—which is a problem in its own right. Too much security or a false sense of security blocks growth.

The unexpected cannot be completely controlled or managed anyway, so why not let nature in to enhance your ability to acclimate? Keeping unwanted, disruptive parents out of one's school, for example, can be handled by improving the building's alarm system or by developing a "neighborhood watch" culture within the building (Mullen and Patrick 2000). The former solution is in mountaineering terms a "tent," the latter, a "tarp."

Tent-like schools value external forms of protection, not seeking ways to significantly change from the interior. In contrast, tarp-like facilities that embrace change will permit a degree of instability to naturally occur, particularly where leaders have committed to the process of improving the culture internally through a shared vision that takes context into account. Change that is produced through inquiry and assessment instead of whimsical ideas is essential (Mullen with Stover and Corley 2001; Mullen 2002a, 2002c, 2002d). One participant in this study who is currently working on a doctorate in education endorsed this message: "Being an administrator gives me much real-world experience. When coupled with the advanced classes I have taken in order to reach this stage, this allows me to share ideas with my faculty that are both workable and research-based."

Multipronged Tarp Constructions

Even a tarp has stabilizers—tabs and lines attached to the grommets for protection during a strong wind or storm (Jardine 2001). Anchors can be used as an analogy in graduate education for offering stability in the stormy winds of leadership acclimation and performance. By valuing stabilizers or anchors, we acknowledge that better approximations of "reality" are possible for preparing aspiring leaders. However, this does not mean that the aspirant's exposure to the lived realities of school administration will produce a glossy, fixed image of what to expect. Students will face the unknown in many forms—complex dilemmas and multiple realities have no one "right" answer. This is the legacy of the postmodern condition in leadership and schools (Diamond and Mullen 1999a; English 2003c).

Nonetheless, most leaders will naturally seek some form of "shelter," in such forms as job security and promotion. Even an office, program, person, or supply kit can be considered shelter. Even if we do not seek "shelter" through our relationships with others per se, the processes of dialogue, cooperation, and collaborative decision making bring us comfort and protection. Sheer survival instinct can often draw us to others, once our cocoons have been shed. Notably, the most experienced trekkers travel in the company of a Sherpa or team—even Sir Edmund Hillary did not trek Mount Everest alone or sleep under a starry ceiling unprotected (NPR 1997). In contrast, a "modernist" trekker who seeks instrumental knowledge only, without regard for learning and growth, would end up artificially separating him- or herself in favor of taking the easiest path with the surest and swiftest gains. Believing that leadership means mastering skills and applying knowledge to inherently knowable or fixed contexts fails to account for the inevitable gaps of the real world—all that is unknowable and uncertain.

Until this point we have imagined a multipronged construction of the tarp that can be applied to leadership. Educational leadership and administration can be viewed as gaining support from five core leadership areas—school organization, school management, supervision of instruction, student services, and community relations—anchors that graduate preparation programs need and aspiring leaders should know (e.g., Mullen and Cairns 2001).

Some researchers have identified only one of these anchors as necessary. Dembowski (1998), for example, proposes that because school administrators tend to focus on the business or managerial side of leadership, graduate programs should do the same. In fact, the recommendation is that future administrators acquire an MBA (master's in business administration) and that preparation programs do much more to address this core leadership area. Although this advice may make sense to some, especially given the prominence of school management and specifically budgeting responsibilities for practicing leaders as indicated by my own data analysis, it is limited as a solution to the more global expectations of the principalship. As my more comprehensive results suggest, it will be crucial that the aspiring leader gain competency across all five of the core areas, which necessitates actively making theory/practice connections. In fact, based on the administrators' selections of core leadership areas, supervision of instruction, not school management, was the most popular category from the perspective of having received the highest ratings for not 10 percent but 50 percent of the leadership tasks (see table 5.3).

While some beginning principals deemed exemplary within their communities, such as Tom Graves (Mullen and Graves 2000), have had the "luxury" of being able to specialize on a school's administrative operations, they nonetheless actively build capacity. Beyond managerial coordinator, they rise to the occasion as an instructional leader, organizational builder, community partner, democratic decision maker, mentor, and collaborator. An extensive literature review conducted of educational administration studies reinforced these images of the highly functioning, multitasking leader who builds school capacity beyond areas of preferred or exclusive focus (Mullen et al. 2002). Curriculum at the graduate level could absorb these points, in order to better inform and strengthen the renewal of leadership preparation.

BACKPACKING TIPS AND LEADER ACTIVITIES

- *Camp out*: Have your faculty/staff build a tarp and tent, literally, at your school, or have the colleagues in your graduate program try this. Then have the group compare the experience of the tarp and tent, extrapolating to lessons learned for leadership, particularly in the areas of risk and security.
- *Simulate*: (1) Analyze documentaries featuring emergencies or disasters that have affected institutions and families, and deconstruct lessons for school leaders. (2) Role-play real-world experiences that focus on topics practicing leaders consider crucial (e.g., relating to youngsters with varying disabilities). (3) Bring in guest speakers or have panel discussions with school- and community-based experts (e.g., public health specialist; disease and poison control analyst; law enforcement agent; weather expert; transportation director).
- *Plan*: Finally, analyze recently developed curriculum for school terrorism planning and diversity awareness (e.g., Jolly, Malloy, and Felt 2001). Construct a set of school safety guidelines or an emergency management plan that integrates all five of the core leadership areas (e.g., supervision of instruction). Write relevant case scenarios, and develop instructions for staff training that relate crisis planning to the goals associated with eliminating racial profiling. Apply national guidelines for safety and security (e.g., American Red Cross (2002) and National School Safety and Security Services (2001) at the building level (as cited in Mullen 2004).

Chapter Sixteen

Lantern: Knowledge Source

Candle lanterns are your best bet if you want to carry a lantern [on your] backpacking trip. The light produced by a candle lantern is not very bright, but it works better than a flashlight for cooking, cleaning, reading, writing, or making camp in the dark. Why? Because the light is more diffuse (it doesn't have to be directed), and candles are cheaper than batteries. The candle lantern is safer and more economical than a candle alone. Housed in metal and glass, it is less likely to start a fire if it tips over, and because it is protected from the wind, it does not burn as quickly.

—V. S. Logue 2000

CASE SCENARIO

It is not easy being the principal of a caution-status school that serves two federal housing projects of rival gangs. But this instructional leader thrives on the challenge. Lynne Patrick's school overlooks a jail on one side and a cemetery on the other. In Alabama, there is a cruel saying, "When the children look out of the windows, they see what their future will be."

Dramatic changes in student achievement have occurred here, a seriously disadvantaged K–6 inner-city elementary school. Improved test scores, together with the new year-round calendar, have caught the media's attention. The school's success has been depicted as a climb from despair to hope, with many praising the school's leadership. The stories of success stimulated local support and donations for the school.

Documented as the lowest-achieving elementary school in the state, this site quickly became recognized as the most improved in its city, regardless of its caution status. By 2000, the grade increased from an F to an A for academic improvement on the Stanford Achievement Test. Although it could still face state takeover if the SAT–9 scores do not increase again this year and if it should fail to obtain clear status, it continues to show the highest improvement. Ironically, the state has reported that this school is a model for others at risk of takeover.

Most of the students at Lynne's school are behind one or two grade levels and struggling with reading. Literacy development is challenged by such serious problems as poverty, unemployment, and an epidemic of crack cocaine, which affects both the neurology and the well-being of the children. Community apathy, violent and withdrawn child behavior, unsafe streets, incarcerated parents, and disintegrated families compound these issues. Lynne perseveres at the dream of creating support structures for the success of the children.

This principal's stories are "littered" not with playgrounds of giggling children but with razor blades that they threaten to swallow (and spit out with the skill of a gang member once police arrive), crayons consumed during hysterical fits, knife scars across the back of the neck, and mothers who damage their children's lives. Mindfulness about school safety is obvious in this leader's daily actions, wellness interventions, and discipline techniques.

Lynne was hired to be a catalyst for change in a school in which 40 percent of the students exhibited problems related to the effects of chemical abuse. Most endured trauma and neglect and some, physical and sexual abuse. Compounding this hardship, the children often repress events that produce major trauma—one girl witnessed her sibling's death but did not tell anyone. Lynne investigates hunches in an effort to build scaffolds that support the children and their needs.

This principal, who has earned a doctorate in education, places much stock in research. For example, she is knowledgeable about diversity and literacy issues, as well as the lasting effects of neglect on children. She has also learned about recovery through wellness intervention. Brownlee's (1996) article helped Lynne understand how violent neighborhoods, constant noise, confusion, and fear influence children. That these conditions can alter the chemical composition of the brain is alarming. Lynne realized the teachers needed to see that such students thrive when treated fairly and with respect and noted that they needed help verbalizing their problems without losing control: "Building trust with our children is the key." Lynne's determination to change the environment is apparent in that specialists work with the children who are born drug-exposed or with fetal alcohol syndrome.

Recasting this inner-city school as a place of possibility and renewal may have helped it improve. This principal hopes her school will become a model to show that poor, inner-city children can learn with all of the appropriate programs in place and with teachers who care and teach effectively. (from Mullen and Patrick 2000, 233–36)

Interpreting the Case

This dramatic educational story illustrates that inner-city schools cannot be rescued per se, but they can certainly be strengthened by the support of a compassionate community. Underlying the case study itself are the theory/practice connections upon which Lynne Patrick's administration depended: She had taken upon herself to authentically connect practice with theory. The principal incorporated a host of sources into her learning and decision making to benefit the school's reculturing process. The foundational strategies this instructional leader used to integrate theory and practice can certainly be adapted more generally. And leadership preparation programs will gain from exposing the strengths of such a visionary leader.

Background

"Hang tough, be loving" is this principal's optimistic message for any school responsible for transforming harsh realities into learning opportunities. Her other message of hope is that disadvantaged children and schools are "at-promise," not "at-risk." If, as mountaineering experts testify, it is during the darkest times of our toughest challenges that we must focus to see the light, then we can certainly imagine the Lynne Patrick story from this angle.

But the light is evident in this story, too, and epitomizes Lynne's philosophy: "Pursue your dream with persistence" (Mullen and Patrick 2000, 248). However, the light Lynne operates by is not powerful enough to

Figure 16.1.   Reflection by Diffuse Candlelight
Source: Nova Development Corporation

change despair into a Disney film with a happy ending. Instead, the light
is diffuse and sanguine. Spread out over a wide surface, light, in the form
of hope, can reach a wider community of families, schools, neighborhoods, and even the nation.

This school's story has appeared in the state's newspapers and even
aired on *Frontline*, the national TV news show. Sometimes innovators like
Lynne must incorporate external alliances before they can build the internal resiliency of their schools. In fact, this strategy has distinguished successful from unsuccessful principals intent on improving a school's culture. The message, then, for new leaders, especially of disadvantaged
institutions, is "[harness] all the human resources you can get" (Hargreaves and Fullan 1998, 11).

Because Lynne's was a 100 percent Title I school, all of the students received free breakfast and lunch. The parents were mostly in the early to
mid-twenties, and other family members and foster care providers raised
many of the children. In total, the school had over four hundred students
and thirty-six certified teachers, with additional personnel and specialists.
No principal was previously drawn to this K–6 inner-city elementary
school in Montgomery, Alabama, but Lynne actively sought a leadership

role there, turning down offers from privileged schools. When we began researching together in 1999, Lynne had been at the helm of the racially segregated school for three years. She was politically and culturally in step with its challenges, having interacted with many minority groups and completed a dissertation on issues of diversity and community building for African American populations.

The urban ghettos of Kozol's (1991) portraits have made us poignantly aware that any study of academic achievement in such schools must incorporate the harsh realities the children face. Aguirre and Turner (1995) add that the bleak conditions of racial disparity that suffuse such a landscape are historic, affecting, on a deeper level, the school's spirit and future. Can white, privileged executives lead schools populated by academically at-risk, low-income students of color? The answer is yes. Lynne herself is white, but she is also highly committed to developing learner-centered practices for African American children. Critical theory questions whether democratic change can occur if led by white leaders of privilege (Chalmers 1997). Instead of making an argument either way here, though, I wish to simply acknowledge the controversial nature of this issue as part of the context of Lynne's leadership.

During our scholar-practitioner collaboration from 1999 to 2000, Lynne was asked, "What action have you taken to improve the climate of your inner-city school?" As it turned out, what had sparked our writing relationship was Lynne's concern that although the school had been spotlighted by the media, this attention had in one way impeded the school's progress. The media had portrayed Lynne's school as successful against all odds and as having overcome its academic alert status, but this was not the case. In fact, she and the staff had been working long hours to ensure the school's survival by attracting resources, donors, partners, volunteers, and afterschool tutoring and athletic services.

Lynne and I saw our joint purpose as reclaiming the story of the school and telling it through the principal's eyes. By challenging the mythical proportions that her school had taken on through the media, our intention was to convey the honest-to-goodness, down-to-earth realities encountered by any leadership team situated in a school like hers and the interventions that slowly made a difference. In mountaineering language, we found the candle lantern to be a more effectual light than the penetrating, costly glare of the kerosene lamp. In today's world of outdoor sports, the kerosene lamp is rarely used—it has gone out of fashion. Kerosene, which is classified somewhere between oil and gasoline, must be purchased. It pollutes the environment with soot, and it has caused fires (Jardine 2001). In a school like Lynne's, misconceptions can damage the fragile capacity to recover and grow. Needed for survival are community buy-in and vigorous support of the school's vision.

As trekking partners, we opted for the appeal of the candle lantern, then, over the inefficient and uneconomical kerosene lamp. Metaphorically speaking, both represent knowledge and vision. However, the lantern accommodates the ability to move around and simultaneously carry out numerous tasks, such as reading, writing, visiting, and stretching. In contrast, the light from the kerosene lamp functions more as a flashlight, providing focused illumination of a limited space. Many principals naturally operate by a more diffuse than penetrating light, which seems in keeping with their multitasking role.

Lynne functioned broadly inside and outside the building, and across the state, endeavoring to strengthen the school's capacities. For example, Abraham Maslow's (1954) Hierarchy of Needs model—physiological, safety, social, and esteem—was with her when she entered the neighborhoods—either to wake up a child who had overslept because there was no alarm clock in the dwelling or to confirm that the instructions for a prescribed medication were properly followed. While this leader possessed boundless energy, she also shared such responsibilities with those trustworthy "messengers" designated at her site. In fact, when *Frontline* attempted to capture Lynne's work, the camera had only a few minutes to spend in the principal's office before being taken out into the ghetto neighborhoods. My own action research within this school made me realize the potency of its vision, involving nothing short of a momentous ascent for the administration and staff and on one of the toughest trails possible.

Lynne's Secret Sources of Knowledge

Lynne combined her research and strategies in creative ways to increase the effectiveness of her decisions. To understand what kindled this individual's leadership spirit, it is important to know that Lynne did not advocate abandoning theory "in favor of a cookbook approach to educational administration." Instead she engaged in an active process of testing theory against practice, and practice against theory. Many educational researchers who teach leadership studies strongly support this position for academics and practitioners alike (e.g., Bratlein and Walters 1999, 101; see also Mullen et al. 2002).

Though this is not an exhaustive list, this Sherpa guide drew heavily upon the following for reflection, engagement, and decision making:

- Intuition
- Child advocacy philosophy and school reform
- Developmental needs model
- Up-to-date, relevant research
- On-site expertise of specialists
- Community-based partnerships
- Survey results from stakeholders

Hunches

Notably, Lynne, a self-confident synergist, trusted her own hunches and those of her team to guide their mutual footsteps. Her model of shared leadership stemmed from a confidence in other people's ideas. Along with the teachers and staff, she tested gut feelings within group contexts where problems were openly identified and solutions explored and decisions made, but only once theory had been consulted and the relevant information obtained. One such example that became newsworthy featured Lynne's intuition that grew into a conviction about the potential value of year-round schooling for her establishment.

Philosophy

Lynne's child advocacy was integral to her philosophy of school improvement in disadvantaged settings. Her actions in this light were viewed as consistent, which helped ensure her acceptance within the school community. Her role as a child advocate–reform catalyst, combined with the investment in Maslow's developmental model, undergirded her primary decision making. Using these tenets, she guided others along the daily trails of work, frequently consulting with her team. She believed wholeheartedly that no one could stray for long if decisions were authentically and steadfastly rooted in the children's best interest. She refused to compromise on this position—no "rope" was given to teachers, staff, and guardians when their needs would have in some way hindered the children's. (The relevant strategies Lynne used for building the school's resources are covered in chapter 13.)

Development

Maslow's theory of human development became the school's guiding philosophy: Children could not be expected to learn, or be taught—including being tested on standardized exams—until their basic needs were met. Curricular and instructional improvements mattered only when basic needs were satisfied on an ongoing basis. One focus group participant criticized that "Florida, with its FCAT testing for all, seems to ignore this basic fact—how lives are qualitatively different from one school unit to another." Lynne believed that without the security of this foundation, students live without purpose and hope and in a perpetual state of despair and despondency. A clothing closet, daily meals, predictable routines, health checkups, counseling, and special programs—not to overlook loving attention and lots of hugs—were all available to the children to help compensate for their family predicaments.

Some would argue that Maslow's theory should also apply to adult populations, including those training to become school leaders, for whom conditions of safety and esteem, for example, are considered vital to performance and for whom the modeling is equally valuable (e.g., Mullen 2002c; Shapiro 2003). But even as this school focused on survival and safety demands, the adults prepared for the higher-level concerns of social acceptance and self-actualization that Maslow's model encompasses.

Research

Lynne Patrick was constantly learning and modeling this value through her contagious enthusiasm, symbolizing a "lantern" to many people. She was an avid reader who believed that concepts were not only powerful tools but also applicable, in some cases, to inner-city school environments in the ongoing process of enacting goals for improvement. Lynne viewed theory as a compass or map providing direction, similar to the spirit of

British dramatist Christopher Hampton, who believes that "those who are enamoured of practice without science are like a pilot who goes into a ship without rudder or compass and never has any certainty where he is going. Practice should always be based upon a sound knowledge of theory" (*Compton's Reference Collection* 1995).

However, Lynne also operated with discernment, judging various theories and practices on the basis of what potentially made sense for her school environment, thus enacting the wisdom in this aphorism: "A thing may look [good] in theory, and yet be ruinous in practice; a thing may look evil in theory, and yet be in practice excellent" (August Bier, *Compton's Reference Collection* 1995). The motivation to connect practice with theory in order to magnify opportunities for producing desirable change may be at the heart of transformational leadership. Transformational leaders like Lynne Patrick are committed to such deep values as child advocacy and social justice, and they seek ways to do not just what works but what is good (Sergiovanni 1992, 1995). How many people realize that the drive to connect theory with practice in informed and compassionate ways may be behind this larger purpose of moral leadership?

This elementary principal from Alabama relentlessly pursued theoretical knowledge and empirical information for insight into the complex questions her school was facing. And she devised strategies for positive change from consulting multiple sources, ranging from research, theory, case study, and the news when seeking answers to her questions. Lynne also talked with content experts from the university system in addition to a broad range of community-based specialists. She was particularly drawn to human psychology, with a focus on multicultural and literacy studies, as well as descriptions of at-risk programs and assessments. For example, she introduced a new program into her school after having read encouraging reports about the use of Peace Works as an effective, antiviolence behavioral intervention for inner-city schools like her own. In one such school in New York the children did not even have housing—they lived in makeshift shelters. Similar schools had already tested the strategies she adopted, which turned into the special programs implemented within her own site.

When her imagination was sparked, she would communicate what she found. One longitudinal study that Lynne shared with me examined how family structure affects serious crime (Harper and McLanahan in Gallagher 1998). The lives of 6,403 boys were tracked, and it was discovered that boys who are raised without fathers are twice as likely to be jailed. Family structure proved to be a more important variable than any other, including poverty and discrimination. Consistent with this research finding, the most severe behavioral problem Lynne's school faced occurred when absent (e.g., incarcerated) parents were released, only to ignore their children. Such insight proved vital to this education officer for whom the politics of her role mattered when it came to arguing for additional resources and monies, as well as the freedom to experiment with alternative calendars and atypical programs.

Brownlee's (1996) study connected unhealthy conditions and abusive circumstances with children's mental functioning in such an environment. An epiphany occurred for Lynne when she learned that while fear released "biological chemicals," distorting a child's mental patterns, the brain has a recuperative capacity from such damage. Helpful interventions include "psychotheraphy, mentoring, and loving relationships" (p. 71). With this knowledge in hand as a new principal, Lynne raised the expectations of her teachers to uniformly exhibit positive feelings and actions toward the children. Because of the difficulties experienced by the student population and the adults within the building, it was hard to find quality teachers. Even so, those who proved inadequate because of their neglectful or abusive patterns were, after being carefully documented, dismissed or transferred and replaced. Lynne also tracked the guardians' whereabouts, confronting individuals when necessary and inviting those exhibiting dysfunctional parental behavior to participate in her school's counseling programs.

Specialists

Lynne relied on the expertise of various specialists at her school, especially the social services coordinator, whom she had herself hired through a grant. The coordinator's awareness of the children's individual circumstances, including their families, neighborhoods, and parents' whereabouts, proved invaluable. Tapping into the knowledge banks of an on-site nurse and caring teachers as well, Lynne created educational and remedial programs that were successfully implemented. The new programming helped both the children and their guardians build the capacity to grow stronger. Highlights included:

- Peace Works training—Promotes social skills and "I Care Rules" that children rehearse daily, such as "Hands are for helping, not for hurting."
- WAIT (Why Am I Tempted)—Teaches kids about sexual abstinence.
- Anger management—Helps kids who have violent outbursts.
- Saturday school—Provides academically strong kids with enrichment.
- Summer school—Gives extra academic attention to kids who need it.
- Read aloud—Teaches young kids to enjoy books and quiet time.

Partners

The process of building capacity within the school was supported through a whole-community effort. A number of key stakeholders—organizations and partners—assumed responsibility for developing and sustaining the school's initiatives:

- Churches
- Strategies to Elevate People (STEP) program (supports public housing residents)
- Community organizations (YMCA)
- Boys and Girls Club of America (academic tutoring and athletic organization)
- University preservice interns and researchers
- Teacher-activists
- Health professionals
- Guardians

Surveys

Lynne regularly surveyed community stakeholders to gain a better grasp of the children's lives and learn others' views on particular issues, often surrounding the school's planning and initiatives. For instance, based on a 1999 survey of the children's guardians, seventy-three parents were incarcerated or had recently been released from jail. Other situational demographics revealed that only 8 percent of the students in this school had two parents at home, which helped explain the family–school crises that pervaded the building, including discipline problems and violent outbursts.

Another survey sought to gain the necessary support from stakeholders for the controversial move to year-round schooling. Lynne and her faculty research team interpreted the survey data, which revealed a favoring of year-round schooling. The respondents clearly wanted the children to be within a loving, caring, and supportive environment all year. The Boys and Girls Club of America was even willing to accommodate Lynne's students during the new intersessions (scheduled breaks) that year-round schooling would introduce. Lynne then prepared a case for year-round schooling as part of her overall school improvement plan and presented the report to the board of education. The request was approved, despite opposition and the recent failure of a nearby white-majority district to win its own case. This leader argued that the alternative calendar is not the best choice for every community, but that it was essential for hers. The plea was supported with the school's philosophy and the research results, securing her position. The change was welcomed by most of the school's parties.

SUMMIT DATA AND ANALYSIS

In my study for this book I learned that theoretical-practical integration appears to have little support in the professional development of many beginning leaders, although there were some budding possibilities. This may be an aspect of leadership that entire school systems, beyond the individual unit of administration, need to work on, in addition to educators who teach and learn within graduate programs and training contexts. The Lynne Patrick story provides inspiration along these lines.

In the administrator survey data I obtained, the emphasis on real-world experience was highlighted as a significant value over any other construct (e.g., knowledge sources). This outcome, in and of itself, illustrates the split between theory and practice within the data and, by way of extension, in the minds of the respondents. Instead of practice (real-world experience) and theory (knowledge sources) being viewed as parts of an integrated whole, these were considered two different, if not irreconcilable, types of knowing and learning. Although this characteristic treatment varied to some extent, the separation of theory from practice was evident across the survey and focus group data.

When theory and practice are assigned different and unequal weights, limits are placed on conceptual and technical ability and even on the capacity to make well-informed decisions. The tendency to separate theory from practice and, more severely, to value one at the expense of the other is problematic in any professional realm, including leadership and administration. Lynne Patrick's philosophy and actions stand in stark contrast with this picture.

It is possible that newly practicing administrators do not necessarily know when theory or conceptual models are influencing their actions. It follows that decisions would be made without consciously knowing which theory is being followed or adapted. This level of inattention in decision making is problematic. If practitioners are only interested in theory when it can be operationalized, their reflective capacity and creative approaches to problem solving may be hindered. Sources of knowledge pieced together to deepen inquiry and answer questions, then, would not be vigorously explored. How many K–12 schools deliberately use multiple sources of knowledge, such as empirical research, proven models, success stories, and case studies, to inform their school improvement planning and implementation?

On the One Hand

The theory/practice split apparent in the data analysis should not be attributed only to the practicing leaders. In fact, this problem was given greater attribution by the respondents themselves. References were made to graduate preparation programs, at the prompt of the survey. The picture that formed, using mountaineering language, was mostly of ineffectual training at base camp. Complaints about the effectiveness of formal educational experiences in Florida were not in short supply. This underscored the schism-like status of formal graduate school preparation, as some participants claimed to have not made any gains whatsoever in the area of real-world experience.

The assessment of formal university learning was that it had been, for the most part, split off from the real world of summit climbing: "My graduate classes prepared me well for my role as an AP in theory; however, it was my hands-on experience as a dean that was most valuable." Harsher renditions of this sentiment were, "The master's classes I took did next to nothing in preparing me for the hectic, fast-paced position I hold," and "In no way did the M.Ed. help prepare me." Disappointment and disillusionment, and perhaps even disapproval, can be heard in such testimonies.

Similarly, one survey respondent testified: "The program at the university where I studied does *not* offer significant practical experiences and skills. It was mostly a 'jump through the hoop' paper education." Less emphatically, another wrote, "Graduate experiences lack tie-in to the real world and are too general." Even more general criticism extended beyond educational leadership to teacher education in a few instances: "My graduate work was in reading, so it did not apply much. My doctoral program can't compare to the *experience* I'm having as an AP, just like the undergraduate education I had as a beginning teacher, which had not trained me for the real world of the classroom."

The respondents who critiqued their preparation provided helpful clues about the deficiencies or areas in which gains had not been made. Some even specified ways to improve formal learning with redesigned components. Notably, the issue of social skills, or human interaction, was stressed: "Knowledge of the day-to-day activities of the job vis-à-vis student and adult interaction were not aided by my graduate studies." Another echoed, "The amount of interpersonal exchanges between students, parents, and teachers were rarely touched upon." Perhaps for this reason, someone recommended that "facilitative leadership training and conflict resolution training should be included in educational leadership programs. They weren't in mine." Role-playing and case study development and critique are examples of how some classes have been engaged in shared decision-making and conflict resolution (Mullen 2002e).

On the Other Hand

Where there was some gain from the formal learning at base camp for this group of respondents, value was attributed to two main areas: the rules of professional practice and basic skills: "I would say that the school law class was the most beneficial class I took, which gave me confidence in knowing what I was and was not allowed to do. The program besides that has not been particularly helpful other than giving you theory and many writing and presentation assignments, which gave some valuable skills." A number of focus group members emphasized that "more of these kinds of graduate classes would be most helpful." The perspective stressed here placed value on skills development (e.g., data collection and analysis) through school-based action research, not assignments devoid of applied learning.

On the more positive end of this sliding scale, preparatory programs had clear value for some of the participants: "My graduate program was very appropriate and helpful. Our district does not have APs at the elementary level, so coursework was my main preparation." This minority viewed the programs they had completed as foundational, and hence essential, to their experience and knowledge. It appears that they did not perceive theory or knowledge building as separate from or inferior to real-world experience.

Overall, perhaps my research participants will gain more value from their graduate programs and training experiences over the span of their professions, but this is not known for certain. Learning within graduate school can be construed as a developmental process that takes precedence over one's career: "My graduate work (Ed.D.) greatly assisted me in the supervision piece as I came to take that on." Another likewise revealed, "The educational leadership program I took in Florida does lay the foundation for this continued learning." The few statements to this effect acknowledge that context can function vicariously as a productive stimulus in one's graduate program. It is as though a context is needed before any deeper connections can be made between theory and practice, before useful and meaningful concepts become relevant, and before the cognitive strategies for continuing the quest of learning become apparent.

It was also recognized that one cannot avoid having to make meaning, exercise sound judgment in the real world, and actively learn many new things, all of which goes beyond what can be formally taught: "Just like in teaching, the theory taught doesn't always mirror the real-life experience. You can't always teach the good judgment needed in crisis situations and everyday problem solving." One respondent reinforced the reality of this sentiment: "Graduate courses prepared me well, but there are so many things specialized to each K–12 school that there's always going to be a huge learning curve."

LESSONS

Students in leadership courses and new principals can benefit from a context without being directly *in* the situation. We all do this—derive value from contexts not directly experienced, transferring the learning to our own lives. Some of us learn vicariously to better our relationships with others and ourselves, for example. Aspects of my mountaineering metaphor were similarly experienced; throughout this book I have been a virtual trekker, using my imagination to map onto leadership contexts the analogies and examples from hiking expeditions.

Lynne Patrick had a great facility for applying what she had read to her own context. In one case, she adapted a child-centered program that proved successful in another impoverished, inner-city elementary school. This is consistent with Miller's (1996) model of conceptual processing that distinguishes between situation and context. Typically we treat them as the same thing, but they are different, and for an important reason. Consider that if you were to read the article about Lynne Patrick's school reform model (Mullen and Patrick 2000) at home in your favorite chair, the context, which is encoded in the text, is independent of your personal situation. In other words, you vicariously learn from what you read and actively make meaning without actually experiencing the context, just as you have with the Lynne Patrick story. This is why when you encounter related situations in your own life, you can figure out what to do— because as an expert learner you can make imaginative leaps and productive connections.

Miller also says that the ability to contextualize—to use context to make meaning—is a conceptual skill. This lends credence to the notion of "being there" as an imaginary process through which reflection and analysis are key. Perhaps for this reason, Miller (1996) believes that "the stage is a place for make-believe; it provides a situation very different from the everyday world" (p. 3). Interestingly, a parallel expressed in the survey data was that "there are a lot of issues to study in university programs but the true lesson is taught on the job."

Perhaps when you read Lynne Patrick's story you were reminded of other great mentors or Sherpa guides. Lynne's talents cover a wide arena, but her ability to be resourceful, or inventive and practical, was best demonstrated as many of us witnessed the threadbare building turn into a dynamic child-centered place of learning that everyone wanted to visit or contribute to. By using multiple sources of knowledge and support, and by not restricting herself to the school's scarce budget, she made the impossible a reality. She reached out into the community and imported its many forms into her building and exported the children into the community's afterschool programs, building capacity. Metaphorically speaking, she and her team had created a school without walls.

When I got to know Lynne I was reminded of the George Washington Carver story. In the early 1920s, this famous inventor, a doctoral graduate of Iowa State University, became known for his association with peanuts. But few realize that he turned the peanut into dozens of products, ranging from beverages to household items. This African American inventor also turned the scientific study of agriculture into a mechanism for helping farmers become more resourceful, developing hundreds of uses for one's own crops (African-American Inventor Series, 2003, online). Similarly, Lynne helped her teachers and staff gradually refine their own "crops" by understanding that "poverty is more about other resources than it is about money," including appropriate role modeling from caring adults (Payne 1998, 38–39).

People like Lynne and George have made great contributions to the creation of our society and its best practices, and their legacies should be shared for the benefit of tomorrow's leaders and children.

BACKPACKING TIPS AND LEADER ACTIVITIES

- Visit the most poverty-stricken school in your district or state and the most privileged school at the same level (e.g., elementary). Take detailed notes. Ask yourself, How do the circumstances of the two schools differ? What are some of the ways in which the leaders are oriented toward issues of theory and practice? Identify the sources of knowledge that are critical to the leadership of the schools as well as the strategies for building the institution. Finally, assess the resourcefulness of the leaders and their teams: What resources can you identify that support the school's programs and initiatives, and what stakeholder groups are committed to making a contribution?

- Reflect on your own processes of using theory and practice and ask yourself some questions: What is the role of "theory" in your job and of "practice" in your studies? Specifically, how do you go about becoming informed about a new program in your area, for example? And, when you teach others, how do you guide them? Also, when you want to "know" something important that is new to you, to what sources do you turn?

- Prepare an argument or rationalization for any initiative that has great significance to you (for Lynne Patrick this was year-round schooling). After you have completed this task, reflect on the process you used to develop the argument and document your new learning. For example, did you: Articulate your underlying philosophy? Consult experts to gain knowledge? Read the relevant literature? Apply the most salient models in education or another field? Conduct action research? Distribute a survey and do an analysis of the data collected? Show your results to the relevant stakeholder groups for feedback?

Part 3

CLIMBING THE SUMMIT USING SIGNPOSTS, SIGNAL FLARES, AND BACKPACKING TIPS

Chapter Seventeen

Charting a Trail That Traverses the Summit

Everest for me, and I believe for the world, is the physical and symbolic manifestation of overcoming odds to achieve a dream.

—Tom Whittaker, mountaineer/trainer and
first disabled athlete to climb Mount Everest

Throughout these pages, a trail to the summit of school leadership has been charted. Here, we review what has been covered and translate the relevant ideas for graduate preparation into summit signposts, signal flares, and backpacking tips. From this research we have obtained pointers for improving the quality of our journey and ultimately for mapping a more empowering experience for leadership aspirants and beginning leaders alike.

What have we learned to enhance preparation contexts for prospective leaders and administrative contexts for beginning leaders? What have *they*—the early career principals and assistant principals from Florida's schools—collectively communicated herein that *we*—the university professors, district coordinators, leadership candidates, mentor principals, and educational policymakers—can all benefit from? We attempt to answer this question by reflecting on the journey as a whole. In this topsy-turvy world, that not-quite-visible entity, the beginning leader, has emerged as a Sherpa guide and teacher.

Let us first remember the most important signposts along the way.

Figure 17.1.   Trekker Mullen Reads Signpost in Cinque Terre, Italy
Source: William Kealy

SUMMIT SIGNPOSTS

Leadership Standards Versus Summit Perspectives

As previously explained, any standards in educational leadership and administration—such as the Interstate School Leaders Licensure Consortium (ISLLC) and the Educational Leadership Constituent Council (ELCC)—should be contextualized (translated into meaningful, workable ideas) and questioned. This is the antithesis of impulsive consumption or blind application. Such critical processes also apply to the summit perspectives I offer: Should the results derived from my administrator study be applied, these would require thoughtful appraisal by the user. The findings were based on feedback from a group of beginning practitioners combined with my appreciative critique. The critique itself has incorporated multiple orientations, lenses, and studies from different fields, not strictly educational leadership and administration.

Four interrelated approaches were pivotal to this leadership study for obtaining meaningful reflections and useful results, with implications for graduate program redesign and policymaking:

1. Solicit the critical reflections of graduates on their university preparation experiences.
2. Assess the current leadership role within schools in terms of the energy, time, and commitment spent on particular tasks and in particular domains.
3. Remap graduate programs from the perspective of what matters to beginning leaders once they have assumed their administrative positions.
4. Interpret the beginning leaders' feedback using such pivotal constructs as "theory/ practice gap" and "expert novice" to guide the inquiry.

From the Mouths of Trekkers

An innovation was pursued here: No prior signpost exists on the leadership summit that describes the work of currently practicing new leaders with such attention from their own perspective. Further, an assessment of the new leaders' duties and functions, in terms of priority areas, was elicited from the workers themselves, not their supervisors or professors. The respondents also provided critical reflection on their previous leadership training. This multifaceted, multilayered study has accommodated the viewpoints of new administrators so the leadership field can potentially make new strides.

Convergence of the Trails

By having climbed the "mountain" while viewing it from different angles, footsteps have been left on Everest, but not arbitrarily and not in just one place. Instead, ten significant and useful trails (e.g., conditioning preparation, inventory survey, direction indicator) have been forged in part 2 of this book and, leading from the south, east, and west, converged, forming an interconnected route:

- Core leadership areas and salient leadership tasks, including weight distribution relative to areas (e.g., instructional supervision) and individual tasks/duties.
- Base camp preparation as a developing practitioner-scholar (e.g., rigorous, ongoing learning sought from making theory/practice connections).

- Socialization patterns and values (e.g., conditioning preparation) for developing the newcomer into a mountaineering team player who is socially, culturally, physically, and conceptually fit and who is able to tie theory to practice.

You can follow this multifarious way to the mountaintop, but you will not "get there" by a linear path. The trails are traverse and the track itself is zigzag, compelling the leadership trekker to configure the journey in a way that works while contending with unfamiliar elements and unknown circumstances. Personalize this mountaineering/imagineering voyage— interpret it in your own terms, apply it to your own context, and improve upon the maps provided or make your own.

Core Leadership Areas

Five core leadership areas mark the trail to the summit of school leadership. Each constitutes a mandatory path, and they intersect just before the summit is reached, so you must be in the expedition for the long haul to make sense of the patterns. Table 5.3 organizes the core leadership areas into primary, secondary, and tertiary tiers. Incorporate it into your own hiking map. The primary tier shows where graduate programs and other base camps (e.g., school administration, district training) can benefit from placing emphasis, time, energy, and resources. The main arteries highlighted in this book were:

- Supervision of instruction (50 percent)
- School organization (10 percent)
- School management (10 percent)
- Student services (20 percent)
- Community relations (10 percent)

By studying the broader map of Everest, we see the primary and secondary tiers as a whole. As covered in chapter 5, the weight distribution given to the five core leadership areas, relative to the twenty priority tasks identified, remains roughly similar, except that school organization certainly takes on greater importance in the bigger picture:

- Supervision of instruction (60 percent)
- School organization (60 percent)

- School management (10 percent)
- Student services (40 percent)
- Community relations (30 percent)

Program designers, professors, and trainers could all reap value from learning that instructional supervision and school organization were viewed as the most noteworthy signposts or categories. This implies that conceptual attention and application in these two areas are "musts" for leadership hopefuls and that graduate programs will need to be redesigned to support these foci.

Instructional supervision was given more weight than school organization, however, relative to its salient tasks (see table 5.3 and chapter 5). From this perspective, supervision of instruction was the most significant area of leadership in this study, which reflects a more recent emphasis for many schools. The shift from the role of manager to instructional leader, whose multitasking competencies include managerial operations, has been reinforced by many current studies. However, the focus on the five core leadership areas and their weights relative to priority tasks is pioneering, especially as an outgrowth of the beginning leaders' assessment.

Based on these research results, approximately 50 to 60 percent of graduate program preparation can consequently be committed to instructional supervision as a focus, but not to the exclusion of the other core areas. Particular emphasis would give authority to the primary and secondary tier, ranging from hiring staff to working closely with teachers to support their efforts at classroom management and standardized testing, for example. In fact, creating an instructional climate that all employees can support is essential.

School organization would also be given a major emphasis, albeit not to the same overall extent. Creating school schedules, attending staff and administrative meetings, planning school activities, and reviewing curriculum documents are all vital functions that aspirants should experience firsthand. School management would focus on the area of finances and budgeting. The other core leadership areas (e.g., student services) would also be featured, but in relation to the weights ascribed and the salient tasks identified (see table 5.3). Of course, context matters, having a shaping influence on this picture.

Base Camp Preparation

During our trek up the summit we have learned some valuable lessons about base camp preparation, namely:

- Create hiking maps, chart unknown territory, and write daily in your journal.
- Practice operating different survivalists instruments (e.g., compass) and interpreting the "direction indicators" received.
- Condition for long periods of time and expect intensive exposure and discomfort.
- Avoid rushing up the summit and experiencing asphyxiation and altitude sickness.
- Learn at base camp (17,500 feet) and know that this will be followed by intermittent training episodes at different campsites and various altitudes (e.g., 19,500 and 26,300 feet), all the way to the summit (29,028 feet).
- Rethink the expectation for a perfect match between training and the job itself.

Importantly, base camp and preparation at base camp are not restricted to graduate school culture. In fact, learning at base camp is typically a cobbled-together experience that incorporates not just graduate school programs, or even administrative learning within school buildings and/or school districts, but also internal training systems that school districts often require of their master's graduates in educational leadership. About learning at base camp, "the skills needed on the steeper slopes are gained only through training and practice. The beginning climber must spend long hours learning the proper use of equipment before attempting any serious climbing." Additionally, "the safety of the individual climber and of the team may someday depend on the rhythms, pacing, and ability to cooperate acquired at this stage" (*Compton's Reference Collection* 1995). Individual and team rhythms of leading, managing, and following all take time to develop.

Socialization Patterns and Values

Analysis of the complete study data (i.e., survey and focus group information) highlighted notable areas of leadership. These broader domains, derived from written and oral exchanges with the study participants, subsume the survey results in tables 5.2 and 5.3. The beginning school leaders experienced socialization in their graduate programs and/or on the job and, importantly, attributed value to the following dimensions (see chapter 5; see also part 2):

1. *Conditioning preparation*—training program and preparation.
2. *Inventory survey*—school inventory and management.
3. *Direction indicator*—instrument, person, document, or process.
4. *Basic know-how*—routine administrative tasks.
5. *Real-world experience*—on-site exposure to schools.
6. *Knowledge source*—operationalized theory and practical knowing.
7. *Mentoring scaffolds*—peer networks, teams, and effective mentors.
8. *Emotional expression*—stress, challenge, and excitement.
9. *Coping skills*—ability to solve problems.
10. *Accountability climate*—professional accountability and high-stakes testing.

We move now from summit signposts to signal flares that communicate vital long-distance messages.

SIGNAL FLARES

Theory/Practice Gap Dysfunction

One critical endurance trial involved in reaching the summit is the ability to test theory against practice, and in illuminating and productive ways. Three major strategies for narrowing the theory/practice gap recommended by the beginning leaders in my study highlight, in the order of importance:

- Mentoring relationships and systems (e.g., principal appenticeship training).
- Simulations (e.g., case study, action research, role play, expert practitioner panels).
- Relevant research perspectives and information (e.g., empirical studies, cases).

Outdoor Emergencies and Discomforts

New leaders should not strive to carry everything needed for an "outdoor emergency" or equivalent in one's school-community, so they need to learn how to improvise with what they do have (Logue 2000). Experienced hikers recommend that first-aid training definitely be taken. Literally and figuratively, this could prove invaluable for administrators: What is available in your school district or community that can help prepare you for school emergencies and what information could you gather from campus medical staff about taking care of youth and adults?

Also, it is important to realize that "backpacking is more than just a walk in the woods." If you do not feel prepared to deal with the discomforts inherent in carrying heavy burdens as a school leader, you will need to seriously reconsider getting into the sport/profession: "When backpacking, the outdoors is your home." However, as stressed throughout this book, you will need to develop perspective relative to such heavy weights as high-stakes testing in order to increase your effectiveness and ability to cope. Similarly, as an educational leader you can expect at most "to have the shelter of a tent over your head at night, but other than that, the sky is your roof and everything beneath it shares its home with you, including poisonous plants and rocks, roots, and mud, all potential accidents waiting to happen" (Logue, 264–65). We are all exposed to the elements in our work—the days of insulated comfort are distant, perhaps gone.

Context Is Crucial

The results from this study are not static or comprehensive; many situations could extend, shift, or even altogether change what has been found. For example, a larger participant population could produce different insights, and so, too, could a location other than Florida, a different timeframe, or even a researcher whose orientation is different. Context is meaningful to this overall picture: Judgments have been made about what core leadership areas need to be emphasized, with implications for graduate preparation programs and district training.

Contextual variables considered for this study and "factored" into the final, overall picture were:

Relevance of school level (e.g., elementary, middle, and secondary)—accounted for in understanding the particular situations that administrators encounter.

Timing and school cycles—some leadership tasks will have priority at different times of the year (e.g., budget management; master schedule design; hiring).

Cultural situation—the administrator survey (appendix C) is a template to
be possibly adapted and changed; it is not to be treated as though exhaustive of all the roles, duties, or even core leadership activities that a
new school leader may perform.

BACKPACKING TIPS

Backpacking tips shared in this guidebook identified the following significant resources:

- *Sherpa guide*—Select a role model (peer leader or mentor) or team to
  guide your footsteps, but remember that these must always be of your
  own making. Develop a body of knowledge to help you make informed
  decisions independent of a guide.
- *Philosophical orientation*—Articulate your philosophy of education
  and relate it to school improvement planning or something else. Herein,
  aspiring and practicing administrators alike shared their philosophies of
  team building, map making, quality preparation, shared leadership,
  democratic accountability, sustained leadership, systemic wellness,
  child advocacy, change agentry, and more.
- *Knapsack assemblage*—Locate and "pack" inspiring and useful materials,
  and especially texts that illuminate the socialization, mentoring, and support systems that enable beginning administrators to be successful. Practice attaining perspective and learn to lighten your cargo for long hauls.
- *Leadership directory*—In Florida, the *FASA Directory* (2002) proved invaluable for identifying and locating beginning administrators and for
  covering all of the school districts in the state. Find an equivalent resource to meet your own needs.
- *Action research*—Conduct a study of any educational issue you think is
  important in your role as a future administrator who will integrate theory

with practice, and passion with research (e.g., collect and analyze data on a "burning" issue and situate your topic within the broader leadership context).

- *Inventory survey*—Use the administrator survey provided in this book or any of the assessment surveys discussed for analyzing your own leadership capacities and those of others—a strategy for developing high-power, synergistic teams.

- *Reflective writing*—Study the underlying patterns of your thoughts and behaviors, or the events in your life, by keeping a practitioner-scholar journal. This will also give you much-needed time to make connections between seemingly disparate events and to resolve lingering issues. Invite others to journal with you. Use this device as a mechanism for problem solving with another person, or for developing a relationship and creating equality.

Epilogue: Leaving Footprints on Everest

As the members of the team climb upward, they must also plan their descent. It is harder to see on the way down, and fatigue can cause a climber to make a careless mistake. A rapid means of descent, particularly useful on nearly vertical slopes, is the rappel. In rappeling, the rope is supported by a piton. It is then wrapped around the climber, who leans back against it and feeds it out gradually, relying on friction to pace the descent. The feet are pressed against the rock face, and the climber in effect walks backward down the wall, supported by the rope.

—Compton's Reference Collection, 1995

THE SUMMIT STONE

Imagine having survived Everest's penultimate test, pulling each other up its ascending ice-steps at sunrise just this morning! Roped together, we would soon have to descend the Himalayas of school leadership. Mythically speaking, amidst members' celebrated shouts and wildly outreached arms stretching around Everest—our glorious mother goddess—I was reminded of the legendary summit stone. It was at our feet, encased in ice for safekeeping. Remember the story of mountaineer Tom Whittaker's leaving behind a stone on the summit as a gift for the next team that successfully ascended Mount Everest? On the peak, worn but elated, we each held the stone in turn, silently intrigued by the magnitude of its meaning.

Figure E.1.   Leaving Your Footprints on Everest
Source: Nova Development Corporation

SHERPA GUIDE AND TREKKING TEAM

Tom Whittaker's incredible story of failed attempts and hard-won success confirmed my need to assemble a strong team for this book journey: "There on the Rhumbok Glacier at 17,000 ft. in Tibet, Whittaker began to plan his final expedition" (Whittaker 2003). A very special Sherpa guide, no doubt an unexpected choice in the minds of many, led our expedition. The newly practicing school leader, with one foot in the present and the other in the future of schools, was our bodhisattva. The expert novice who serves as an inspiration to aspirants and educators alike symbolizes hope and renewal.

These Sherpa guides were tucked deep within the infrastructure of their school communities, a barely visible entity within the educational system. Once found through a directory search, as a professional group they openly shared the nature of their work and environments. In addition to their duties, they reflected on their own adjustment period as new leaders. And, importantly, they offered insight into how to improve the preparation of teachers as leaders for future generations. They proved willing to lead and to learn.

Yet these beginning administrators naturally turned to the more experienced trekkers for ongoing consultation and feedback. References were made in their written disclosures to mentors from whom they sought advice, and during the conversational circles the newcomers looked to the more seasoned professionals for insight. This process of simultaneously following while leading is what survivalists are trained to do on the heights: "Caution and cooperation are essential; a lapse on the part of one climber endangers the whole team. Teamwork does pay off, and for the successful team the thrill of standing at the summit of a challenging peak with the world spread out beneath its feet more than amply repays it for the risk and effort involved" (*Compton's Reference Collection* 1995).

In addition to the new school leaders, our team consisted of various highly committed and engaging professionals—experienced teachers, aspiring leaders, mentor principals, district trainers, superintendents, university professors, program designers, and legislators, as well as parents and community activists. With this guidebook it is hoped that all of these parties will listen to the stories of our Sherpa guide and respond with their own appreciative critiques.

MOUNTAINEERING EQUIPMENT SELECTIVITY

After putting together a synergistic comentoring team, we had to figure out what equipment to bring along. From a wide array of trekking equipment, we selected for our purposes mountaineering boots, a map, compass, Swiss army knife, tarp, lantern, rope, journal, first-aid kit, and ax—for the dual purposes of support and critique. These particular items and provisions served us well because they were meaningful in relation to the data collected. Specifically, these mountaineering tools/constructs were mapped onto the results of the administrator survey, focus group transcripts, and research journal entries. For instance, the emphasis on academic accountability for new school leaders was interpreted as an ax, and the focus on mentoring scaffolds was translated into a rope. None of the metaphorical (and, to some degree, literal) equipment choices were arbitrary, and all provided additional substance to the developed themes.

REFLECTING AT BASE CAMP

Cozy and warm, we fell like children into the comforts of our base camp. With our comrades the summit team talked late into the night around a campfire. The highlights of our discussion, recorded in my journal, follow.

Passing Along the Stone

One of our Sherpa guides shared that in 1995 Tom Whittaker had come "within 1,500 feet of the summit before being beaten back."

> On returning to base camp, teammate Greg Child gave Tom a stone, saying "I picked this up on the summit and I want you to put it back where I got it from." The gauntlet was cast. The trekking team all looked at one another. . . . we were wondering who should inherit the stone as an inspiration to continue the climb. The members looked in my direction. I handed the stone to someone whose time was spent preparing at base camp, a seasoned teacher who was dreaming about leading a school in the near future. Passing along the summit stone, I remarked, "We will only get quality principals in numbers if we have quality teachers in numbers, because it is from teacher ranks that future leadership derives. (Fullan 2003, 106)

Recognizing Complex Travel Routes

This research story can offer guidance to base camp educators and leaders within both school and university settings. However, there is no formula or recipe; context varies, defeating the notion that answers to complex issues are simple and straightforward (English 2003c; Fullan 1999). Consequently, no absolutes were anticipated or derived from this journey. Instead, routes and intersections that eventually led to the summit were constructed through an intensive inquiry process that occurred at a particular time and place. The caveats, sidebars, fluxes, and serendipitous moves at play along the way underscored how the journey was by no means linear, sequential, or even replicable. Those seeking direction can benefit with the willingness to actively interpret this journey and chart new and better routes as they traverse the Himalayas of school leadership.

Not only paths (e.g., core leadership areas and salient tasks) but also methods (e.g., mentoring scaffolds) used to reach goals will differ in many critical ways. Similarly, in the world of mountaineering, "climbing techniques vary according to the terrain," ranging from "cutting steps in ice slopes" to "climbing a vertical wall or getting by an overhang" (*Compton's Reference Collection* 1995).

Empowerment through Critical Reflective Inquiry

As a professor who teaches in an educational leadership program, I operate in a kind of base camp. With this awareness, I decided to conduct this quasicomprehensive study to deepen my own understanding in an effort to improve our graduate school operations. By seeing through the eyes of practicing leaders, I felt I that I could "trek" vicariously, anticipating being able to construct empowering connections between theory and practice within the leadership and administration field. This journey was influenced by my pedagogical goal to continuously improve upon the conditions in which my own students (aspiring and practicing leaders) learn.

According to Fullan (2003), our collective goal is to create the conditions for leaders to thrive and make a lasting impact, and not just by competently fulfilling expectations. To this end, Sergiovanni (1992) has also called for more attention to "successful leaders of leaders" (p. 273), shedding light on the role of capacity-building and mentoring beyond isolated school contexts to systemwide contexts. Tomorrow's leaders will need to know how to develop leaders around them and, by this virtue, the ability of organizations to strengthen in ways not previously attained (Mullen 2002d).

Interestingly, in this sense the theory/practice gap can be construed as desirable. The case scenarios and action research by my graduate students shared on such topics as diversity awareness in school emergency planning were produced not through school contexts but at university base camp, which supported traveling differently along K–12 school trails. It was in this space that the leadership aspirants were able to pursue their deeper questions and with ongoing feedback from educators in the same evening course. This meaning of theory/practice gap, as I have depicted, underscores the creative integration of thinking and doing, theory and practice, and academic and practitioner through action research (Mullen 2004). Nonetheless, as argued throughout, a more conscientious effort is collectively needed in the creation and delivery of graduate preparation programs. And our goal must go beyond viable connections with schools to helping site-based teams develop conditions for fostering unrealized capacities through a new generation of mentoring leaders: This is a summit climb for us to make together.

Distinguishing the "Real" and "Not So Real"

Another impression I have more clearly formed from this study is that the closer preparation programs can get to "the real thing" (i.e., school leadership practice within actual settings), the higher the value to aspiring and practicing administrators and school districts. Implicit in this notion is that "the real thing" exists, meaning that life in schools is a mirror to reflect. This may be a modernist as opposed to a postmodernist notion. However, understandably, my participants typically called for more intensive training through internships and other means as a solution for addressing the theory/practice gap: "I completed a three-hundred-hour internship at a Florida university, which was a wonderful experience." "More practical experience such as an internship in a master's program would have been helpful." Perhaps an imitation model would be attractive to many for bridging the theory/practice gap.

Along these lines, a fantasy notion is that the university could be reinterpreted as the school's base camp. Only the most relevant and timely skills would be learned and the school systems would do the hiring, training, and assessment of professors. I personally see great promise in experimental models that bring theory and practice, and universities and schools, into closer accord. However, I also believe that although the notion that school life can be imitated is very limiting, we can do a better job within universities of simulating pivotal operations of schools. Importantly, ongoing learning necessitates that theory and practice be constantly connected and reconnected in various contexts. This process requires a lifelong commitment to inquiry on the leader's part. In this sense, there is no summit to reach. Perhaps the best example offered in this book was the Lynne Patrick story, centering on a beginning leader who actively researched complex questions that arose out of her conviction to improve conditions for at-risk children.

It seems unrealistic, then, to imagine our collective work as trying to produce a one-on-one correspondence between school and university. How can this kind of experience be manufactured at base camp anyway? Unforeseen variables, contextual idiosyncrasies, and changing conditions all make the gap inevitable to some extent. Further, the cultures of "school" and "university" are rooted in different values, as my graduate students often attest and site-based action researchers echo. Some of my research respondents—new school leaders—supported this view, arguing that schools vary to such an extent in their internal cultures that professors should not assume that a norm exists—in the case of curriculum to be reviewed, for example.

In this postmodern era, we at the university cannot hold up a mirror to the reality of schools, even where patterns and rhythms of schooling do exist. Instead of striving to imitate that elusive animal called "reality," I believe it is our calling to create the conditions for reflective engagement and critical inquiry, with constant input from educational stakeholders, so our contexts can be better traversed and our worlds, deeply understood. Functioning at a very high speed, schools typically cannot effectively develop or sustain reflective spaces that promote informed action. Universities pride themselves on offering this kind of sanctuary. Ironically, in this particular sense the theory/practice gap that makes universities and schools different places of learning can be construed as desirable, as long as our goals are mutually supportive.

Just as our mission at university base camp is to help create new realities and to interrogate those that limit positive change, we must also see our function as producing leaders who can manage systems while building capacity for change. According to Fullan (2003), school leaders must not only thrive but also make a lasting impact, and not just by competently fulfilling expectations. Insights have been shared along these lines through the stories of Tom Graves, Elaine Sullivan, and Lynne Patrick, all change agents who created conditions for leadership to be shared and sustained while managing systems and implementing improvements. All three leaders shared a deep passion for their schools and a strong willpower, beyond technique and ability, as well as the drive to make a difference. And they found it invaluable to integrate practice with theory as a fundamental approach to making significant decisions about programming, staffing, scheduling, curriculum, and more.

IT'S YOUR TURN

As many leaders have testified, the more glorious the prospect, the greater the uncertainty. The mountaineer brings to this challenge deep passion and a strong will to make a difference in ways that are both profoundly theoretical and vigorously practical: "Technique and ability alone do not get you to the top—it is the willpower that is the most important. This willpower you cannot buy with money or be given by others—it rises from your heart." Junko Tabei spoke these words in 1975 after becoming the first woman to climb Mount Everest (Wiesel 2003).

The summit stone is now in *your* hands, ready for *your* footprints to be left on Everest. The lessons learned on this backpacking expedition should come in handy. Share with us your own wonderment of life's mountain climb and ineffable summit.

Figure E.2.   Surpass Your Own Summit Dreams
Source: Nova Development Corporation

Appendix A

School Leadership Expedition Glossary

The terms and meanings contained in this glossary are central to the metaphor of the trekking expedition used throughout this book. The definitions selected for each term have been extracted from a number of sources, primarily *Compton's Reference Collection* (1995) and *New Webster's Dictionary and Thesaurus of the English Language* (1993). Where other sources have been used, the citational information is provided. In some instances, a number of sources have been combined to provide the nuances of meaning that this book exploits. Each particular term and description has been selected for its relevance to the context of school leadership, as depicted within these pages. *Note*: The definitions have been edited in order to highlight the purposes and nuances expressed throughout. While some of the terms have multiple meanings and definitions, only those that align with the meanings of this book have been included.

Ax, also, *ice ax*. A small pickax carried by mountaineers especially for cutting footholds in the ice. Logue (2000) adds that the ice ax, in winter hiking, can be used for cutting steps in ice or snow, and for self-arresting and braking if you start to slide downward.

Backpack, also *knapsack*. A canvas bag that is strapped to the back for carrying necessaries and supplies. By reducing the weight of your backpack and the items in it, particularly the quantity and size, you will be better prepared to experience what one expert hiker calls "synergy in motion," or freedom of movement (Jardine 2001, 40).

Binocular, or *binoculars*. Means adapted for both eyes or requiring the use of two eyes. Also known as field glasses, binoculars are a portable telescope for using with both eyes at once and for viewing distant objects

259

outdoors. This optical instrument focuses both objectives simultaneously, while the focus of the eyepieces is independent. Distant objects are magnified so that they can be seen more clearly. Unlike the monocular, or single, telescope, they also allow the user to see depth or perspective. They accomplish this because they make possible the stereoscopic effect of the two eyes seeing an image from slightly different angles. Field glasses usually enlarge an image no more than five times the size it appears to the unaided eye. The field of view, or the area that can be viewed through field glasses or binoculars, decreases as the magnification power increases. Thus it is more difficult to locate a bird or other objects with a high-power instrument.

Bodhisattva. See *Sherpa,* also *Guide* and *Porter.*

Compass. Any of various instruments for showing direction, especially one consisting of a magnetic needle swinging freely on a pivot and pointing to the magnetic north. Before the development of sophisticated electronic and sound detection systems, navigators calculated directions from objects in the sky: the sun, the North Star, and the moon. A much more reliable guide for finding direction is a magnetic compass, which works at all times and in most places. When a piece of magnetized iron is placed on a splinter of wood and floated in a bowl of water, the wood will swing until the iron is pointing north and south. Any other direction can be found. The compass works because the Earth itself is a huge magnet.

A compass card usually has direction pointers consisting of thirty-two points. The four principal, or cardinal, points are north, east, south, and west. They are marked N, E, S, and W. Between these lie the intercardinal points, such as northeast (NE). Further division gives such points as north-northeast (NNE). A final division is by points, such as north by east (N by E). Naming all the points of a compass in their order is called boxing the compass. When surveyors, navigators, and similar technicians need more exact directions they use degrees. The compass card has 360 degrees marked on it. North is 0 (or 360); east, 90; south, 180; and west, 270.

Everest, Mount. (See also *Himalayas.*) Peak of the Himalayas, on the border of Nepal and Tibet: Highest known mountain in the world: 29,028 ft. Known in Tibet as *Chomolungma* or "Goddess Mother of the World," and also *Sagarmatha,* meaning "Forehead in the Sky." Mount Everest was known as Peak XV until 1856, when it was named for Sir

George Everest, the surveyor general of India from 1830 to 1843. The naming coincided with an official announcement of the mountain's height, taken as the average of six separate measurements made by the Great Trigonometrical Survey in 1850.

The summit reaches 5.5 miles above sea level to heights where oxygen is thin. Everest has seven individual glaciers—ice sheets fed by frequent avalanches that cover the slopes down to the base. The mountain climbs began with the opening of the Tibetan route in 1920. Ten tries from 1921 to 1952 failed because of the cold, dry air, fierce winds, difficult terrain, and high altitude. The peak was finally reached in 1953 by an expedition sponsored by the Royal Geographical Society and the Joint Himalayan Committee of the Alpine Club. Edmund Hillary of New Zealand and Tensing Norgay of Nepal climbed the southeastern ridge to the summit. Numerous treks sponsored by various countries have since been undertaken, many of them successful. (Nova Online/PBS, "Lost on Everest," 2003, http://www.pbs.org/wgbh/nova/everest)

First-Aid Kit. The main purpose of first aid is to provide proper care to suddenly ill or injured persons until medical help becomes available or, for problems that do not need a physician's attention, until complications have been prevented. Even a child can save a life by knowing what to do. For example, by rolling an unconscious person's head to one side, anyone can save that person from drowning in his own saliva or choking on his tongue. Many first-aid techniques are as simple. Others require preparation in advance of a crisis, but almost anyone can learn most of the important rules and methods. Training in first aid, which a hundred years ago was almost exclusively connected with war and large-scale disaster, is now taught in many schools, beginning with the fifth grade, and is available in almost every community. People who wish to be rescuers should study first-aid rules beforehand because there is little time to learn in an emergency.

Hike, also *hiking* and *hiker.* To take a long, vigorous walk; tramp or march, especially through the country, woods, etc.; a moving upward; rise. Distance walking for exercise or pleasure is called hiking. Hiking is one of the easiest and least expensive ways to promote physical fitness. Many individuals go walking alone on a regular basis, and there are clubs that sponsor group hikes. The Appalachian Trail Conference has member organizations in fourteen states and maintains campsites and a trail more than two thousand miles (3,200 kilometers) long from Maine to Georgia. The normal length of a hike is from twelve to twenty miles (19 to 32 kilometers) for a full day. Most American states and European countries have set aside hiking trails in the countryside surrounding densely populated areas. Hiking, in addition to being a sport in itself, is basic to several other sporting activities. It constitutes a large part of mountain climbing. The most tiring hours of mountaineering are spent on the lower trails, climbing slowly and steadily upward. Backpack camping is another sport in which hiking plays a significant role. In some countries, hiking is used as a test of fitness.

Those who take hiking seriously wear well-made boots or shoes and carry such supplies as first-aid kits, flashlights, rain gear, accurate topographical maps, food, water, and a compass. These can be carried in a backpack, leaving the hands free for getting through forests and wilderness areas. Good hikers will adjust their walking to the weather and climate: One does not hike the same way in a hot desert region as along the foothills of a cool, mountainous terrain. Heat exhaustion can be a problem in high-temperature areas, while colder places may induce hypothermia, or an abnormally low body temperature. An informative international guide is Michael Kelsey's (1981) *Climbers and Hikers Guide to the World's Mountains* (Kelsey Publishing).

Himalayas. The mountain system of South Central Asia, extending along the India–Tibet border and through Pakistan, Nepal, and Bhutan: highest peak, Mount Everest: also Himalaya Mountains. The highest mountain range on Earth, the Himalayas form the northern border of the Indian subcontinent in Asia. The mountain ranges extend in a massive arc for about 1,550 miles. Several Indian states and the kingdoms of Nepal and Bhutan lie along the southern slopes of the Himalayas, and the Tibetan Highlands border them in the north. The width of the mountain system varies from 125 to 250 miles (200 to 400 kilometers) from south to north, and the average height is twenty thousand feet (6,100 meters). The Himalayas extend over about 229,500 square miles (594,400 square kilometers), and India has sovereignty over most of them; Pakistan and China also occupy parts. The Sanskrit name *Himalayas*, meaning "of snow," characterizes the vast permanent snowfields above the snow line. These mountains pose the greatest challenge in the world to mountaineers.

Imagineering. The art or science of using imagination to intuitively make practical applications from knowledge (O'Callahan 1999). A cross between *engineering* and *imagination*, this is a perfect word for mountaineering or summit climbing, as this type of journey requires both practical sense and risk-taking sensibilities.

Journal. A diary, a narrative of transactions; a record of events, personal experiences and thoughts, kept day by day.

Kindle. To awaken, as in the spirit; to light, excite.

Map, also *mapping*. A representation of the surface of the earth or any part of it. A drawing or other representation, usually on a flat surface, of all or part of the earth's surface, ordinarily showing countries, bodies of water, cities, mountains, etc; to draw in a map, arrange or plan in detail: to "map out" a project; to survey or explore for the purpose of making a map; to transform, as by a mapping; put on the map [Colloq.] means to make well known, whereas to wipe off the map means to put out of existence.

Navigate. To plot a course or route, follow a map, steer, or find one's way.

Porter. A person employed in hiking, mountaineering, and other contexts to carry baggage or other loads.

Rope. A thick, strong cord of some thickness, made of intertwisted strands of fiber, thin wires, or leather strips; to connect or tie together (especially by mountain climbers) by a rope. The type of rope used in mountain climbing is made of nylon; "know the ropes" means to be fully acquainted with the details or procedures of something; "the end of one's rope" connotes being at the end of one's endurance, resources, and so forth.

Sherpa. A member of a Buddhist people living in northeast Nepal, in the foothills of the Himalayas, many of whom are noted as being expert porters or guides on mountaineering expeditions.

Signpost. A post at a crossroad or juncture, with arms showing directions and sometimes distances to places.

Signal (flare). A sign to communicate intelligence or orders at a distance.

Swiss army knife, also *all-in-one gadget*. Specialized multitools are used by hikers, rock climbers, and other outdoors adventurers. Such tools typically contain a knife, pliers, screwdriver, wire cutter, bottle opener, chisel/scraper, wire bender, can opener, ruler, and more, such as a shield mechanism for displaying altitude and temperature (Swiss Knives Express, http://www.swissknivesexpress.com/swisarswisrs [accessed May 27, 2003]).

Tarp. A shelter made of canvas, nylon, or another material, supported by a pole or poles and secured by ropes. A tarp is to be distinguished from a tent, which is a heavier and more sturdy, hence more secure, piece of equipment.

Topocentric. Perceived from a specific point on earth.

Topography. A description of a surface's features, natural and artificial, of a particular region; the science of drawing maps and/or diagrams that represent these features, as in topographic surveying.

Trailblaze, n. *trailblazer.* The process of marking out a new path. The first person to mark out a path for others to follow is a trailblazer or pioneer in some enterprise.

Train. To bring into proper bodily or mental condition. To cause to respond to discipline and instruction. To make a person efficient in some activity by repeated practice, and to make one's own body more efficient by exercise and diet, or one's intelligence and memory by application.

Appendix B

Annotated Bibliography on Early Career Socialization

Adkins, C. 1990. "A Longitudinal Examination of the Organizational Socialization Process." PhD diss., University of South Carolina, Columbia.

In a longitudinal study of organizational socialization, Adkins found that having similar previous job experience as well as friends in a new position had little effect on the process of socialization being facilitated for the entrant. As suggested, role conflict might explain this effect. This finding is contrary to some studies, which predict that positive transfer effects are present in this situation. Adkins's results proved consistent, however, with other literature indicating that role definition and social support in the workplace are associated with job satisfaction, organizational commitment, tenure, and, consequently, less job turnover. The author also found that internal motivation (being a self-starter) was predicted by the process variables of socialization (seen as a sign of successful socialization). In this study, as subjects became more aware of all they did not know about their new job, role ambiguity increased and self-rated performance decreased.

Begley, P. T., and G. Campbell-Evans. 1992. "Socializing Experiences of Aspiring Principals." *Alberta Journal of Educational Research* 38 (4): 285–99.

Assistant principals are viewed in this study as having varied backgrounds, experiences, and strengths, to the point of challenging any "standardized" principalship program. Such programs were viewed as unable to address all the various needs of their candidates, yet formal training programs continue to be the primary means of socialization for assistant principals.

For this research, eighty-seven aspiring principals were involved in data collection using surveys, interviews, and dialog journals. Findings indicate that internal processes, such as desire for promotion (financial goals) or career advancement (or stability), emerged as the strongest influence on the decision to enroll in a formal principalship training program. The decision to pursue training as a principal was less informed by one's relationships (collegial contact), ranking second as an influence on a person's decision. These results appear to contradict earlier research concerning the degree of influence superordinates have in influencing aspirants' career decisions through nominations and so forth. The third most important factor in deciding to enroll was encouragement by others (colleagues, family, and friends). Financial support and stability emerged as important factors in finalizing the decision to pursue the principalship.

Bloom, G., and M. Krovetz. 2001. "A Step into the Principalship." *Leadership* 30 (3): 12–13.

A brief but interesting report of a program implemented at the New Teacher Center at University of California, Santa Cruz, is highlighted. Because of the shortage of principals across the nation, time as an assistant principal can be too fleeting for many. A team initiated breakfast meetings with principals, assistant principals, and resource teachers to facilitate discussion of apprenticeship programs for aspiring school leaders. Pairs of mentors/apprentices signed an agreement to participate in a mentoring relationship over a one-year period. One participant found tremendous benefit from implicit and explicit learning with her mentor and described the interaction as a "team." The participating principals apparently did not find this relationship to be a burden. Benefits to principals were mentioned: the opportunity to build leadership in others; encourage reflection and growth for the principals; and develop an awareness of how teams offer strength and increase the effectiveness of principals.

Bush, T., and M. Coleman. 1995. "Professional Development for Heads: The Role of Mentoring." *Journal of Educational Administration* 33 (5): 60–73. Online at www.peer.ca/cgi-bin/ms2/rcarr/search (accessed January 26, 2003).

Mentoring, which involves an experienced colleague supporting the development of a new principal, is an important mode of professional development. The findings are reported by a major national research project on mentoring and teacher education in England and Wales. The nature and purpose of mentoring are considered, and the "match" between mentor and new head teacher is examined. The benefits are reported for new principals, mentors, and the educational system, and certain limitations of this approach to professional development are discussed. Several conceptual models of the mentor relationship are presented, and it is reported that the dominant normative conception is peer support. It is concluded that mentoring is valuable in supporting principals as they adapt to their new role, but it may lack the rigor to be a really effective mode of professional development.

Cantwell, Z. M. 1993. "School-Based Leadership and Professional Socialization of the Assistant Principal." *Urban Education* 28 (1): 49–68.

Assistant principals and principals (seventy-two in all) were surveyed regarding their perception of time spent by the former in seven administrative functions. Results from the two groups were similar, except that the assistant principals indicated that, ideally, they would prefer to devote more time to curriculum development and less time to discipline. Principals' perceptions of the assistant principals' time spent on these tasks were significantly lower and higher, respectively, than the perceptions of the assistant principals themselves.

It is argued that the socialization processes typically in place in schools reinforce a custodial orientation toward the assistant principalship, making an unfavorable environment for innovation. The author suggests that an alternative process of socialization can remove impediments to innovation and "professional socialization to a team leadership role for the assistant principal" (p. 50).

Crow, G. M., and C. Glascock. 1995. "Socialization to a New Conception of the Principalship." *Journal of Educational Administration* 33 (1): 22–43.

Seventeen candidates were selected for a cohort principal preparation program focusing on women and minorities. Data were gathered via surveys and interviews. The cohort seemed to represent genuine solidarity, and the members progressed together through the program. Innovative practices were used in the program: outdoors leadership experiences, advisement conferences emphasizing group cohesiveness, internship with a mentor, and frequent conferences with faculty.

Crow, G. M., L. J. Matthews, and L. E. McCleary. 1996. *Leadership: A Relevant and Realistic Role for Principals.* Larchmont, NY: Eye On Education.

This book places leadership within the context of schools, society, and organizations. Leadership literature and controversies are explicated and summarized. The book provides small case studies or "reflective vignettes" at the end of chapters, including course-related activities involving self-reflection and peer-reflection.

The authors suggest a framework for *principal leadership*—principals as "leaders of leaders" (p. 32). They suggest that a principal leads by developing a relationship of influence with all sectors of education, both in and outside of the school environment. The authors also discuss principal leadership in relation to three major areas: school culture, leadership for vision (especially collective vision), and school change or improvement. The book concludes with coverage of relevant and realistic leadership issues for today and for the future, such as purpose and methods of leadership, systemic leadership, and leadership for responsibility. Finally, the authors aver that peer-reflection, self-reflection, and formal training offer paths to a "realistic and relevant leadership role" (p. 134) for contemporary and future principals.

Daresh, J. C., and M. A. Playko. 1992. *The Professional Development of School Administrators' Preservice, Induction and Inservice Applications.* Boston: Allyn and Bacon.

A focus here is on the topic of mentoring as applied to beginning principals within the context of induction. Two applications are noted for improving ways to become a school administrator: (1) identify individuals who would be appropriate role models for beginners; and (2) engage in mentoring as an essential dimension of "formation," defined as the process by which an individual becomes aware of his or her personal values and assumptions regarding the formal role of school administrator.

Recommendations for establishing formal mentoring programs for administrative leaders in school systems are also provided: create a mentoring "team," observe the apprentice in "action," and share insights. Structured support systems that include induction programs are endorsed. Graduate-level university programs, which represent a "traditional model of inservice," are viewed as a method for providing ongoing inservice education to administrators.

Daresh, J. C. 2001. *Leaders Helping Leaders: A Practical Guide to Administrative Mentoring,* 2nd ed. Thousand Oaks, CA: Corwin.

Here, some attention is given to structured mentoring programs that guide practical experiences for novices. The idea that mentoring can help a novice fit into a new social and professional setting is identified. General discussion of mentoring is emphasized, with focus on how mentors should approach empowering novices, share experiences that establish limits, and promote self-directed learning. The mentor should also serve as a role model "by consistently demonstrating professional and competent performance on the job" (p. 41).

The advocacy of establishing a structured plan for mentoring is thought to be most effective where an informal quality is upheld: "Mentors and new administrators must have the opportunity to meet concerning socialization issues. These are things that will help a person who is in a position of visible authority feel more comfortable for the first time. Discussions along these lines are best handled on an ongoing basis and as new administrators come forward with concerns . . . during face-to-face discussions" (p. 84).

Daresh, J. C. 2001. *Beginning the Principalship: A Practical Guide for New School Leaders,* 2nd ed. Thousand Oaks, CA: Corwin.

The need to build a support system is underscored for new principals who are encouraged to find a mentor, develop a network, participate in professional associations, and maintain personal and family support. Importantly, the author maintains that it is not always the case that people with many years of experience make good mentors. The implication is that mentors can be newer principals and that good mentors are not necessarily of the same gender or race as their mentees.

The discussion of socialization is communicated via survey material regarding critical skills, without stories of personal mentoring.

Effective Leaders for Today's Schools: Synthesis of a Policy Forum on Educational Leadership. 1999 (June). Policy brief. Online at www.ed.gov/pubs/ EffecitveLeaders/policy-forum.html (retrieved October 15, 2002).

Those participating in a policy forum on educational leadership expressed the view that university preparation programs were doing an inadequate job. The report suggests that prospective school leaders should be trained by having more time with actual school leadership opportunities, which incorporate reflection on events and discourse about the process with others. The writers consider learning though engagement with real challenges, interacting with successful leaders, and conducting grounded research and guided inquiry into real-life problems all to be invaluable solutions to the problem of principal preparation.

Ehrich, L. C. 1995. "Professional Mentorship for Women Educators in Government Schools." *Journal of Educational Administration* 33 (2): 69–83. Online at www.peer.ca/cgi-bin/ms2/rcarr/search on (retrieved January 26, 2003).

This article examines mentorship as a policy mechanism to promote the career development and advancement of women in educational administration in Australian government schools. Mentorship has been identified to assist women educators' careers because, over the last decade, there has been a general consensus among academic and managerial researchers that mentorship is a significant career tool and a prerequisite for career success for both males and females. Because women experience difficulties in securing traditional mentoring relationships, it is argued that a mentorship policy will positively influence the career prospects of female educators by enabling them to be part of the power structures in educational administration that they can then change.

Franklin, J. 2000 (December). "Evaluating the School Principal: Changing Processes for Changing Roles." *Education Update* 42 (8): 1. Online at www .peer.ca/cgi-bin/ms2/rcarr/search on (retrieved January 26, 2003).

The pressures on principals to be educators, managers, accountants, supervisors and a myriad of other roles often outpace the resources available to handle challenges. One way principals can improve their chances of keeping pace is to find a mentor, particularly during their first year in the role. The author stresses that mentorship is more than a buddy system, where an individual might be available to help out during a crisis. Mentoring involves creating an ongoing relationship dedicated to the higher purpose of professional growth that is itself sustained.

Gibble, J. L., and J. D. Lawrence. 1987. "Peer Coaching for Principals." *Educational Leadership* 45 (3): 72–73. Online at www.peer.ca/cgi-bin/ms2/rcarr/ search on (retrieved January 26, 2003).

Principals in a Pennsylvania district voluntarily observed one another in order to improve their supervisory skills. Two principals jointly observed a teacher, compared notes, labeled the data, conducted the teacher postconference, and then held the principal postconference.

Glickman, C. D., S. P. Gordon, and J. M. Ross-Gordon. 1998. *Supervision of Instruction: A Developmental Approach*, 4th ed. Boston: Allyn and Bacon.

This textbook formally deals with task-specific examples of how to perform the role of a new school principal. The issues addressed focus on the practical question of how to implement critical learning as a whole-school cultural commitment with one's staff. The specific areas receiving attention involve how to facilitate peer coaching among one's teaching staff; how to assist teachers to maximize their performance within the context of adult learning and social role development; and how to implement successful mentoring programs that both value and support teacher growth.

Goldring, E. B. 1992. "System-wide Diversity in Israel: Principals as Transformational and Environmental Leaders." *Journal of Educational Administration* 30 (3): 49–62.

This article sets some context for contemporary leaders regarding the influence of diversity and global change on the role of the principalship and the skills required for success. The principal, who must address increased diversity and the political climate surrounding many urban schools (e.g., turbulence, immigration patterns), is "being retrained to manage schools as professional work settings, rather than bureaucratic service organizations" (p. 56). Today principals are moving toward a more dynamic view of themselves as transformational leaders. The ability to adapt their role to current, changing realities is seen as essential.

Goldring, E. B., and S. F. Rallis. 1993. *Principals of Dynamic Schools: Taking Charge of Change.* Newbury Park, CA: Corwin.

The socialization process that enables leadership development is "both formal and informal, and the content is both technical and moral" (p. 113). The authors define informal processes as ambiguous by nature, in that "the role of the learner" and the material to be understood are not defined. However, "these natural learning and development situations occur informally as one discovers and learns norms, traits, attitudes, and orientations in a given job setting, or in moving from one position to another" (p. 113).

The role of "leadership training as a continuous process" is considered essential: "Preparing leaders is not a linear path with a single starting point and ending point. Rather, the process is more of a revolving door that includes both formal and informal activities and that has multiple entry and exit points" (p. 128).

Hart, A. W. 1993. *Principal Succession: Establishing Leadership in Schools*. Albany: State University of New York Press.

This book is a study of the succession of experienced principals in a new setting within the context of organizational socialization frames. Various frameworks (e.g., Duke and Greenfield, 1984) illuminate features of a principal's professional socialization, notably the duration of a socialization period, the mechanisms of adaptation, relationships between expectations and realities of the job, and formal and informal preparation for school administration. The organizational socialization themes discussed include tactics used in the transitional process, socialization stages, personal and social contexts, and outcomes or effects of adaptation practices.

Hart, A. W., and P. V. Bredeson. 1996. *The Principalship: A Theory of Professional Learning and Practice*. New York: McGraw Hill.

A principal will experience socialization either in close contact with or in the absence of role models. The authors write, "She will feel more or less pressure to divest herself of the emerging professional self-concept shaped by early formal experiences and years as a teacher, or she may find her early values and professional self-image affirmed and supported" (p. 17). Structured, formal opportunities for principals to regularly meet with other new principals are called for. Peer-assisted leadership (Barnett, 1985) is described as a professional growth stimulus whereby well-trained peer coaches shadow and question each other, and provide informed feedback on each other's administrative practice. It is argued that new entrants need time to talk about shared experiences and learn from those experienced principals who are "models for exemplary practice" (p. 13).

Formal socialization can prove problematic where mentors "constrain innovation" and expect that existing roles will be reproduced. While *informal socialization* can increase creativity and innovation, it has been known to produce more excessive responses in innovative directions than formal socialization.

Heck, R. H. 1995. "Organizational and Professional Socialization: Its Impact on the Performance of New Administrators." *The Urban Review* 27 (1): 31–49.

Findings of this study underscore that organizational socialization may have a greater influence in shaping a new administrator than formal socialization (training). One's working conditions in the school, then, appear to moderate the effects of previous training. An administrator's performance is largely considered a function of the socialization experienced, especially by the informal transition that takes place on the job, in the school. In addition, women administrators were rated as performing more effectively than men, a difference that was ascribed to female teachers having more experience in the classroom.

Lumsden, L. S. 1992. "Prospects in Principal Preparation." Eugene, OR: ERIC Clearinghouse on Educational Management. (ERIC Document Reproduction Service No. ED350726.)

The author asserts that "administrator training has failed to keep pace with changing times and changing expectations of leaders" (p. 1). It is thought that internships and mentorships can prove to be insufficient training experiences for students because of poor program planning and inadequate supervising. It is suggested that principals need more training in group process skills, problem-solving strategies, conflict management skills, strategic thinking skills, and recognition of their values as related to education and leadership and prioritization of goals.

Marshall, C. M. 1985. "Professional shock: The Enculturation of the Assistant Principal." *Education and Urban Society* 18 (1): 28–58.

This article raises questions not about how the principal's tasks are learned and attitudes developed, but rather about the issue of culture shock. The assistant principal's story centers on how administrators seem to select and nurture those types of personalities that do not pose "threats," or those that can be "relied upon to defend fellow administrators, to keep trade secrets, to cooperate in coalitions" (p. 41). Those with "alternative" or strong personalities or styles often find a diminished mentoring system available to them.

Milstein, M. M., B. M. Bobroff, and L. N. Restine. 1991. *Internship Programs in Educational Administration: A Guide to Preparing Educational Leaders*. New York: Teachers College Press, Columbia University.

The researchers provide what they consider to be the desired characteristics of mentors (e.g., demonstrated desire to help others extend present levels of performance and aspiration), as well as functions of mentoring (e.g., modeling). These concepts are applied to the context of beginning administrator socialization. The authors claim: "Clearly there are two kinds of site administrators in an internship—those who provide opportunities to attain the necessary skills as site administrators and those who go beyond imparting skills and knowledge to become mentors" (p. 72). Those who go beyond and become mentors approach their relationship with interns as more than teacher and professional advocate—they instead attempt to engage reciprocity and mutual growth.

Nalls, F. 1994. "The Middle School Assistant Principalship: Organizational Socialization and Preparation for the Principalship." PhD diss., University of South Florida, Tampa.

In this study, middle school assistant principals had both formal and informal socialization experiences. Formal experiences centered on university classes and training programs, contrasted with the primary training received, which was on-the-job trial and error, or informal adaptation.

The majority of participants indicated that there is no specific sequence of steps (hierarchy) to achieve assistant principalship. The process instead depends upon random socialization, as opposed to one that is more sequential. Accordingly, the process was viewed as other than "fixed," in that there was not an experience requirement. The majority of assistant principals indicated that there were seasoned administrators who "groomed them for the position, serving as role models/mentors" (p. 122). This process is called *serial* (versus disjunctive) *socialization*, whereby experienced organizational members groom or prepare newcomers for similar positions within the organization. Most of the assistant principals reported that they were "able to pursue the role as they saw fit within their own personal characteristics when they assumed the AP" (p. 123).

Parkay, F. W., and G. E. Hall, eds. 1992. *Becoming a Principal: The Challenges of Beginning Leadership*. Boston: Allyn and Bacon.

The authors define *socialization* as the "processes by which an individual selectively acquires the knowledge, skills, and dispositions needed to perform adequately a social role (in this case the school principalship)" (p. 286). Socialization can consist of formal training programs, less formal—working with a mentor, or quite informal, such as unplanned on-the-job experiences. Additionally, four dimensions of socialization are identified: relationships (with superordinates and peers); school system policies, procedures, and control mechanisms; formal training; and one's role, skills, norms, and values.

Results highlight that (1) female principals consistently perceived their transitional apprenticeship activities as more helpful than did their male counterparts; (2) independent of socialization, new principals considered interpersonal, managerial, and legal tasks more important than instructional leadership tasks; and (3) formal preparation programs for aspiring principals "vary widely in perceived value. They are capable of being extremely helpful or not helpful at all, presumably depending on their quality. Such variation may also be the case, in a less pronounced way, for relationships with superordinates and nonleadership, school experiences" (p. 301).

Scanlon, K. C. (1997, Fall). "Mentoring Women Administrators: Breaking through the Glass Ceiling." *Initiatives* 58: 39–59.

Mentoring in higher education involves a variety of functions on the part of the mentor and concomitant responsibilities on that of the mentee. Mentoring may lead to role entrapment or submissiveness for the mentee, and finding a mentor can be difficult. Persons in higher education who wish to encourage and reward the mentoring process for women administrators will find many useful sources of information in the fields of business administration, as well as elementary and secondary education.

Schmieder, J. H., C. Z. McGrevin, and A. J. Townley. 1994. "Keys to Success: Critical Skills for Novice Principals." *Journal of School Leadership* 4: 272–93.

For this study, 450 principals and superintendents were surveyed. When asked to rank their preparation for the principalship, socialization emerged as the second most important critical skill. Both principals and superintendents identified providing longer and more rigorous internships, providing training in human relations, establishing opportunities to shadow a principal, and facilitating conflict management/resolution skills among the most important aspects of preparation program in need of improvement.

When principals were asked how they would change principal training programs, they responded as follows: "provide longer and more rigorous internships," "enable mentoring and shadowing experiences," and "introduce instruction by practicing school leaders": "Principals suggested that their [graduate] class work . . . did not adequately address the reality they encountered on accepting the position of principal; they wanted more time to socialize with practitioners" (p. 290). Toward this end, the authors suggest that more effective collaboration between training programs and K–12 schools is seriously needed.

Shackelford, J. 1992. "An Uphill battle: Socialization of a Novice Elementary Principal." PhD diss., Oklahoma State University, Stillwater.

Shackelford reports that six super domains emerged as major forces in her own transition as a new principal: personal vision, stories, written artifacts, existing norms, battles, and level of acceptance. The author further categorizes stories as historical, organizational, humorous, and inspirational. Oral stories were gathered from students, teachers, parents, and administrators in informal school settings (e.g., the playground), and written artifacts encompass formal documents and personal correspondence. Shackelford found that a significant amount of socialization occurred in interaction with parents and teachers, which at times could be negative or coercive (as in complaints and pressure), and that this process is affected by gender, worldview, and leadership style. She also asserts that any principal who operates reflectively can choose whether to be shaped by a situation, event, or occurrence and by doing so actively participates in her own socialization.

Stanton, D. 2001 (April 15). "A Lifeline for School Principals [La Bouée des directeurs d'école]. *L'Actualité Magazine*. Online at www.peer.ca/cgi-bin/ms2/rcarr/search (retrieved January 26, 2003).

Mentoring that combines the wisdom of experience with the enthusiasm of beginners has appeal for the school administration world. Within the next five years (by 2006) in Quebec, approximately half the school principals will be newcomers. Canadian school boards have had great difficulty filling principal positions, worsened by the increasing requirements associated with responsibilities of the role and the demands of educational reform. No guidelines for this job exist. Teachers turned principals will often suddenly find themselves sitting on the other side of the fence, but in isolation.

Appendix C

Survey Questions for Early Career Administrators

Research question: What Matters Most for Florida's School Administrators to Know?

Instructions: Please take a few minutes to respond to each of these items based on your own knowledge and experiences. Your completed form can be returned via e-mail or fax to the Principal Investigator.

Basic demographics (please mark the categories that apply to you, as appropriate; check to the left of your choices or circle them):

Geographic area of your school: ___urban ___rural

Level of your school: ___elementary ___middle ___secondary

Your administrative title or role: ___assistant principal ___principal ___other

Months or years in rank: ___months ___one year ___two years ___more (specify)

Gender: ___male ___female

Age: ___25–30 ___31–35 ___36–40 ___41–45 ___46–55 ___over 56

Your professional goal(s):

___assistant principal
___principal
___county office administrator
___superintendent
___other (specify): _____

Formal degree and program accomplished:

___master's degree in educational leadership
___master's degree in liberal arts field w/ed. leadership certification
___master's degree in curriculum w/ed. leadership certification
___doctor of education
___doctor of philosophy
___other (specify): _____

For the survey:
Please write a number for each item below from 0 to 5, ranging from of no importance to most important, that best represents the nature of the work and tasks you perform as a beginning school administrator.

Hopefully a picture will emerge from the survey data that answers the pertinent question, What matters most for Florida's school administrators to know?, so that leadership preparation programs can benefit from the results.

For the purposes of this survey, a "beginning administrator" is anyone transitioning into a new job or anyone in the first two years of a new job.

No Importance	*Least Important*	*Some Importance*			*Most Important*
0	1	2	3	4	5

E.g., Attending relevant conferences _0_
School Organization:

• Design master schedule, including specials ___
• Plan staff orientation/school-opening activities ___
• Review and plan nursing services ___
• Review and plan media center services ___
• Review student and faculty handbooks ___
• Design a school profile ___
• Conduct a school climate audit ___
• Review curriculum documents ___
• Attend a school board meeting ___
• Attend faculty meetings selectively ___

- Attend principal/assistant principal meetings ___
- Attend different school committee meetings ___
- Serve on a school committee ___

School Management:

- Manage budget (e.g., for instructional supplies) ___
- Write and submit a grant application ___
- Review attendance/tardy policies (discipline) ___
- Explore programs to improve student attendance ___
- Investigate plans for substitute (sub) coverage when teachers are absent ___
- Process student admissions/withdrawals ___
- Assess and analyze work of support personnel, paraprofessionals, and custodians ___
- Coordinate inservice training for secretaries ___
- Evaluate facilities maintenance (of buildings and grounds) ___

Supervision of Instruction:

- Assist teachers with instructional plans ___
- Advise teachers regarding classroom management ___
- Advise teachers on proper, effective documentation ___
- Interpret standardized test results with/for teachers ___
- Develop instructional guides/resource materials ___
- Check instruction against curriculum guidelines ___
- Observe levels of questions used in instruction ___
- Develop a monthly bulletin, spotlighting effective teaching ___
- Observe teacher–student interaction ___
- Communicate *every* school employee supports instruction ___
- Assist in interviewing and hiring potential faculty and staff ___
- Improve how instruction and achievement is celebrated ___

Student Services:

- Mediate teacher–student/student–student conflicts ___
- Work with Protective Services ___

- Mediate parent–teacher conferences ___
- Investigate disciplinary cases ___
- Supervise student transport to and from school ___
- Study student retention ___
- Review and enforce Americans with Disabilities Act ___
- Relate to youth with disabilities ___
- Supervise behavior in cafeteria ___
- Attend parent–principal conferences ___
- Supervise and assess evacuations, fire, and tornado drills ___
- Review and enforce school safety program ___
- Review and enforce field trip policies and activity forms ___
- Supervise student social activities ___
- Form a parent advisory group and meet ___

Community Relations:

- Plan open house ___
- Newsletter (student/staff accomplishments) ___
- Participate in PTSA*/SAC** involvement ___
- Assist with community surveys ___
- Supervise community/parent volunteers ___

*PTSA = Parent–Teacher–Student Association
**SAC = School Advisory Council

Commentary (open response)

1. (a) Expand on your experiences as a beginning school administrator in terms of your actual work on the job, and/or (b) reflect on how well your graduate experience prepared you for the role of Assistant Principal.

   (a)_____

   _____

   _____

   _____

(b)_____

_____

_____

_____

2. Critique this survey instrument—is anything missing or worth noting?

_____

_____

_____

Appendix D

Matrix Results of Administrator Survey for All Florida Counties

RESEARCH QUESTION: WHAT MATTERS MOST FOR FLORIDA'S SCHOOL ADMINISTRATORS TO KNOW?

Basic Demographics   *Date: 6/03*   *Number of Surveys: 91*

Geographic area: _61_ urban   _30_ rural

Level of school: _33_ elementary   _30_ middle   _28_ secondary

Administrative title: _46_ assistant principal   _41_ principal   _4_ other

Months or years in rank: _41_ months   _17_ one year   _33_ two years

Gender: _36_ male   _55_ female

Age: _9_ 25–30   _9_ 31–35   _24_ 36–40   _13_ 41–45   _31_ 46–55
   _5_ over 56

Professional goal: _2_ assistant principal   _47_ principal
   _17_ county office administrator   _11_ superintendent
   _14_ other (e.g., curriculum supervisor)

Formal degree and program:_57_Master's Degree in Educational
    Leadership
_1_ Master's Degree in Liberal Arts Field w/ Ed. Leadership
    Certification
_10_ Master's Degree in Curriculum w/ Ed. Leadership
    Certification
_1_ Doctor of Philosophy
_2_ Doctor of Education
_20_ Other (not specified by respondents)

School Organization   *Date: 6/03*   *Number of Surveys: 91*

	No Importance	Least Important	Some Importance			Most Important
Design master schedule, including specials.	2	3	5	19	24	38
Plan staff orientation/school-opening activities.	1	1	7	14	31	37
Review and plan nursing services.	7	25	29	21	4	5
Review and plan media center services.	5	12	31	31	11	1
Review student and faculty handbooks.	0	2	8	26	33	22
Design a school profile.	4	4	13	26	17	17
Conduct a school climate audit.	3	2	11	32	20	22
Review curriculum documents.	0	5	3	15	35	33
Attend a school board meeting.	10	24	17	20	17	3
Attend faculty meetings selectively.	6	3	3	9	21	48
Attend principal/ assistant principal meetings.	1	1	7	15	28	40
Attend different school committee meetings.	1	1	6	20	41	22
Serve on a school committee.	3	4	4	17	34	30
	0	1	2	3	4	5

School Management *Date: 6/03* *Number of Surveys: 91*

	No Importance	Least Important	Some Importance			Most Important
Manage budget (e.g., for instructional supplies)	6	15	23	39	53	47
Write and submit a grant application.	4	15	16	29	20	7
Review & enforce attendance/tardy policies (discipline)	11	13	23	54	53	28
Explore programs to improve student attendance.	2	5	10	29	31	13
Investigate plans for substitute ("sub") coverage when teachers are absent	4	6	9	31	25	10
Process student admissions/withdrawals.	7	26	20	20	11	7
Assess and analyze work of support personnel, paraprofessionals, & custodians.	9	15	10	22	12	4
Coordinate inservice training for secretaries.	11	11	19	22	16	4
Evaluate facilities maintenance (of buildings & grounds).	8	6	12	18	34	12
	0	1	2	3	4	5

Supervision of Instruction *Date: 6/03* *Number of Surveys: 91*

	No Importance	Least Important	Some Importance			Most Important
Assist teachers with instructional plans.	2	1	3	21	21	43
Advise teachers regarding classroom management.	1	0	1	8	34	47
Advise teachers on proper, effective documentation.	1	0	4	16	28	24

	No Importance	Least Important	Some Importance			Most Important
Interpret standardized test results with/for teachers.	1	3	4	13	12	45
Develop instructional guides/ resource materials.	3	6	17	24	23	18
Check instruction against curriculum guidelines.	1	4	6	13	24	43
Observe levels of questions used in instruction.	2	3	6	13	32	35
Observe teacher–student interaction.	1	2	3	13	25	47
Develop a monthly bulletin, spotlighting effective teaching.	3	6	14	22	20	26
Communicate *every* school employee supports instruction.	1	1	9	14	21	47
Assist in interviewing and hiring potential faculty and staff.	1	1	2	12	18	57
Improve how instruction and achievement is celebrated.	1	0	6	16	27	43
	0	1	2	3	4	5

Student Services　　　　*Date: 6/03*　　　　*Number of Surveys: 91*

	No Importance	Least Important	Some Importance			Most Important
Mediate teacher–student/ student–student conflicts.	1	1	9	11	37	32
Work with Protective Services.	2	1	11	34	27	16
Mediate parent–teacher conferences.	1	1	6	25	39	19
Investigate disciplinary cases.	2	1	7	15	36	30
Supervise student transport to and from school.	5	8	17	24	21	16
Study student retention.	1	5	8	26	32	20
Review and enforce Americans with Disabilities Act.	2	3	8	41	23	24
Relate to youth with disabilities.	0	2	7	8	37	37
Supervise behavior in cafeteria.	2	6	11	15	26	21
Attend parent–principal conferences.	0	2	2	15	25	47
Supervise and assess evacuations, fire, & tornado drills.	1	1	5	17	21	46

	No Importance	Least Important	Some Importance			Most Important
Review and enforce the school safety program.	0	1	10	14	31	43
Review and enforce field trip policies & activity forms.	1	6	16	23	21	16
Supervise student social activities.	1	3	11	24	27	25
Form a parent advisory group and meet.	2	4	10	15	25	35
	0	1	2	3	4	5

Community Relations   *Date: 6/03*   *Number of Surveys: 91*

	No Importance	Least Important	Some Importance			Most Important
Plan open house.	1	4	6	21	23	36
Newsletter (student staff/ accomplishments).	0	4	7	22	25	35
Participate in PTSA*/SAC** involvement.	7	9	17	42	43	57
Assist with community surveys.	4	6	10	22	33	16
Supervise community/parent volunteers.	0	7	19	36	19	10
	0	1	2	3	4	5

*PTSA = Parent–Teacher–Student Association
**SAC = School Advisory Council

Appendix E

Focus Group Questions for Early Career Administrators

Research question: What Matters Most for Florida's School Administrators to Know?

For the focus group:

Instruction: Please note that the following agenda will be adjusted as the study takes shape and in relation to your questions and contributions. Folders containing the agenda and handouts on the survey data and reflective analysis exercises will be provided at the session. Written responses will not be required—verbal commentary will be elicited, and audiotaping accompanying note taking will occur. You will be asked to anonymously complete the Focus Group Participant Form within one week of this session and submit your demographics at that time via e-mail or fax. (Carol Mullen, principal investigator)

Generic agenda (to be adjusted for each focus group session)

1. Critique both the survey instrument and the results with the goal of developing insight into the most important items selected by a pool of beginning school administrators.
2. Clarify the tasks and roles most representative of school leadership revealed both through the survey results and the focus group members' relevant experiences in administration. Five categories of administrative school responsibility—school organization, school management, supervision of instruction, student services, and community relations— will serve to launch a deeper, more complex conversation concerning core areas of school leadership for beginners.

3. Identify and discuss the most critical elements (e.g., team building and collaborative leadership) needed for socializing beginning school leaders. Each of these areas will reflect a deeper synthesis or new creative focus from the survey; the function of the survey is to promote a more reflective conversation about the underlying, critical areas that define the work and development of new school leaders. On the surface, such areas as school organization and management are essential, but on a deeper level learning about the school culture and its hidden rules may be more challenging.

4. Elicit critique and suggestions in graduate principal preparation, with implications for program improvement and policy reform.

Appendix F

Focus Group Workshop
Evaluation Form

Dear School Practitioner/Graduate Student: Thank you for participating in the workshop seminar!! This session focused on the development of a school-based study that looked at the experience of new administrators and their work-related functions. With your help, we analyzed the relevant qualitative research data in a focus group context. The objective of this session was twofold: to model key qualitative processes that you might use in your own research and projects within schools, and to validate the interpretation of the preliminary data that I have collected thus far for my book, *Climbing the Himalayas of School Leadership*.

Please respond to the following two-part form (basic demographics and short response questions).

—Carol Mullen, Principal Investigator

Basic Demographics (Mark the categories that apply to you, as appropriate; check to the left of your choices or circle them)
Geographic area of your school: ___urban ___rural
Level of your school: ___elementary ___middle ___secondary
Your title or role: ___assistant principal ___principal ___teacher ___other (specify)
Months or years in rank: ___months ___one year ___two years ___more (specify)
Gender: ___male ___female
Age: ___25–30 ___31–35 ___36–40 ___41–45 ___46–55 ___over 56

Professional Goal(s): ___assistant principal ___principal ___county office administrator___superintendent ___curriculum supervisor ___other (specify below)

_____

_____

Formal degree & program accomplished:
   ___Master's Degree in Educational Leadership
   ___Master's Degree in Liberal Arts Field w/ Ed. Leadership
   Certification
   ___Master's Degree in Curriculum w/ Ed. Leadership Certification
   ___Doctor of Education
   ___Doctor of Philosophy
   ___Other (specify)

Short Response Questions:

1. What did you like the best about the actual workshop seminar?
2. What could be improved upon for the next time the researcher/professor does this workshop?
3. Did you learn anything new about qualitative data analysis that you did not already know, or did you gain any new insights? If so, what exactly?
4. What new ideas or tools might you apply to your own graduate research and/or projects within schools?
5. What contributions did you personally make or did the group make to the research project and to its possible improvement?
6. Do you have any suggestions for how the workshop might be best delivered to make it as effective as possible for teachers and leaders in school districts?

Final comments:

Appendix G

Application of Florida School District Structure to Study

NORTH SCHOOL DISTRICTS

Alachua, Baker, Clay, Duval, Jackson, Levy, Nassau, and Santa Rosa from the northern region responded to the survey. Of the state's smallest school districts, none governs more than two hundred schools. Duval County is the largest district, with 177 educational institutions and 126,919 students, and Baker the smallest, with eight schools and 4,490 students. Most of the northern districts have a graduation rate of approximately 60 percent; Santa Rosa's graduation rate of 75.5 percent makes it the highest. The dropout rates vary more widely than the graduation numbers, with most districts averaging between 2 and 6 percent. Some outlying districts include Jackson's, with the lowest dropout rate, 1.5 percent, and Duval's, which at 8.3 percent is the highest. The ethnic makeup of the northern districts is predominately white, but some counties are more diverse than others. Baker, Clay, Nassau, and Santa Rosa have a white majority student population, whereas two of the counties have ethnic diversity: In Alachua, 54 percent of the student body is white, and 37 percent black. Duval, with the highest dropout rate, has 48 percent white students, 43 percent black, and 5 percent Hispanic. Overall, the Hispanic population remains under 10 percent in those northern districts surveyed for this study.

SOUTH SCHOOL DISTRICTS

Broward, Collier, Miami-Dade, Lee, Monroe, and Palm Beach comprise the southern districts that returned the survey. Three districts in

this geographic region are the largest: Broward County with 246
schools and 262,027 pupils, Dade County with 418 institutions of
learning and 374,806 students, and Palm Beach containing 217 educational facilities and 159,862 children. As the largest district in terms of
school size and students served, Dade County (which was not represented in the study) is unique in terms of its ethnic mix, with white as
the minority race (11 percent of the student population), and the majority, 57 percent, Hispanic, and 30 percent black. The counties that have
a majority of white students are Collier (53 percent), Lee (64 percent),
and Monroe (66 percent). Graduation and dropout rates are similar
from district to district. Based upon these six southern counties, the average graduation rate is 65 percent, and the average dropout 3.5 percent. There are some notable exceptions: Monroe County, the smallest
in this southern region, has the highest graduation rate, 68.5 percent.
Lee County, one of the smaller districts, has the highest dropout rate at
5.6 percent.

WEST SCHOOL DISTRICTS

A number of counties from the west coast—including Charlotte, Citrus,
Hillsborough, Manatee, Pasco, Pinellas, and Sarasota—returned completed surveys. This district has a diverse group of counties in terms of
size and racial makeup. Hillsborough is the largest district in this
group, with 242 schools and 169,682 students. Also, it is the only
county that does not have a white majority being served in its educational centers, with a student population that is 49 percent white, 23
percent black, and 22 percent Hispanic. The other counties, Charlotte,
Citrus, Manatee, Pasco, Pinellas, and Sarasota, serve a majority of
white students, 80 percent and higher. The smallest counties, Citrus and
Charlotte, have not more than 10 percent black or Hispanic students.
The lowest dropout rate, 2.7 percent, is found in Hillsborough, the
largest county. The highest graduation rate is in Charlotte County with
74.7 percent, just three-tenths of a percent higher than Hillsborough's
graduation rate. Conversely, the highest dropout rate, 4.5 percent, is in
Manatee County.

EAST SCHOOL DISTRICTS

The eastern counties that returned survey data were Brevard and St. Lucie. The two districts appear similar, statistically speaking. A major variation, however, is the total number of schools in the districts: Brevard is the larger county, with 117 schools, whereas St. Lucie has 45. Apart from this difference, both districts have high graduation rates, between 70 and 80 percent, and their dropout rates do not exceed 5 percent. Also, both districts are predominantly white, 56 percent of the student population in St. Lucie County and 77 percent in Brevard County.

CENTRAL SCHOOL DISTRICTS

Central Florida has five counties that returned surveys: Desoto, Marion, Orange, Osceola, and Putnam. The largest counties in this region are Orange County, with 156,905 students and 202 schools, and Marion County, with 39,319 pupils and 66 institutions. Osceola has 51 educational centers and serves 37,744 young people. The smallest counties are DeSoto and Putnam. The central districts in Florida vary widely in size, with some counties serving fewer than ten thousand students, while others accommodate over a hundred thousand. All of these counties have a graduation rate of approximately 60 percent, with the highest rate of matriculation at 63 percent from Putnam County. Putnam is the smallest student population. Florida's central region also varies widely in its ethnic makeup: Marion, Desoto, and Putnam Counties' student populations are predominantly white (over 50 percent). Desoto and Putnam school districts have large Hispanic populations, 20 percent and 27 percent, respectively, and Orange County has a diverse mix of ethnicities—42 percent white, 29 percent black, and 24 percent Hispanic.

References

Acker-Hocevar, M., and D. Touchton. 2002. How principals level the playing field of accountability in Florida's high-poverty/low-performing schools—Part I: The intersection of high-stakes testing and effects of poverty on teaching and learning. *International Journal of Educational Reform* 11 (2): 106–24.

Adkins, C. 1990. *A longitudinal examination of the organizational socialization process.* PhD diss., University of South Carolina, Columbia.

AdvisorTeam. 2002. *Keirsey Temperament Sorter II Personality Instrument.* Online at http://www.advisorteam.com.

African-American Inventor Series. 2003. Online at http://www.ehhs.cmich.edu.

Aguirre, A., Jr., and J. H. Turner. 1995. *American ethnicity: The dynamics and consequences of discrimination.* San Francisco: McGraw-Hill.

Aidelbaum, J., J. Crabtree, V. Jeffers, L. Johnson, and M. Miller. 2003. *Case study in bioterrorism: An anthrax attack on a Florida elementary school.* Unpublished manuscript.

Amatt, J. 2000. *All-star agency: John Amatt.* Online at www.allstaragency.com/cgi-bin/speaker2001 (accessed June 1, 2003).

American Red Cross. 2002. *Homeland Security Advisory System recommendations,* www.redcross.org/services/disasterbeprepared/busiindustry (accessed May 25, 2003).

Arnone, M. 2003. Watchful eyes: The FBI steps up its work on campuses, spurring fear and anger among many academics. [Special report]. *Chronicle of Higher Education* 49 (31), April 11, A14.

Bailey, S. M. 1996. Shortchanging girls and boys. *Educational Leadership* 53 (8): 75–80.

Bailin, S. 1988. *Achieving extraordinary ends: An essay on creativity.* Norwell, MA: Kluwer Academic Publishers.

Banks, C. 2000. Gender and race as factors in educational leadership and administration. In *The Jossey-Bass reader on educational leadership*. ed. Jossey-Bass Publishers, 217–56. San Francisco: Jossey-Bass.

Barber, E., S. Chandler, and E. C. Collins. 2001. Using Monet to teach leadership: Integrating the arts into educational administration preparation. *Journal of Curriculum Theorizing* 17 (2): 27–38.

Barksdale-Ladd, M. A., and K. F. Thomas. 2000. What's at stake in high-stakes testing: Teachers and parents speak out. *Journal of Teacher Education* 51 (5): 384–97.

Barnett, B. 1985. Peer-assisted leadership: A stimulus for professional growth. *Urban Review* 17: 47–64.

Barr, R., and M. Bizar, eds. 2001. *School leadership in times of urban reform.* Mahwah, NJ: Lawrence Erlbaum Associates.

Bayless, L. K. 2004. A turnover tale: The effect of excessive leadership turnover in an elementary school. *International Journal of Educational Reform.*

Begley, P. T. 2002. Western-centric perspectives on values and leadership. In *School leadership and administration: Adopting a cultural perspective*, ed. A. Walker and C. Dimmock, 45–59. New York: RoutledgeFalmer.

Begley, P. T., and G. Campbell-Evans. 1992. Socializing experiences of aspiring principals. *Alberta Journal of Educational Research* 38 (4): 285–99.

Benjamin, W. 2003 (June). Personal communication.

Bereiter, C., and M. Scardamalia. 1993. *Surpassing ourselves: An inquiry into the nature and implications of expertise.* Chicago: Open Court.

Berry, K. S. 2002. Color me white: Dismantling white privilege with young students. *Taboo: Journal of Culture and Education* 6 (10): 85–96.

Blacker L. V. S., J. Buchan, and P. F. M. Fellowes. 1933. *First over Everest! The Houston–Mount Everest Expedition.* New York: Robert M. McBride.

Blasé, J., and J. Blasé. 2000. Effective instructional leadership: Teachers' perspectives on how principals promote teaching and learning in schools. *Journal of Educational Administration* 38 (2): 130–41.

Bloom, G., and M. Krovetz. 2001. A step into the principalship. *Leadership* 30 (3): 12–13.

Bogotch, I. 2002 (Fall). Emerging trends in teaching and learning educational leadership. *Educational Leadership and Administration* 14: 93–111.

Bolman, L. G., and T. E. Deal. 1993. *The path to school leadership: A portable mentor.* Newbury Park, CA: Corwin Press.

———. 1997. *Reframing organizations: Artistry choice and leadership.* San Francisco: Jossey-Bass.

Bouleris, S., D. E. Collett, M. Mauntler, and S. Ray. 2003. *McCormick's mayhem: "The time to learn to dance is not five minutes before the party."* Unpublished manuscript.

Bowers, C. A. 1998. Toward a balanced perspective on the educational uses of computers: Advantages, myths, and the responsibilities of educators. *International Journal of Leadership in Education* 1 (1): 75–83.

Boyer, N. 2003. Leaders mentoring leaders: Unveiling role identity in an international online environment. *Mentoring and Tutoring: Partnership in Learning* 11 (1): 25–41.

Bratlein, M. J., and D. L. Walters. 1999. The superintendency: Preparing for multi-dimensional roles in complex and changing environments. In *A thousand voices from the firing line*, ed. F. K. Kochan, B. L. Jackson, and D. L. Duke, 87–102. Columbia, MO: University Council for Educational Administration.

Britton, E., S. Raizen, L. Paine, and M. A. Huntley. 2001 (March). *More swimming less sinking: Perspectives on teacher induction in the U.S. and abroad.* Online at www.wested.org/online_pubs/teacherinduction (accessed July 5, 2003).

Brownlee, S. 1996. The biology of soul murder. *U.S.News and World Report*, November 11, 71–73.

Bruner, D. Y., and M. Livingston. 2002. Out of the mouths of babes. *Journal of Cases in Educational Leadership* 5, (1) (winter). Online at www.ucea.org/cases (accessed June 25, 2003).

Brunner, C. C. 2002. Professing educational leadership: Conceptions of power. *Journal of School Leadership* 12 (6): 693–720.

Bundros, Zoe. 2000. *Women Climbing.* Online at www.womenclimbing.com.

Buntin, J., C. Rovellada Gutierrez, and C. Spires. 2003. *For the love of our country: A case study in bioterrorism preparedness.* Unpublished manuscript.

Burrell, B. 2002. Strategies to reduce racial biases in education. In B. Burrell, D. Faysash, K. King, M. Miller, and K. Sutton, *It ain't fair! Racial disparities in special education,* 7–11. Unpublished manuscript.

Cantwell, Z. M. 1993. School-based leadership and professional socialization of the assistant principal. *Urban Education* 28 (1): 49–68.

Centers for Disease Control and Prevention. 2001. *Bioterrorism and public health.* Online at www.cdc.gov (accessed May 30, 2003).

———. 2003. *Sheltering in place during a radiation emergency.* Online at www.cdc.gov (accessed May 30, 2003).

Chalmers, V. 1997. Whiteout: Multicultural performances in a progressive school. In *Off white: Reading on race, power, and society,* ed. M. Fine, L. Weis, L. C. Powell, and L. M. Wong, 66–78. New York: Routledge.

Champy, J., and N. Nohria. 2000. *The arc of ambition: Defining the leadership journey.* Oxford, UK: Perseus Publishing.

Clark, D. L. 1999. Searching for authentic educational leadership in university graduate programs and with public school colleagues. In *Educational administration: A decade of reform*, ed. J. Murphy and P. B. Forsyth, 228–36. Thousand Oaks, CA: Corwin Press.

Clement, M., and R. Vandenberghe. 2001. How school leaders can promote teachers' professional development: An account from the field. *School Leadership and Management* 21 (1): 43–57.

Cole, A. L., F. A. Squire, and E. P. Cathers. 1995. *Supporting beginning teachers: A handbook for school administrators.* Toronto, ON: University of Toronto Press.

Compton's Reference Collection. 1995. Carlsbad, Calif.: Compton's NewMedia: A Tribune New Media/Education Company.

Connecticut Department of Public Health. 2003. *Bioterriorism preparedness fact sheet*, 1–4. Online at www.dph.state.ct.us/Agency_News/FCT_bioterror. (accessed February 15, 2003).

Connelly, F. M., and D. J. Clandinin. 1985. Personal practical knowledge and the modes of knowing: Relevance for teaching and learning. In *Learning and teaching the ways of knowing*, ed. E. W. Eisner, E174–98. Eighty-fourth Yearbook of the National Society for the Study of Education. Chicago: University of Chicago Press.

———. 1986. Rhythms in teaching: The narrative study of teachers' personal practical knowledge of classrooms. *Teaching and Teacher Education* 2 (4): 377–87.

Creighton, T. 2003. *It's time to take back our profession.* Paper presented at the annual meeting of the National Council of Professors of Educational Administration, Sedona, AZ.

Crow, G. M. 1992. The principal in schools of choice: Middle manager, entrepreneur, and symbol manager. *Urban Review* 24 (3): 165–74.

Crow, G. M., and C. Glascock. 1995. Socialization to a new conception of the principalship. *Journal of Educational Administration* 33 (1): 22–43.

Crow, G. M., and L. J. Matthews. 1998. *Finding one's way: How mentoring can lead to dynamic leadership.* Thousand Oaks, CA: Corwin Press.

Danielson, C. 2002. *Enhancing student achievement: A framework for school improvement.* Alexandria, VA: ASAD Publications.

Daresh, J. C. 2001a. *Leaders helping leaders: A practical guide to administrative mentoring*, 2nd ed. Thousand Oaks, CA: Corwin Press.

———. 2001b. *Beginning the principalship: A practical guide for new school leaders*, 2nd ed. Thousand Oaks, CA: Corwin Press.

Daresh, J. C., and M. A. Playko. 1992. *The professional development of school administrators: Pre-service induction and in-service applications.* Boston: Allyn and Bacon.

de Gues, A. 1997. *The living company*. Cambridge, MA: Harvard Business School Press.

Della-Giustina, D. E., S. E. Kerr, and D. L. Georgevich. 2000. Terrorism and violence in our schools. *Professional Safety* 45 (3): 16–21.

Dembowski, F. L. 1998. What should we do now? Suggested directions for school administration programs. *The AASA Professor* 22 (1): 1–7. Online at www.aasa.org (accessed June 3, 2002).

Diamond, C. T. P. 1991. *Teacher education as transformation: A psychological perspective*. Milton Keynes, UK: Open University Press.

Diamond, C. T. P., and C. A. Mullen, eds. 1999a. *The postmodern educator: Arts-based inquiries and teacher development*. New York: Peter Lang.

Diamond, C. T. P., and C. A. Mullen. 1999b. "Roped together": Artistic forms of comentoring in higher education. In *The postmodern educator: Arts-based inquiries and teacher development*, ed. C. T. P. Diamond and C. A. Mullen, 315–40. New York: Peter Lang.

Dorn, S., and R. Papalewis. 1997. *Improving doctoral student retention*. Paper presented at the Annual Meeting of the American Educational Research Association, Chicago.

Doud, J. L., and E. P. Keller. 1998. The K–8 principal in 1998. *Principal Magazine*. Online at www.naesp.org/comm/p0998d (accessed July 18, 2002).

Duke, D. L., N. S. Isaacson, R. Sagor, and P. A. Schmuck. 1984. *Transition to leadership: An investigation of the first year of the principalship*. Portland, OR: Lewis and Clark College, Transition to Leadership Project.

Edmonds, R. 1979. Some schools work and more can. *Social Policy* 9: 32–36.

Elkind, D. 2001. *The hurried child: Growing up too fast too soon*, 3rd ed. Boulder, CO: Perseus Publishing.

Effective Leaders for Today's schools: Synthesis of a policy forum on educational leadership. 1999 (June). Online at www.ed.gov/pubs/EffectiveLeaders/policyforum (accessed January 11, 2003).

English, F. W. 2003a (March). Cookie-cutter leaders for cookie-cutter schools: The teleology of standardization and the de-legitimization of the university in educational leadership preparation. *Leadership and Policy in Schools*, 1–20.

———. 2003b (Spring). PERSPECTIVE: About the policing functions of ELCC/NCATE and the standardization of university preparation programs in educational administration. *AERA Division A Newsletter*, 5–8.

———. 2003c. *The postmodern challenge to the theory and practice of educational administration*. Springfield, IL: Charles C. Thomas.

———. 2003d. Tsar Khorosh, Boyary Polkhi: The ISLLC standards and the enshrinement of mystical authoritarianism as anti-change doctrine in educational leadership preparation. In *Shaping the future: Policy partnerships and emerging perspective* (NCPEA Yearbook), ed. F. C. Lunenburg and C. S. Carr, 112–33. Lanham, MD: ScarecrowEducation.

eSchool News staff and wire service reports. 2003 (April 9). The role of weather information in disaster response and recovery. National Weather Service Online at www.aws.com (accessed April 13, 2003).

Farley, J. 2003. Field guide story: How to use a map and compass. *Cabela's World's foremost outfitter*. Online at www.cabelas.com/cabelas/en/templates/community/inthefield/fieldguides (accessed May 11, 2003).

Fede, H., and R. Flanary. 2003 (August). *NCATE/ELCC*. Special session presented at the annual meeting of the National Council of Professors of Educational Administration, Sedona, AZ.

Federal Emergency Management Agency. (n.d.). *Emergency management guide for business and industry*. Online at www.fema.gov/library/biz2.

Finn, C. E. 1999. *Why testing experts hate testing*. Dayton, OH: Thomas B. Fordham Foundation. Online at www.edexcellence.net/topics/standards (accessed July 11, 2003).

Fishman, A., and E. J. Raver. 1989. "Maybe I'm just NOT English teacher material": Dialogue journals in the student teaching experience. *English Education* 21 (2): 92–109.

Florida Association of School Administrators. (FASA). 2002. *Florida education directory by FASA 2002–2003 school year*. Tallahassee, FL: Florida Board of Education/CMD Publishing Corporation.

Florida Department of Education. Online at http://osi.fsu.edu/data.nsf.

———. [Self-study aids, "Data in a Day."] Online at http://osi.fsu.edu/data.nsf.

Florida Department of Education, Florida Information Resource Network (FIRN). Online at http://www.firn.edu.

———. [Accommodations for students with disabilities]. Online at http://www.firn.edu/doe/commhome.

———. Florida Educational Leadership Exam (FELE). Online at http://www.firn.edu/doe.

———. School Improvement and Accountability. Online at http://www.firn.edu/doe/schoolgrades.

———. Sunshine State Standards. Online at http://www.firn.edu/doe/curric/prek12.

Florida Department of Education (FIRN). Online at http://www.firn.edu/doe/eias/flmove/eias.

———. Florida's A-Plus Program. 2001. Online at http://firn.edu/doe/choice/excellence.

Fullan, M. G. 1999. *Change forces: The sequel.* London: Falmer Press.

———. 2001. *The new meaning of educational change*, 3rd ed. New York: Teachers College Press.

———. 2003. *Change forces: With a vengeance.* London: Falmer Press.

Gallagher, M. 1998. Fatherless boys grow up into dangerous men. *Wall Street Journal*, December 1, A22.

Glaser, R., A. Lieberman, and R. Anderson. 1997. "The vision thing": Educational research and AERA in the 21st century. Part 3: Perspectives on the research-practice relationship. *Educational Researcher* 26 (7): 24–25.

Glickman, C. D, S. P. Gordon, and J. M. Ross-Gordon. 1998. *Supervision of instruction: A developmental approach*, 4th ed. Boston: Allyn and Bacon.

Glickman, C., S. Gordon, and J. Ross-Gordon. 2001. *SuperVision and instructional leadership.* Boston: Allyn and Bacon.

Glines, D. 2001 (March). Creating educational futures through imagineering. *Wingspan: The Pedamorphosis Communiqué* 13 (2): 9–14.

Goldring, E. B. 1992. System-wide diversity in Israel: Principals as transformational and environmental leaders. *Journal of Educational Administration* 30 (3): 49–62.

Goldring, E. B., and S. F. Rallis. 1993. *Principals of dynamic schools: Taking charge of change.* Newbury Park, CA: Corwin Press.

Goodson, I., and C. Anstead. 1998. Heroic principals and structures of opportunity: *Conjoncture* at a vocational high school. *International Journal of Leadership in Education* 1 (1): 61–73.

Greenfield, W. D., Jr. 1985. *Being and becoming a principal: Responses to work contexts and socialization processes.* Paper presented at the Annual Meeting of the American Educational Research Association, Chicago.

Hackmann, D. G., D. M. Schmitt-Oliver, and J. C. Tracy. 2002. *The standards-based administrative internship: Putting the ISLLC standards into practice.* Lanham, MD: Scarecrow Press.

Hargreaves, A., and M. Fullan. 1998. *What's worth fighting for out there?* New York: Teachers College Press.

Hargreaves, A., L. Earl, and M. Schmidt. 2002. Perspectives on alternative assessment reform. *American Educational Research Journal* 39 (1): 69–95.

Hart, A. W. 1991. Leader succession and socialization: A synthesis. *Review of Educational Research* 61 (4): 451–74.

———. 1993. *Principal succession: Establishing leadership in schools.* Albany: State University of New York Press.

Hart, A. W., and P. V. Bredeson. 1996. *The principalship: A theory of professional learning and practice.* New York: McGraw-Hill.

Hatch, T. 2000. What does it take to break the mold? Rhetoric and reality in new American schools. *Teachers College Record* 102 (3): 561–89. Online at http://80firstsearch.oclc.org.ezproxy.lib.usf.edu (accessed May 18, 2002).

Hay, J. 1995. *Transformational mentoring: Creating developmental alliances for changing organizational cultures.* London: McGraw-Hill.

Heck, R. H. 1995. Organizational and professional socialization: Its impact on the performance of new administrators. *Urban Review* 27 (1): 31–49.

Helfrich, F. 2004. Going deeper to change teachers' health habits. *International Journal of Educational Reform.*

Hemingway, E. 1987. *The complete short stories.* New York: Collier.

Henke, R. R., S. P. Choy, S. Geis, and S. P. Broughman. 1996. *Schools and staffing in the United States: A statistical profile, 1993–94* (NCES No. 96–124). Washington, DC: U.S. Department of Education, National Center for Education Statistics. Online at http://nces.ed.gov/pubs/96124. (accessed July 3, 2003).

Hobson, A., and J. Clarke. 1997. *The power of passion: Achieve your own Everests.* Calgary, Alberta: The Everest Effort Inc.

Hoffman, D. D. 1998. *Visual intelligence: How we create what we see.* New York: W. W. Norton & Company.

Hom, P. W., and R. W. Griffeth. 1995. *Employee turnover.* Cincinnati, OH: South-Western.

Hoover, E. 2003 (April 11). Closing the gates: A student under suspicion. [Special report]. *Chronicle of Higher Education* 49 (31), A12.

Hopkins, G. 2000. From the principle files: The principle shortage—what can schools do to attract a new generation of school leaders? *Education World, School Administration Article*: 1–6. Online at http://www.educationworld .com/a_admin/admin197.a.

Horn, R. A. 2001. Promoting social justice and caring in schools and communities: The unrealised potential of the cohort model. *Journal of School Leadership* 11: 313–34.

Humanetrics. 2003. *Jung Typology Test.* Online at http://www.daviddeck.com/ cgi-bin/tests/tests.cgi.

Information Resources. 2003. *Anthrax.* Online at http://banthrax.com/glossary.

Internet Mental Health. 2003. Online at http://www.mentalhealth.com/dis1/ p21-an06.

Jardine, R. 2001. *Beyond backpacking: Ray Jardine's guide to lightweight hiking.* Arizona City, AZ: AdventureLore Press.

Johnson, D. W., R. T. Johnson, and E. J. Holubec, eds. 1993. *Cooperation in the classroom,* 6th ed. Edina, MN: Interaction.

Jolly, E. J., S. M. Malloy, and M. C. Felt. 2001. *Beyond blame: Reacting to the terrorist attack. A curriculum for middle and high school students.* Newton,

MA: Education Development Center. Online at www.edc.org/spotlight/ schools/beyondblame. (accessed June 8, 2003).

Jones, T. 2003. Top of the world: Climbing Everest. *The Times*, May 25, C1, C8–9.

Jossey-Bass Publishers. 2000. *The Jossey-Bass reader on educational leadership*. San Francisco, CA: Jossey-Bass Publishers.

Kealy, W. A. 2003. Personal communication.

Kealy, W. A., and J. M. Webb. 1995. Contextual influences of maps and diagrams on learning. *Contemporary Educational Psychology* 20: 340–59.

Kincheloe, J. K., and D. Weil, eds. 2001. *Standards and schooling in the United States: An encyclopedia*. Vols. 1–3. Santa Barbara, CA: ABC-CLIO.

Kochan, F. K., B. L. Jackson, and D. L. Duke, eds. 1999. *A thousand voices from the firing line: A study of educational leaders, their jobs, their preparation, and the problems they face*. Columbia, MO: University Council for Educational Administration.

Kosseff, A. 2003. *AMC guide to outdoor leadership*. Guilford, CT: Globe Pequot Press.

Kozol, J. 1991. *Savage inequalities: Children in America's schools*. New York: HarperCollins.

Labaree, D. F. 2003 (May). The peculiar problems of preparing educational researchers. *Educational Researcher* 32 (4): 13–22.

Lanahan, L. 2002 (April). *Beyond school-level Internet access: Support for instructional use of technology*. [Brief report from the National Center for Education Statistics.] Washington, DC: U.S. Department of Education Office of Educational Research and Development. Online at http://nces.ed.gov/ pubsearch (accessed July 6, 2002).

LeBoeuf, M. 1980. *Imagineering: How to profit from your creative powers*. New York: McGraw-Hill.

Leithwood, K. A., D. Jantzi, H. Silins, and B. Dart. 1993. Using the appraisal of school leaders as an instrument for school restructuring. *Peabody Journal of Education* 68 (2): 85–109.

Leithwood, K. A., D. Jantzi, and R. Steinbach. 1999. *Changing leadership for changing times*. Buckingham, UK: Open University Press.

Lick, D. W. 1999. Proactive comentoring relationships: Enhancing effectiveness through synergy. In *New directions in mentoring: Creating a culture of synergy*, ed. C. A. Mullen and D. W. Lick, 34–45. London: Falmer Press.

Lieberman, A., and M. Grolnick. 1997. Networks, reform, and the professional development of teachers. In *Rethinking educational change with heart and mind*, ed. A. Hargreaves, 192–215. Alexandria, VA: Association for Supervision and Curriculum Development.

Lincoln, Y. S. 1997. Self, subject, audience, text: Living at the edge, writing in the margins. In *Representation and the text: Re-framing the narrative voice*, ed. W. G. Tierney and Y. S. Lincoln, 37–55. Albany: State University of New York Press.

Lippek, M. 2003. *Teacher perception of high-stakes testing and the FCAT*. Unpublished manuscript.

Llewellyn, P. E. 2004. Will I be ready as an administrator for school emergencies? *International Journal of Educational Reform*.

Logue, V. S. 2000. *Backpacking: Essential skills to advanced techniques*. Birmingham, AL: Menasha Ridge Press.

Lortie, D. C. 1998 (Summer). Teaching educational administration: Reflections on our craft. *Journal of Cases in Educational Leadership* 1 (1): 1–12. Online at www.ucea.org/cases (accessed July 6, 2003).

Lumsden, L. S. (1992). Prospects in principal preparation. *ERIC Digest 77*. ERIC Clearinghouse on Educational Management. ED350726. Online at www.ed.gov/databases/ERIC_Digests. (accessed August 6, 2003).

Malone, Jay. 2001. Principal mentoring. *Research Roundup* 17 (2): 1–8. Online at http://eric.uoregon.edu/publications/roundup/Winter_2001 (ERIC Clearinghouse on Educational Management, OR) (accessed August 9, 2002).

Marsh, D. D. 2000. Educational leadership for the twenty-first century. In *The Jossey-Bass reader on educational leadership*, ed. Jossey-Bass Publishers, 126–45. San Francisco: Jossey-Bass.

Marshall, C. M. 1985. Professional shock: The enculturation of the assistant principal. *Education and Urban Society* 18 (1): 28–58.

Maslow, A. H. 1954. *Motivation and personality*. New York: Harper & Row.

Mayer, D. P., J. E. Mullens, and M. T. Moore. 2000. *Monitoring school quality: An indicators report* (NCES No. 2001–030). Washington, DC: U.S. Department of Education, National Center for Education Statistics. Online at http://nces.ed.gov/pubs2001/2001030 (accessed July 3, 2003).

McCarthy, M. M. 1999. How are school leaders prepared? *Educational Horizons* 77 (2): 74–81.

McCarthy, M. M., and G. D. Kuh. 1997. *Continuity and change: The educational leadership professoriate*. Columbia, MO: The Universiy Council for Educational Administration.

McDaniel, E. L. 1999. The principal as mentor: From divergence to convergence. In *New directions in mentoring: Creating a culture of synergy*, ed. C. A. Mullen and D. W. Lick, 116–24). London, England: Falmer Press.

McNabb, M., M. Hawkes, and U. Rouk. 1999. *Critical issues in evaluating the effectiveness of technology*, 1–12. Online at www.ed.gov/Technology (accessed July 14, 2003).

Meadows, L. L. 2003. *Going deeper into diversity initiatives: A Band-Aid or the miracle cure?* Unpublished manuscript.

Mendis, P. 2001 (Winter). Teaching in the information age: Leadership aspects of integrated learning with technology in democratic environments. *Academic Leadership* 1 (2): 1–5. Online at www.academicleadership.org. (accessed July 3, 2003).

Merriam, S. B. 1998. *Qualitative research and case study applications in education.* San Francisco: Jossey-Bass.

Miles, M. B., and A. M. Huberman. 1994. *Qualitative data analysis: An expanded sourcebook,* 2nd ed. Thousand Oaks, CA: Sage.

Miller, G. A. 1996. Contextuality. In *Mental models in cognitive science,* ed. J. Oakhill and A. Garnham. 1–18. East Sussex, UK: Psychology Press.

Milstein, M. M., B. M. Bobroff, and L. N. Restine. 1991. *Internship programs in educational administration: A guide to preparing educational leaders.* New York: Teachers College Press, Columbia University.

Montgomery, M. A., and A. Krutulis. 2002 (November). *Climb it! A Webquest.* Online at www.plainfield.k12.in.us/hschool/webq (accessed June 18, 2003).

MountainZone.com 2002 (September/December). *Everest: Both sides now; with little fanfare Ellen Miller summits from both sides in same year; Siemens action Asia Himalayan mountain bike series.* Online at http://climb.mountain-zone.com/2002/story (accessed December 22, 2002).

Mullen, C. A. 1999. Birth of a book: A narrative study of a synergistic comentoring process. In *New directions in mentoring: Creating a culture of synergy,* ed. C. A. Mullen and D. W. Lick, 48–70. London: Falmer Press.

———. 2000. Constructing co-mentoring partnerships: Walkways we must travel. *Theory Into Practice* 39 (1): 4–11.

———. 2001. Disabilities awareness and the preservice teacher: A blueprint of a mentoring intervention. *Journal of Education for Teaching: International Research and Pedagogy* 27 (1): 39–61.

———. 2002a. Editorial: Emerging from our cocoons to take action. *Teacher Development: An International Journal of Teachers' Professional Development* 6 (1): 5–14.

———. 2002b. Mentoring aspiring school leaders in scholarly writing through case studies of diversity. In *The organizational and human dimensions of successful mentoring programs and relationships 1,* ed. F. K. Kochan, 83–102. Greenwich, CT: Information Age Publishing.

———. 2002c. The original ten: A multisite case study of Florida's Millennium High School reform model. *Education Policy Analysis Archives* 10 (40): 1–23. Online at http://epaa.asu.edu. (accessed November 18, 2002).

———. 2002d. Teacher activism in education reform. [Special issue]. *Teacher Development: An International Journal of Teachers' Professional Development* 6 (1).

———. 2002e. Web-enhanced instruction: A mixed bag of contradictions and possibilities for doctoral education. *Journal of Academic Leadership* 2 (2): 1–37. Online at www.academicleadership.org.

———. 2003a. The WIT cohort: A case study of informal doctoral mentoring. *Journal of Further and Higher Education 27* (4): 411–26.

———. 2003b. *New administrator research journal.* Researcher's personal log. Tampa, FL: University of South Florida.

———. 2004. *(Bio)terrorism top secret! Challenges, omissions, and tensions in exploring crisis management with teacher-leaders.* Unpublished manuscript.

Mullen, C. A. (with A. R. Kohan). 2002. Beyond dualism, splits, and schisms: Social justice for a renewal of vocational–academic education. *Journal of School Leadership* 12 (6): 640–62.

Mullen, C. A. (with L. Stover and B. Corley). 2001. School accreditation and teacher empowerment: An Alabama Case. *Teacher Development: An International Journal of Teachers' Professional Development* 5 (1): 101–17.

Mullen, C. A. (with E. C. Sullivan). 2002. The New Millennium High School, tomorrow's school today? *International Journal of Leadership in Education* 5 (3): 273–84.

Mullen, C. A. (with E. Tuten). 2004. A case study of adolescent female leadership: Exploring the "light" of change. *Journal of Educational Thought.*

Mullen, C. A., and J. H. Applegate. 2002. The deanship inside out: Conversations on a college's adjustment to top-tier research status. *Scholar-Practitioner Quarterly* 1 (2): 41–56.

Mullen, C. A., and S. S. Cairns. 2001. The principal's apprentice: Mentoring aspiring school administrators through relevant preparation. *Mentoring & Tutoring: Partnership in Learning* 9 (2): 125–52.

Mullen, C. A., S. P. Gordon, B. Greenlee, and R. H. Anderson. 2002. Capacities for school leadership: Emerging trends in the literature. *International Journal of Educational Reform* 11 (2): 158–98.

Mullen, C. A., and T. H. Graves. 2000. A case study of democratic accountability and school improvement. *Journal of School Leadership* 10 (6): 478–504.

Mullen, C. A., and F. K. Kochan. 2000. Creating a collaborative leadership network: An organic view of change. *International Journal of Leadership in Education* 3 (3): 183–200.

Mullen, C. A., and D. W. Lick, eds. 1999. *New directions in mentoring: Creating a culture of synergy.* London: Falmer Press.

Mullen, C. A., and R. L. Patrick. 2000. The persistent dream: A principal's promising reform of an at-risk elementary urban school. *Journal of Education for Students Placed At Risk* 5 (3): 229–50.

Murphy, J. 1999. *The quest for a center: Notes on the state of the profession of educational leadership.* Columbia, MO: University Council for Educational Administration.

Murphy, J., and P. B. Forsyth, eds. 1999. *Educational administration: A decade of reform.* Thousand Oaks, CA: Corwin Press.

Nalls, F. 1994. *The middle school assistant principalship: Organizational socialization and preparation for the principalship.* PhD diss., University of South Florida, Tampa.

National Association of Elementary School Principals. 2002. *Leading learning communities: Standards for what principals should know and be able to do.* [Executive summary]. Alexandria, VA: Collaborative Communications Group.

National Association of Elementary School Principals/Nova Southeastern University (NAESP/NSU). 2003. NAESP Principal Online. Online at http://www.naesp.org/misc/edweek_article_4-9-03.

National Center for Fair and Open Testing. 2003. *The dangerous consequences of high-stakes standardized testing.* Online at www.fairtest.org/facts/Dangerous %20Consequences (accessed May 28, 2003).

National Commission on Excellence in Education. Online at http://www .ed.gov/pubs/NatAtRisk.

National Mental Health Information Center. 2002 (October). *After a disaster: A guide for parents and teachers.* Online at www.mentalhealth.samhsa.gov (accessed May 16, 2003).

National Policy Board for Educational Administrators for the Educational Leadership Constituent Council. 1995. *Technology Standards for School Administrators (TSSA).* Online at http://cnets.iste.org/tssa.

National Public Health Leadership Institute. 2003 (April). *Public health grand rounds: Bioterrorism revisited—leadership lessons learned?* 1–4. Online at www.phli.org:9018/biorevisited (accessed May 3, 2003).

National Public Radio (NPR). 1997 (May 30). *Climbing Everest.* [Ira Flatow, host; Peter Hackett, Founder, Himalayan Rescue Association].

———. 2003a (April 25). *Mount Everest commentary: Fiftieth anniversary of Edmund Hillary and Tenzing Norgay's climb to the top of Mount Everest.* [Bob Edwards, host; Elizabeth Arnold, reporter].

———. 2003b (May 28). *Mount Everest commentary: Fiftieth anniversary of Edmund Hillary and Tenzing Norgay's climb to the top of Mount Everest.* [Bob Edwards, host; Frank Deford, Sports Illustrated].

National School Safety and Security Services. 2001. *Terrorism and school safety*, 1–8. Online at www.schoolsecurity.org/resources/nasro_survey_2002. (accessed April 3, 2003).

Neale, J., J. Saltzgaver, and K. Sutton. 2003. *Being prepared for an unexpected biological attack and the effects of racial profiling and discrimination*. Unpublished manuscript.

New Webster's Dictionary and Thesaurus of the English Language. 1993. Danbury, CT: Lexicon Publications.

Nieto, S. 2000. *Affirming diversity: The sociopolitical context of multicultural education*, 3rd ed.. New York: Longman.

Nowicki, E. 2002. Racial profiling problems and solutions. *Law and Order* 50 (10): 16–18.

Oakes, J. 1998. Tracking, inequality, and the rhetoric of reform: Why schools don't change. In *Critical social issues in American education: Transformation in a postmodern world*, ed. H. S. Shapiro and D. E. Purpel, 127–47. Mahwah, NJ: Lawrence Erlbaum.

Oberg, A. 1990. Methods and meanings in action research: The action research journal. *Theory into Practice* 29 (3): 214.

O'Callaghan, J. 1999 (May 20). *WebRing: Imagineering.* http://home.attbi .com/~jeffocal/Imagineering (accessed June 5, 2003).

Oliver, R. 2003. Assistant principal job satisfaction and desire to become principals. *NCPEA Education Leadership Review* 4 (2): 38–46.

O'Neil, J. 1995 (October). Teachers and technology: Potential and pitfalls. *Educational Leadership* 53 (2). Online at www.ascd.org/readingroom/edlead/ 9510/oneil2 (accessed May 5, 2003).

Orozco, L. 2003. CAPEA president's message: The evolving profession of school leader and leadership preparation. *Educational Leadership and Administration* 14:3–9.

Paladin Executive Services. 2003. Online at http://www.paladinexec.com/mbti.

Paquette, B. S. 2004. Are today's beginning school administrators prepared for their jobs? A case study. *International Journal of Educational Reform*.

Parkay, F. W., and G. E. Hall, eds. 1992. *Becoming a principal: The challenges of beginning leadership*. Boston: Allyn and Bacon.

Parkay, F. W., and B. H. Stanford. 2004. *Becoming a teacher*, 6th ed. Boston: Allyn and Bacon.

Payne, R. K. 1998. *A framework for understanding poverty*. Highlands, TX: RFT Publishing.

Petrides, L. A., and S. Zahra Guiney. 2002. *Teachers College Record* 104 (8): 1702–17.

Polanyi, M. 1962. *Personal knowledge: Towards a post-critical philosophy*. Chicago: University of Chicago Press.

Posise, R. D. 1999. Strategic planning for school administrators. *Phi Delta Kappa Fastbacks* 457: 7–37.

President's Council on Physical Fitness and Sports (PCPFS). 2001 (March). http://www.Indiana.edu/~preschal.

Rallis, S. F., and E. B. Goldring. 2000. *Principals of dynamic schools: Taking charge of change.* Thousand Oaks, CA: Corwin Press.

Rizvi, F. 2003. Democracy and education after September 11. *Globalisation Societies and Education* 1 (1): 25–40.

Romero, A. D. 2001. *ACLU joins with Broad New Coalition in Defense of Freedom: America must not cede democracy to terrorism.* Online at http://search.aclu.org/AdvancedSearchResults.

Sarason, S. B. 1990. *The predictable failure of educational reform: Can we change before it's too late?* San Francisco: Jossey-Bass.

———. 1993. *The case for change: Rethinking the preparation of educators.* San Francisco: Jossey-Bass.

Schechter, C. 2002 (April–June). Marching in the land of uncertainty: Transforming school culture through communal deliberative process. *International Journal of Leadership in Education* 5 (2): 105–28.

Schein, E. H. 1985. *Organizational culture and leadership: A dynamic view.* San Francisco: Jossey-Bass.

———. 1992. *Organizational culture and leadership.* San Francisco: Jossey-Bass.

Schmidt, L. 2002. *Gardening in the minefield: A survival guide for school administrators.* Portsmouth, NH: Heinemann.

Schmieder, J. H., C. Z. McGrevin, and A. J. Townley. 1994. Keys to success: Critical skills for novice principals. *Journal of School Leadership* 4: 272–93.

Schön, D. A. 1987. *Educating the reflective practitioner: Toward a new design for teaching and learning in the professions.* London: Jossey-Bass Publishers.

Schumaker, D. R., and W. A. Sommers. 2001. *Being a successful principal: Riding the wave of change without drowning.* Thousand Oaks, CA: Corwin Press.

Scott, C., and S. Dinham, S. 2002. The beatings will continue until quality improves: Using carrots and sticks in the quest for educational improvement. *Teacher Development: An International Journal of Teachers' Professional Development* 6 (1): 15–31.

Sergiovanni, T. J. 1992. *Moral leadership: Getting to the heart of school improvement.* San Francisco: Jossey-Bass Publishers.

———. 1995. *The principalship: A reflective practice perspective.* Boston: Allyn and Bacon.

Shapiro, A. 2000. *Leadership for constructivist schools.* Lanham, MD: Scarecrow Press.

———. 2003. *Case studies in constructivist leadership and teaching.* Lanham, MD: Scarecrow Press.

Short, P. M., and J. P. Scribner. 2002. *Case studies of the superintendency.* Lanham, MD: Scarecrow Press.

Sills, C. K. 1994. Paths to leadership: Building middle school girls' self-esteem. *Feminist Teacher* 8 (2): 61–67.

Skrla, L., J. J. Scheurich, J. F. Johnson, Jr., and J. W. Koschoreck. 2001. Accountability for equity: Can state policy leverage social justice? *International Journal of Leadership in Education* 4 (3): 237–60.

Slater, C. L., M. W. McGhee, R. L. Capt, I. Alvarez, C. Topete, and E. Iturbe. 2003. A comparison of the views of educational administration students in the USA and Mexico. *International Journal of Leadership in Education* 6 (1): 35–55.

Snyder, K. J., M. Acker-Hocevar, and K. M. Snyder. 2000. *Living on the edge of chaos: Leading schools into the global age.* Milwaukee, WI: Quality Press.

Spencer, W. A., and F. K. Kochan. 2000. Gender related differences in career patterns of principals in Alabama: A statewide study. *Education Policy Analysis Archives* 8 (9): 1–12. Online at http://epaa.asu.edu/epaa/v8n9. (accessed July 3, 2003).

Stiggins, R. J. 2002. Assessment crisis: The absence of assessment for learning. *Phi Delta Kappan* 83 (10): 758–65.

Sullivan, A. 2004. A plea for infusing communications technology in the middle school environment: A case study. *International Journal of Educational Reform.*

Swiss Knives Express. 2003. Online at http://www.swissknivesexpress.com.

Texas School Safety Center. Online at www.txssc.swt.edu.

Twale, D. J., and F. K. Kochan. 2000. Assessment of an alternative cohort model for part-time students in an educational leadership program. *Journal of School Leadership* 10: 188–208.

U.S. Senate. *Racial profiling education and awareness act of 2002.* 107th Congress, 2nds sess., S. 2114. (April 11, 2002) *theorator.com.* Online at http://www.theorator.com/bills107/s2114.html.

Verma, G. K., and K. Mallick. 1999. *Researching education: Perspectives and techniques.* London: Falmer Press.

Waite, D., M. Boone, and M. McGhee. 2001. A critical sociocultural view of accountability. *Journal of School Leadership* 11 (3): 182–203.

Walker, A., and C. Dimmock, eds. 2002. *School leadership and administration: Adopting a cultural perspective.* New York: RoutledgeFalmer.

Wasley, P. A. 1992. When leaders leave. *Educational Leadership* 50 (3). Online at www.ascd.org/readingroom/edlead/9211/wasley (accessed July 29, 2002).

Webb-Johnson, G. 2000. My emerging destiny: Mentoring from an African-American perspective. In *Breaking the circle of one: Redefining mentoring in the lives and writings of educators*, ed. C. A. Mullen, M. D. Cox, C. K. Boettcher, and D. S. Adoue (2nd ed.), 3–19. New York: Peter Lang.

Weil, D., and J. L. Kincheloe, eds. 2003. *Critical thinking and learning: An encyclopedia*. Greenwood Publishing Group.

Whittacker, T. 2003. *A footprint on Everest*. Online at www.tomwhittacker.com/evstory.

Wiesel, E. 2003. *Daily celebrations*. Online at www.dailycelebrations.com/101401 (accessed June 1, 2003).

Williams, E. J., J. Matthews, and S. Baugh. 2004. Developing a mentoring internship model for school leadership: Using legitimate peripheral participation. *Mentoring and Tutoring: Partnership in Learning.*

U.S. Department of Justice. 2001 (September). *OVC handbook for coping after terrorism*. Online at www.ojp.usdoj.gov/ovc/publications (accessed April 17, 2003).

Zerubavel, E. 1981. *Hidden rhythms: Schedules and calendars in social life.* Chicago: University of Chicago Press.

Ziegler, W. 2001. School partnerships: Something for everyone. *Principal Leadership* 2 (1): 1–3.

Index

About the Author

Carol A. Mullen, Ph.D., is an associate professor of leadership studies at the University of South Florida and a graduate of the Ontario Institute for Studies in Education, University of Toronto. She specializes in graduate student development, innovative forms of mentorship and collaboration, the process of principal preparation, and exemplary leadership within challenging school contexts. She teaches a variety of master's and doctoral courses, in addition to supervising a large group of dissertation writers within a thriving cohort called the Writers-in-Training (WIT).

Dr. Mullen has published almost a hundred journal articles and book chapters, and, as guest editor, eleven special issues of academic journals (most recently, *Journal of School Leadership*, *Journal of Curriculum Theorizing*, *Teacher Education Quarterly,* and *Qualitative Inquiry*). One of her four previously published books, *Breaking the Circle of One: Redefining Mentorship in the Lives and Writings of Educators* (Peter Lang, 1997/2000, 2nd edition), received the Exemplary Research in Teacher Education Award from the American Educational Research Association (Division K) in 1998. Her other three books are *New Directions in Mentoring: Creating a Culture of Synergy* (1999, Falmer Press), *The Postmodern Educator: Arts-Based Inquiries and Teacher Development* (1999, Peter Lang), and *Imprisoned Selves: An Inquiry into Prisons and Academe* (University Press of America, 1997).

Dr. Mullen is editor of the refereed international journal *Mentoring & Tutoring: Partnership in Learning,* online at http://www.tandf.co.uk/journals/carfax/13611267.html.